The Making of a Nuclear Peace

The Making of a
Nuclear Peace

The Task of Today's Just War Theorists

Marcia Sichol, S.H.C.J.

GEORGETOWN UNIVERSITY PRESS
Washington, D.C.

Library of Congress Cataloging-in-Publication Data

Sichol, Marcia W., 1940-
    The making of a nuclear peace : the task of today's just war
theorists / Marcia W. Sichol.
        p. cm.
    Includes bibliographical references.
    ISBN 0-87840-482-1. -- ISBN 0-87840-483-X (pbk.)
    1. Nuclear warfare--Moral and ethical aspects.   2. Just war
doctrine.   3. Ramsey, Paul--Contributions in just war doctrine.
4. O'Brien, William Vincent--Contributions in just war doctrine.
5. Walzer, Michael--Contributions in just war doctrine.   6. Ramsey,
Paul--Contributions in nuclear warfare.   8. Walzer, Michael-
-Contributions in nuclear warfare.   9. Peace.   I. Title.
U263.S53 1989
172'.422--dc20   89-23688
                                                         CIP

I DEDICATE THIS BOOK TO
MY MOTHER AND FATHER

RUTH AND ADAM

Contents

Foreword   xi

Acknowledgements   xiii

CHAPTER 1

The Nuclear Age: Questions of War and Peace

Politics and the Role of Ethics in the Nuclear Age   1
The Quantity and Quality of the Threat   2
The Arms Race: The Quantitative Threat   4
The Arms Race: The Qualitative Effects   5
Toward an Ethical Framework   6
Nuclear War Deterrence and the Churches   13
Three Contemporary Just War Theorists   22

CHAPTER 2

The Principle of Proportionality in Classic and Contemporary Just War Theories

Introduction   25
Classic Just War Theories and
    the Principle of Proportionality   25
Comparison with Contemporary Just War Theories   29
Three Contemporary Theorists and
    the Principle of Proportionality   30

PAUL RAMSEY 30
WILLIAM O'BRIEN 38
MICHAEL WALZER 49

CHAPTER 3

The Principle of Noncombatant Immunity and Contemporary Just War Theories

Introduction 59
Classic Just War Theories and
    the Principle of Noncombatant Immunity 60
Religious Sources 61
Secular Sources: Chivalry 63
Definitions 64
    AUGUSTINE 64
Classic Just War Theorists 65
    AQUINAS 65
    VITORIA 68
    SUAREZ, GROTIUS, GENTILI 68
Contemporary Just War Theorists and
    the Principle of Noncombatant Immunity 73
    PAUL RAMSEY 74
    WILLIAM O'BRIEN 82
    MICHAEL WALZER 93

CHAPTER 4

The Military and Political Uses of Nuclear Weapons

Introduction: "Use" and "Non-Use" Defined 107
Nuclear Weapons in War Fighting 107
Deterrence 109
Bargaining Chips 112

The Contemporary Just-War Theorists and
the Military and Political Uses
of Nuclear Weapons   113
    PAUL RAMSEY   113
    WILLIAM O'BRIEN   126
    MICHAEL WALZER   146

CHAPTER 5

Nuclear War, Nuclear Peace, and the Bondedness of Peoples

Introduction: "In a Different Voice"   157
In Search of Progress   158
Discovering an Old Principle   158
Classic Just War Theorists:
    Foundations and Methodologies   163
Contemporary Just War Theorists   166
The Bondedness of Peoples and
    Jus ad Bellum Doctrines   167
    PAUL RAMSEY   167
    WILLIAM O'BRIEN   169
    MICHAEL WALZER   171
The Bondedness of Peoples and
    Jus in bello Doctrines   172
    PAUL RAMSEY   173
    WILLIAM O'BRIEN   175
    MICHAEL WALZER   177
A "New-Clearing" for Nuclear War
and Nuclear Peace   180

ENDNOTES   185

SELECTED BIBLIOGRAPHY   209

Foreword

JOHN LANGAN, S.J.

In their celebrated pastoral letter on war and peace, *The Challenge of Peace* (1983), the U.S. Catholic bishops refer to 'two principles which have special significance today precisely because of the destructive capability of modern technological warfare,' which they then proceed to identify as 'proportionality and discrimination.'[1] Precisely because of the extensive work and various church documents but also in the general debate over the moral problems that modern warfare and nuclear weapons in dispassionate study of the way these principles are used and understood by three of the most eminent just war theorists of our time: Paul Ramsey, William O'Brien, and Michael Walzer. The three come from the three most influential American religious traditions (Protestant, Catholic, and Jewish) and from three different academic disciplines (theological ethics, international law, and political philosophy). The corpus of their writings on the morality of modern warfare covers a wide range of issues and spans the period from the debate over nuclear weapons in the late 1950s to the present. They have engaged in mutual criticism and dialogue. They have all been widely read by scholars and those concerned with moral questions about public policy in this area. So they provide an overlapping set of perspectives on some of the issues about nuclear weapons that have most troubled the American conscience during this period.

The special value of this study of their views by Sister Marcia Sichol, S.H.C.J., lies in her careful comparative study of their understanding and use of these two basic moral principles governing the conduct of modern warfare, and of the conclusions that they reach about the possible use of nuclear weapons in warfare and about nuclear deterrence. Their conclusions, as she presents them, show both the strains that the development of weapons of mass destruction has put on the classic formulations of just war theory and the continuing fruitfulness of just war theory in the development of complex arguments and assessments that are sensitive to the demands of the moral life and of international politics. This study provides an important benchmark for evaluating both the work of these three moralists and the contributions of a new generation of scholars which includes James Turner Johnson, David

Hollenbach, Bryan Hehir, George Weigel, David Fischer, Gregory Kavka, and John Finnis. It draws light and conviction from her own concern for the preservation of peace among all peoples and for the comprehensive principle of humanity that she regards as fundamental. The U.S. Catholic bishops stated with clarity the double task confronting those who have to make the difficult decisions about the development, the deployment, and the possible use of nuclear weapons in the following lines from *The Challenge of Peace*: 'The moral duty today is to prevent nuclear war from ever occurring *and* to protect and preserve those key values of justice, freedom and independence which are necessary for personal dignity and national integrity.'[2] The achievement of these goals imposes a heavy task which requires both careful thought and informed virtue. Marcia Sichol's scholarly insight and moral sensitivity provide one example of how the scholarly community can contribute to the resolution of the most difficult problem of our time.

Notes

1. National Conference of Catholic Bishops, *The Challenge of Peace* (Washington, D.C.: U.S. Catholic Conference, 1983), par. 101.
2. Ibid., par. 175.

Acknowledgements

No one writes a book alone even though much of one's research and writing time is spent in solitude. I have been helped and supported by many colleagues and friends. I am especially grateful to Martha Dudley in the Philosophy Department at Georgetown University and to Linda Turbyville in the Graduate Dean's office. Without their patience and assistance, I could never have mastered the rudimentary techniques of word processing that I needed to begin this project. I am also especially grateful to those Sisters of the Holy Child and Sisters of St. Joseph with whom I have lived and shared much of the research and production experience.

I am grateful, too, to the U.S. Arms Control Agency, whose funding through the Hubert Humphrey Fellowship in Arms Control and Disarmament has enabled me to do my research uninterrupted by the claims of other commitments, and whose public relations officer, Matt Murphy, has been especially helpful in leading me to pertinent information on weapons systems and U.S. nuclear policy. Others in related fields have also talked with me and pointed out new avenues to explore: David Hollenbach, S.J., Rev. J. Bryan Hehir, Francis X. Winters, S.J., Gerald Mara, Professors LeRoy Walters and Jesse Mann.

I have also had the opportunity to speak with the three just war theorists who are the focus of this study: Michael Walzer, Paul Ramsey, and William V. O'Brien, and I am grateful to them for their encouragement. During the writing of this book, Paul Ramsey passed away, and we shall all miss his quick wit and insightful critique.

There are two persons to whom I owe greatest thanks. The first is John P. Langan, S.J., who was my mentor, and who has tirelessly, faithfully, and incisively critiqued my various drafts. Without his constant advice and encouragement, I could neither have begun nor finished the writing of this book. The second is my mother whose understanding and support have given me periods of respite when the research and writing became especially wearisome.

The study that follows is the result of the contributions of all these people. It is my hope, and I know it is theirs, that the contents of the following pages will contribute to an understanding of the place of the Just War Tradition in the current nuclear debate, and that in doing so, this analysis will contribute even more to the building of a more just and peace-filled world—to the making of a real peace.

Chapter 1

The Nuclear Age: Questions of War and Peace

Politics and the Role of Ethics in the Nuclear Age

Rationality ... dictates reflection on peace despite the uproar of melee, and on war when weapons are silent.[1]

Though so-called small wars continue to rage about the world, this is a time of "nuclear silence," at least in the sense that the nuclear bombs are silent even if the voices of protest are not. It is, therefore, an age particularly suited to reflection on the use of nuclear force, its consequences and its possible justification.

Force as an instrument of policy is as old as humankind and so, too, are the moral questions regarding its use. Many today, however, conclude that ethics and politics simply do not mix, that the ethicist and the politician are playing different games with different rules. Recent wars have brought about unprecedented amounts of suffering and death and have tended to obscure the role of ethics in matters like national security. Western moral codes prior to the twentieth century would have condemned as indiscriminate and unjustifiable the level of violence and killing engaged in by both sides in the Second World War. They would have found morally abhorrent the present structure of peace as resting on the capacity to commit genocide. This apparent divorce between ethics and politics has "prompted a variety of responses from a confused public." These responses are identified by Francis X. Winters, S.J., as (1) withdrawal from the political arena, (2) engagement in a kind of "theatrical politics," (3) living with a sense that ethics and military strategy can never be squared but somehow believing that everything will turn out all right in the end, (4)or making an effort to influence national security policy in ways that will be consistent with ethical and political values.[2]

Those who accept this last option engage in a challenge to join in a highly worthy human endeavor, a task some have called the most creative action of humankind. They are also immediately confronted with a plurality of outlooks, and they find it necessary to search for some kind of objective moral tests against which to measure the morality of political decisions. Raymond Aron has said that "The theory of international relations starts from the plurality of autonomous centers of decisions, hence from the risk of war, and from this risk it deduces the necessity of the calculation of means."[3] In the twentieth century, modern weapons create precisely the situation Clausewitz has termed "absolute war"--a situation which, Aron maintains, has never been the case until the present.

The fourth option has also led today's moral theorists to draw on long-standing moral traditions for guidance. The form these traditions take in the post-World War II world is greatly affected by the presence of arsenals of nuclear weapons. Theorists are forced to search for answers which no longer allow for the 'unexamined patriotism' so often accepted in the past. They are faced not only with changes in the political landscape of a more global and interdependent society but also with new weapons, weapons which, for the first time in history, possess the capability of obliterating societies.

The Quantity and Quality of the Threat

The twentieth century reveals a vastly different political landscape from any that humanity has ever confronted. The globe is now made up of more than 150 theoretically independent and sovereign nations. At least five possess nuclear arsenals capable of mass destruction--a fact which demands an ethical inquiry into issues that none of the former just war theories has addressed. One such issue is the right of self-defense. Theoretically if any nation believes it needs nuclear weapons to defend itself, it ought to have the same right to those weapons as any other nation; this claim, of course, assumes nuclear self-defense is a moral option. Yet with the proliferation of such weapons comes the greater risk of destabilization in the balance of power. Limits to the right of self-defense must be examined more carefully than in past centuries. Perhaps today's most perplexing moral issue relating to war and its conduct is the present policy of nuclear deterrence, whereby a nation builds up its nuclear arsenal in order to prevent its use. Where formerly nations armed themselves to fight, today they arm themselves so that they will not have to fight.

An understanding of the evolution of modern weapons may help to explain how and why humanity now finds itself involved in such paradoxes. This evolution has made rapid progress in the twentieth century. The very rapidity of weapons development has made it difficult to absorb the implications trailing in its wake; much less has this rapidity of change allowed time to integrate these implications into existing moral codes.

World War I saw the advent of the first of the modern weapons capable of mass destruction, namely, the chemical warfare agents. These threatened widespread, uncontrollable effects in large and unpredictable areas. Possession of chemical weapons was considered by some to be the only counterbalance to stop unpredictable and indiscriminate suffering and death. The Geneva Protocol of 1925 eventually outlawed their use, and it is of interest to note that they were not in fact used in the Second World War. The reasons for this may be speculative. Despite violations of moral codes in other areas, perhaps Nazi Germany feared retaliation in kind or feared being ostracized from the rest of the world community. James Johnson points out that in fact the Washington Treaty of 1922 and the 1925 Protocol banning gas warfare were actually conscious reactions to the experience of World War I. The concern was not discrimination so much as the practical problem of the threat of "retaliation in kind."[4]

Another more recent limitation on weapons worth noting is the unilateral decision of the United States in 1969 to renounce its stockpiles of biological weapons. This would be followed two years later by sixty nations which agreed to the Biological Weapons Convention signed by sixty nations prohibiting the development, production and stockpiling of biological agents, toxins and weapons designed to employ them. Though nations are periodically accused of violations, nevertheless, the pressure of world opinion prevents any transgressor from admitting violations openly. Public opinion may be expected to curtail the use of such weapons. Had nuclear disarmament followed a similar pattern, the present proliferation of weapons could not have occurred.

The use of aircraft during the First World War has blurred the distinction between soldier and civilian more than any other modern development. The airplane has made the traditional condition of noncombatant immunity difficult, if not impossible, to observe. The incendiary bombs dropped on Dresden and Hamburg led to fire storms that consumed entire cities: total populations made up not only of workers in arms factories, but also of butchers, bakers, candlestick makers, babies, the elderly, children, waitresses, cooks, the many who actually *are* the majority--noncombatants.[5]

The use of incendiary bombs and the use of nuclear bombs on Hiroshima and Nagasaki may have violated both the traditional principle of discrimination and the principle of proportionality to an unprecedented degree. A utilitarian justification is often offered for the nuclear bombings emphasizing the *price* and *time* of victory, but their use has posed serious problems for moral theorists. The proliferation of nuclear weapons since the Second World War has raised three fundamental questions: 1) Can the *possession* of such weapons be justified? 2) If so, what is the proper *declaratory policy* regarding their use? 3) What *actual* use might be justified?[6] Some argue that nuclear weapons are so different from previous weapons that they should be treated under a whole new set of moral categories. For example, just as a whole new set of physical laws was needed to explain subatomic particles when the law of the planets proved insufficient to account for certain physical phenomena, so some believe a whole new set of criteria is needed to determine the morality of contemporary warfare.

The Arms Race: The Quantitative Threat

The Stockholm International Peace Research Institute has recently addressed the effects of nuclear weapons and has warned that any arms race is intrinsically unstable. Reflecting on history, it concludes that "circumstances . . . taken cumulatively and over a period of time . . . make the outbreak of a nuclear war highly probable especially in light of the fact that over the past few decades we have averaged three to eight wars per year."[7]

The institute has not been able to learn the exact size of the present stockpiles but estimates these to be more than 13,000 megatons. Some nuclear warheads today have an explosive yield greater than the total of all explosives ever used since gunpowder was invented. The development of means of delivery has resulted in weapons that can travel at such rapid speed that they can reach their target anywhere in the world within a half-hour and with a 50 percent probability of landing within two hundred meters of their objective. Missiles now have multiple warheads with the capacity of being fired separately and aimed at different targets while in flight (MIRVs: "multiply independently targetable re-entry vehicles"). The U.S. and the USSR now have more than 50,000 warheads in total.[8] These include intercontinental ballistic missiles launched from underground silos (ICBMs); submarine launched ballistic missile (SLBMs), and missiles launched from aircraft. Many are equipped with ten warheads each.[9]

While the U.S. and the USSR are currently observing the SALT I and SALT II provisions, NATO is not a party to these and has become increasingly concerned with the balance of power. China, France and the U.K. have smaller arsenals, and there has been horizontal as well as vertical proliferation of nuclear weapons in other parts of the world. India has had nuclear capability since 1974; Pakistan has ostensibly procured nuclear material for peaceful purposes but is concerned about its neighbor, India; Libya and Iraq have made known their desire for an "Islamic" bomb; South Africa has conducted clandestine tests, probably in the Indian Ocean. Argentina, Brazil and Chile are all potential nuclear weapons states (they have not signed the non-proliferation treaty). The potentiality for escalation to nuclear war from smaller conflicts is, therefore, very real. People throughout the world are concerned about the proliferation of nuclear weapons. The Stockholm Institute shows that proliferation has led to an average of five tons of high explosive for each inhabitant on earth. The Stockholm report questions the effectiveness of the deterrence strategy amid such an abundance of nuclear destructive capacity.

Those who supported the Mutually Assured Destruction policy (MAD), prevalent until the last few years, viewed deterrence by nuclear weapons in a similar manner as they viewed deterrence by conventional weapons: nuclear warheads are weapons on a "weapons continuum," and are therefore not different in kind from other weapons. After 1962, ICBMs reduced delivery time to one-half hour but they proved not so accurate as bombers; therefore entire cities had to be targeted, and necessarily, the civilians unconnected with the military force were utterly defenseless. Accuracy gradually improved. The declaratory policy was that the United States would concentrate on military targets; but if low-level response to an attack failed, massive retaliation remained an "ace in the hole."[10]

The official U.S. policy has been shifting from MAD, a countervalue policy (CV), to a counterforce policy (CF) since the time of the Carter administration.[11] This strategy envisages an attempt by one side to knock out the fighting potential of the other, aiming at the destruction of all known missile bases but not centers of population. Counter-city targeting remains a part of America's Single Integrated Operational Plan (SIOP). Whether the idea of a "limited nuclear war" is a viable moral option or a dangerous fallacy is the concern of contemporary just war theorists.

The Arms Race: The Qualitative Effects

Some maintain that there is a qualitative difference in the *kind* of weapons involved in nuclear war as opposed to the kind of weapons used in conventional warfare. This claim is made not only because of the amount of damage that can result from the use of nuclear weapons but also because of the suffering and death that accompany a nuclear explosion. The argument is supported by the following findings of the Stockholm Institute.

Acute effects from radiation occur within one or two hours after exposure to a very high dose of radiation, with death not occurring for some time. It is generally believed that death will occur within two months, though in Japan it took up to several years in some cases. There is no clear-cut distinction between acute and long-term effects: early symptoms include anorexia, nausea, and headache; when the exposure is up to 1 Gray, recovery is nearly complete (normal radiation exposure in a year is one thousandth of a Gray). Five Grays exposure leads to 100% mortality, and this is mainly due to damage to the blood-forming organs. Radiation sickness affects the gastro-intestinal/neuro-muscular systems: anorexia, nausea, vomiting, diarrhea, cramps, salivation, dehydration, and loss of weight ensue. Neuromuscular effects include fatigue, apathy, sweating, fever, headache, hypotension, and hypotensive shock. Seeing similar symptoms in others is also thought to lead to the induction of the same symptoms in oneself.[12]

Among the effects on the blood-forming system is a shortage of dividing cells. The reduction in white cells leads to infection; in platelets, to hemorrhaging; in red cells, to severe anemia. Effects on the gastro-intestinal system cause the villi cells to degenerate and become ulcerative, and lead to gangrenous inflammation. Effects on the central nervous system result in muscle tremors which lead to lack of muscle coordination and to coma, convulsions and to shock. The victim is immediately disoriented and incapacitated because of degeneration of brain cells and cerebral oedema (inflammation of the cerebral vessels). These effects will also occur where the amount of radiation is equivalent to that emitted by neutron bombs proposed for use against tank crews. Acute lung effects are lethal at 10 to 20 Grays. Short-term effects occur to the skin, hair, and reproductive organs. Dosage of more than 2 Grays may result in permanent sterility.[13]

Knowledge of these effects helps to induce the fear that lies behind the policy of deterrence. The dictionary definition of "deter" is, "To discourage and stop by fear; to stop or prevent from acting or proceeding, by danger, difficulty, or other consideration which disheartens or countervails the motive of an act."[14] The policy is well named, for nations, well aware of the effects of nuclear blasts, use deterrence as the rationale for maintaining and increasing their stockpiles of weapons of mass destruction.

Throughout changes in policy, the same ethical questions return with increasing urgency: questions about the continued possession of nuclear weapons, declaratory policy regarding their use, their *actual* use, efforts to control, reduce, and eliminate them. At the very minimum, it would seem that in determining the morality of any alternative, one would do well to hold that alternative up against the principles of the Western tradition, especially the principles of discrimination (who is targeted?) and proportionality (is the good to be achieved commensurate with the harm allowed?). Having done this one will be in a better position to judge whether contemporary just war theories provide an adequate ethical framework to deal with nuclear war and deterrence.

Toward an Ethical Framework

The Tradition of the Western World

Weapons change, the "political landscape" assumes a new shape, but parts of the moral "landscape" endure: war vs. perceptions of a people's interests, costs of weapons vs. gains, disregard for noncombatants vs. military gain. In acknowledging the superiority of justice, moralists deny "the finality of politics ...[and] affirm the indispensability of ethics."[15] James Johnson identifies six moral principles at work throughout the history of warfare: Christian charity; distributive justice, which, Johnson says, is embodied in the concept of proportionality and which implies that the evils and goods of war be distributed according to the relative guilt and innocence among the people affected by war; vindicative justice, which requires the setting right of wrongs suffered; mercy, the secular version of charity; civilization, the principle having to do with the direction of the values resident in a total culture, and humanity, the principle related to mankind abstracted from a cultural setting (Johnson sees these two principles as particularly opposed to military necessity and as often forming a single principle). To these Johnson adds the *prima facie* duty not to kill. He claims that moral theorists deal with all of these and differ on their choice of emphasis, combinations, and on whether they tend to be non-absolute or absolute.[16] People often rely on their leaders' assimilation of basic common values; yet in World War II demands for unconditional surrender and policies such as indiscriminate firebombings by Allied leaders have shown that reliance on statesmen's observing a common moral tradition is not sufficient to guarantee an ethical public policy.

Though it is true that the nations of the world are diverse in culture and religion, and some may question the objectivity to be found among these nations, one may be justified in focusing on the Western nations, which do reflect a common heritage. Keeping in mind that controversy exists over whether the Soviet Union, with its Marxist-Leninist doctrine, is to be counted as a Western nation, it may be said that the Soviet bloc does share much with Western nations, including the Christian roots planted centuries before Marx wrote *Das Kapital*. At any rate, it is the Western nations, including the Soviet Union, that must bear the burden of justifying the waging of wars in the present day, for if Raymond Aron is correct, the globe is politically bipolar: the United States enjoying hegemony among certain nations and the Soviet Union among others. It is, then, the Western nations who provide most of the weapons and financing of war efforts. They are the nations with perhaps not the most to win, but certainly the most to lose (at least in terms of wealth and material productivity) should nuclear conflict break out. Among the Western nations, one becomes aware of a certain moral agreement persisting throughout the history of the Western world both in identifying justifiable causes of war (*jus ad bellum*) and in conducting wars once they are underway (*jus in bello*). This is true even though the means by which wars have been waged over the centuries have changed quantitatively and qualitatively. Not only have the means changed, but there have been changes in the kinds of wars that are justified and those which are not. Wars waged to punish an unjust aggressor were common prior to the sixteenth century, for example, but are not accepted as justified by the majority of nations in the world today.[17]

The issue of *jus ad bellum* has been the occasion of renewed controversy among twentieth century just war theorists. Contemporary just war theory, by and large, emphasizes *jus in bello* while paying little attention to questions of just cause or *jus ad bellum*. James Johnson, in fact, has called the *jus ad bellum* "morally truncated and politically ineffective" in this twentieth century.[18] William O'Brien, too, has been especially critical of the scant attention paid to *jus ad bellum* in the 1983 U.S. Bishops' Pastoral, *The Challenge of Peace: God's Promise and Our Response.*[19]

This change in emphasis can be partly traced back to a kind of 'bifurcation' in the so-called "classic just war doctrine" that dominated the Western world during the Middle Ages. This Western world was the world of Christendom, a world far more unified geographically, theologically and philosophically than the present Western world. Although medieval Christendom is not the focus of the present study, it will be helpful to dwell briefly on its history since that age provides the roots for both the agreement and the disagreement that characterize the contemporary debate on nuclear war and deterrence.

Christianity, War and Peace

The just war 'tradition' is distinct from the various just war 'theories' within that same tradition. Despite the fact that the theorists share a basic agreement on moral principles governing the just war, they differ in their interpretation of these same principles. Prior to the fourth century, it is not just war, but pacifism that characterizes the attitude of most Christians. However, even the 'pacifist tradition' reveals 'extraordinary diversity and incompatibility' in its different forms among Christians.[20] Louis Swift cautions one not to make the writings of this period carry more weight than they can bear. It is difficult to know from the writings, for example, whether Christians were being martyred for their anti-militaristic ideals or for their anti-idolatry.[21] Like the Just War tradition, pacifism has persisted from the time of the Stoics through the Christian era and has reached the forefront of debate again today. Though the pacifist tradition endures in the present age, it will not be within the scope of this book to address its strengths and weaknesses at length. Even a pacifist like Roland Bainton claims that if peace is preserved today, it will be through the efforts of peaceminded nonpacifists rather than through pacifists themselves that the limitation of war will be achieved.

The Christian pacifism that marks the period prior to the fourth century is not an *absolute* pacifism. Christian soldiers, for example, are allowed to continue in military service and are not excommunicated. Bainton describes this period as an age of pacifism "to the degree, that during this period, no Christian author . . . approved of Christian participation in battle." By the fifth century, under Theodosius II, a real reversal occurs; pagans are the ones excluded from the army and only Christians may serve.[22]

Pacifism has never really disappeared from the Christian tradition. It appeared in the twelfth century with the Cathari, in the thirteenth century with the Franciscan Tertiaries and the Waldensians, in the fifteenth century with the Hussites, who had two branches, one pacifist, one crusading.[23] It also dominated several medieval sects during the sixteenth and seventeenth centuries: the Anabaptists (now the Mennonites and Hutterites), the Quakers, and the Brethren, all known as 'historic peace churches.' The twentieth century has witnessed a resurgence of interest in pacifism. The American pacifist churches have long been outspoken in their criticism of war; however, as L. Bruce van Voorst notes in his article, "The Churches and Nuclear Deterrence," they have met with little success.[24] The motivation for the pacifist position is well stated by van Voorst in his commentary on the Society of Friends' statement made in 1948, claiming that no plea of necessity or policy, however urgent or peculiar, can avail to release either individuals or nations from the paramount allegiance they owe to Him who said, 'Love your enemies.'"[25] The Church of the Brethren, another pacifist church, has stated more bluntly, "[A]ll war is sin."[26]

Stanley Hauerwas points out that the pacifist tradition, like the just war tradition, takes many different forms, as has been mentioned. The notion of "peace" that Hauerwas says characterizes Christian pacifism is eschatological; and does not assume that this peace will ever be achieved in history. Rather, as John Howard Yoder suggests, he describes peace as a hope or an ideal according to which Christians model their actions. Christian nonresistance, then, is a form of discipleship to Jesus; it is a form of acting and suffering as Jesus suffered unresisting on the cross.[27]

Not all Christians reach the pacifist conclusion. Some reason instead that love of neighbor sometimes demands defense even by armed force, or that injustice can sometimes only be countered by the use of armed force. Nevertheless, pacifism continues to emerge even among contemporary mainstream Christian churches. This is evident, for example, in the recent U.S. Catholic Bishops' Pastoral, which speaks of "two distinct moral responses" to unjust aggression: pacifism and engaging in just war. Though both are options the Bishops believe to be open to individuals, they nevertheless insist that *governments*, in contrast to individuals, must sometimes defend their people against armed, unjust aggression by the use of armed force if all else fails.[28]

The fact that the U.S. Bishops speak only of just wars of *defense* harks back to Johnson's observation that the nature of "just cause" has gone through significant change since the Middle Ages. Johnson claims that as the Roman Catholic Church in the nineteenth and early twentieth centuries became more involved in the social and political concerns of international society, it abandoned its traditional stance on just cause and joined its Protestant brethren in identifying just cause with whatever positive international law recognizes as just cause. Johnson maintains this position actually reaches its climax in the nineteenth century, when just cause became *competence de guerre*, i.e., it is the sovereign right of every state to determine when it might engage in war.[29]

At the root of this change in just war tradition is another Christian attitude toward a particular type of war: the crusade or "holy war." In order better to understand contemporary just war theories, then, it is necessary to consider the crusade in its relation to the just war tradition.

The Crusade

Roland Bainton describes the crusade as differing from the just war "primarily in its intensely religious quality." The crusade went beyond the "holy wars" of Moses' day, in which God Himself was considered the leader who would deliver the enemy into His people's hands. The crusade, on the other hand, "was fought not so much with God's help as on God's behalf, not for a human goal which God might bless but for a divine cause which God might command."[30]

The true crusade, then, did not take place before the period of the Maccabees, as Bainton claims, for it was not until the establishment of a monarchy that war could be waged under the auspices of the ruler. This crusading ideal survived in the Christian church, not only in the famous crusading expeditions to the Holy Land but also, according to Bainton, in the inspiration they provided to the Reformed Churches, to Zwinglianism, Calvinism and especially to the Puritan Revolution in England in the seventeenth century.

Bainton claims that the Puritans were "loath to exceed the traditional ethics of the just war," not wanting to disrupt the British constitution or to introduce general chaos. However, Oliver Cromwell, according to Bainton, grew impatient with the quest for the authority of a prince as a guarantee for the justice of the cause. If the cause were holy, then it did not matter who said what to the contrary:

Bainton then offers four characteristics of the crusading idea: "that the cause shall be holy (and no cause is more holy than religion), that the war be fought under God and with his help, that the crusaders shall be godly and their enemies ungodly, and that the war shall be prosecuted unsparingly.[31] This last provision, especially, opens up the possibilities for great atrocities to be committed by crusaders so that *jus in bello* is eclipsed by the overwhelming importance of the "holiness" of the cause.

Both James Johnson and LeRoy Walters take exception to Bainton's "pacifism-just war-crusade" typology. Johnson calls it a "misleading conceptual tool" for understanding just war doctrine as it developed in the West. Instead, Johnson tries to show that the crusaders actually considered themselves as acting in the just war tradition--especially the Puritans who, Johnson claims, directly derive their thought on war from "Classic Just War Doctrine." It is precisely the crusade-just war conjunction during the Post-Reformation period which marks a crucial point in the development of just war doctrine for Johnson. Walters also claims that the "parallelism of political and religious was reasserted . . . in post-Reformation Protestant ethical thought," and that "the general tendency of the just-war tradition was toward a single, universalizable standard for military conduct."[32]

The Just War Tradition

Walters' and Johnson's claim is important to consider because the religious or "holy cause" behind the crusading ideal is analagous to the "ideological cause" that characterizes the bipolarity at the root of so many conflicts today. Appeals made to a particular ideology seem in the minds of many to justify overriding all *jus in bello* restraints and result in as much unprecedented suffering, death and damage as technological development permits. What contemporary just war theorists are seeking are the principles that will limit the conduct of war to prevent such atrocities and to preserve justice. In the analysis of the *jus in bello* principles of discrimination and proportionality which follows in the ensuing chapters, more attention will be given to the particular details of the just war tradition. For now, however, it may prove useful to consider some of the history of this tradition. One may be helped in this backward glance by using Johnson's schema of tracing modern just war doctrine back to its sources.

Just war theories have formed part of the Christian tradition from the time of Augustine in the fourth century. Aquinas articulated his particular theory in the thirteenth century. His position, and that of the scholastics who further developed it, are often summed up as laying down the following six conditions: (1) the decision to go to war must be made by a duly constituted authority; (2) the intention must be a good one; (3) the use of force must be proportionate to the aims of war; (4) force must be used in a discriminate fashion; (5) the expected result must be better than if no force were used; and (6) all other means to resolve the dispute must have been tried and failed.[33]

The general position of any just war theory has always been an abhorrence of the use of force; the conditions are not permissive, but point out limitations; they are also jointly necessary and sufficient. They were first articulated during a period when no one could foresee how weapons would develop in the next few centuries. Weapons of mass destruction did not exist; the question of whether the right to possess and have a declaratory policy on their use was not addressed. These are questions that remain to be posed by contemporary just war theorists before they can determine whether the just war tradition is still applicable to problems of war in the nuclear age.

Johnson identifies two medieval sources of modern just war doctrine: church doctrine, largely concerned with *jus ad bellum*, as Aquinas' writings are; and secular doctrine, which focuses on *jus in bello*. The religious base is composed of the writings of Aquinas and the scholastics, and the canon lawyers. The secular base is made up of the chivalric code and the *jus gentium*, or agreements between peoples which had been made up until that time. Both the religious and secular bases are "ideological" in the neutral sense, as Johnson defines it, of referring to belief structures that are discretely based and different from one another, and no value judgment as to their contents is implied.[34] These two sources, the religious and the secular, are brought together to form the "Classic Just War Doctrine" at the end of the Middle Ages. Together they offer, according to Johnson, "the best possible expression for the case of war, of the synthesis of many factors that forms the ideology of medieval Christendom."[35]

Johnson deliberately calls the just war doctrine an ideology of Christendom and not of Christianity because it pervades not that Christianity which extends throughout the world, but the geographical entity within the boundaries of Europe where Christendom was an ideological unity. Just war doctrine emerged from the community as a whole and not simply from Christian theology. He concludes that within that community the developing just war doctrine did effectively limit conflicts.

The unity which once characterized Christendom was broken first by the destruction of theological unity through the Catholic/Protestant break. With this break comes the rending of the idea of just cause: for one group it became the holy cause of the crusader, but among others, there was an attempt to secularize the *jus ad bellum,* to find a more inclusive concept of justice. As the split in the European community took hold, the naturalist-international lawyers began conceiving *jus ad bellum* as *competence de guerre.*

A second stage in the destruction of classic just war doctrine was reached when international exchange took place not only in Europe but also in countries beyond its geographical limits. Johnson notes especially the colonial era as a time when this occurred. Nations began relating to each other according to a "law of reciprocity," writes Johnson, with each believing it received as much as it was given. What emerged concerning the right to resort to war were the treaties and alliances which outlawed all first use of force while allowing second use only for purposes of defense. In so doing, the nations avoided the pitfalls of ideology. However, as the notion of justice is a peculiarly ideological component of the classic just war doctrine of Christendom, whether the emerging doctrine will provide for a truly *just* war is questionable.

According to Johnson, then, the just war doctrine that finally emerged at the end of the Middle Ages excluded all wars of religion. *Jus ad bellum* was deemphasized and *jus in bello* given new emphasis. This last consequence could have resulted from reflection on the unbridled cruelty and destruction of religious wars which revealed the violation of more basic moral principles. These violations have been excused and even encouraged by the former crusader mentality. The "modern just war doctrine" which emerges admits the possibility of justice on both sides. Theorists like Hugo Grotius began basing their just war theories entirely on nature and on the agreements between human beings (the *jus gentium*), and their theories are therefore seen as universal and nonideological.

Johnson also notes that the just war doctrine of Protestant Christianity (except for the pacifist churches) has taken on the identity of the "wholly man-derived" doctrine, i.e.,, of international law just war doctrine; Roman Catholic just war doctrine has remained more closely joined to the classic just war doctrine that emerged from the synthesis of scholastic theology and canon law, on the one hand and the chivalric code *jus gentium*, on the other. This remained true until the late nineteenth and early twentieth centuries when the Roman Catholic Church, too, began to identify its just war doctrine with international law just war doctrine. Johnson believes the Church has weakened its own war doctrine through this conformity.[36] The weakening seems to be in the area of *jus ad bellum* and just cause. This is an area as yet inadequately addressed by the Churches. In the area of *jus in bello*, however, the Churches appear to be reemerging as a powerful influence in secular decision making on matters of war and peace. The Churches are once again expressing themselves with increasing urgency to the moral questions of war and peace in the nuclear age. It is to these expressions that attention must now be given.

Nuclear War, Deterrence and the Churches

The Jewish Community

The official Jewish community has published few statements on the issue of nuclear weapons, although certain individuals have been outspoken: Albert Einstein and Hannah Arendt, to name just two. This situation is changing. Donald Davidson points out that the position taken by American Jews in support of Israel and their reaction to the Beirut massacre suggests they subscribe to a just war position. Davidson singles out several resolutions supporting the SALT treaties and a ban on nuclear testing, as well as various statements made by the Union of American Hebrew Congregations, the Union of Orthodox Jewish Congregations of America and others. In summary he finds the Jewish bodies "reluctant to criticize defense policies, including nuclear weapons policies;" however, in *official* statements, Davidson concludes that "Jewish bodies have taken a firm, though somewhat general, position against nuclear war and the continuing arms race."[37]

L. Bruce Van Voorst offers two reasons for the lack of a strong pacifist tradition among Jews. These have to do, first, with the ambivalence in the Hebrew Scriptures: Micah 4:1-4, for example, speaks of turning swords into plowshares, while Joel 3:9-11 urges turning plowshares to swords. In addition, Deuteronomy 20 has been called a "manual of war." A second factor affecting Jewish attitudes toward war and peace concerns the establishment in modern times of the Jewish state of Israel. Israel's security, van Voorst suggests, is a cause of major concern among all Jews, and may be one reason why some have identified Jewish thought with a certain kind of "militarism." The endorsements of SALT, START, of the nuclear freeze movements and other such actions have indicated, however, that the Jewish position is not static.

Currently, movements are underway to explore the significance of the threat of war in the nuclear age for Jewish law, and manuals are being distributed to synagogues by the UAHC to guide participation in debates. These movements are relatively new, however, and so it is to the Christian churches that one must turn to examine more closely the state of the current debate on nuclear war and deterrence.

The Protestant Churches

The Protestant churches began to speak out on nuclear war long before the Roman Catholic Church. However, certain leaders in the Roman Catholic Church, beginning with Pope Pius XII, have been addressing nuclear issues ever since their use in World War II. Of the larger Protestant denominations affiliated with the National Council of Churches, Davidson finds much similarity in their position, literature and even in their language. In general, they retain the "language and logic of just war theory," but Davidson notes, "the Protestant churches have not always done their work well." He cites "elements of a religious crusade," "slogans and motive imagery" substituted for facts in many of their statements, and an emphasis on the effects of nuclear weapons rather than on relations and problems of international negotiations.[39]

Paul Ramsey also cites the Calhoun Commission report, *Atomic Warfare and the Christian Faith* (Federal Council of Churches, March 1946) in his own book, *War and the Christian Conscience*. He finds the report in fundamental agreement with Jesuit John Ford's article, "On the Morality of Obliteration Bombing."[40] Ford's article emphasized the principle of discrimination, one of the key *jus in bello* principles to which nearly all the churches begin to appeal when they join the debate on the atomic bombings of 1945 and on the massive conventional bombings of World Wars I and II. Such indiscriminate bombing looked as though it would characterize the conduct of all contemporary warfare. Ramsey claims that the Calhoun Report, "[t]hough not an official pronouncement of the Federal Council, comes ... closer to being an expression of top-level ecclesiastical opinion in the churches ... than was the place accorded by the Roman church to expressions of opinion like Ford's during wartime."[41]

The immunity of noncombatants from direct attack was also a focus of the Dun Commission Report in 1950: "The destruction of life clearly incidental to the destruction of decisive military objectives ... is radically different from mass destruction, which is aimed primarily at the lives of civilians, their morale, or the sources of their livelihood."[42]

Ramsey and Davidson are in apparent agreement regarding the lack of force and clarity of the early Protestant statements, for Ramsey calls the Dun Report "very confused and confusing throughout," especially through its imprecision in the use of terms. Ramsey submits the Commission's use of the term "noncombatant" to particularly severe criticism. The Dun Report seems to make noncombatancy status applicable only to those totally uninvolved with their nation's public life, i.e., noncombatants are those who "stand outside." In addition, the report speaks of all contemporary war as "total war," which is taken to mean a casting aside of all moral restraints. As Ramsey views the report, the only limitations incumbent on belligerents, according to such definitions, would be the requirements of proportionality. Ramsey concludes: "Unfortunately, it may be true that apologists for the just-war doctrine today, especially in Protestant circles, have formulated their position too exclusively in terms of prudence."[43]

Despite its limitations, however, the Dun Report did speak out on the issue of noncombatant immunity at a time when the official Roman Church, as John Courtney Murray said, "failed to make the tradition relevant."[44]

The United Methodist Bishops' pastoral, *In Defense of Creation: The Nuclear Crisis and a Just Peace: Foundation Document* was the object of the same type of criticism by Ramsey as well as by Stanley Hauerwas of the pacifist tradition. While both remained loyal members of their church, they called it the "occasion for deep disappointment" becuase of theological, ethical and political inadequacy. Ramsey believed the bishops' writers did insufficient work in unearthing the foundations for their argument and in its doctrine of "Last things/Ultimate Things," that is, its eschatology. Ramsey accused the writers of "leveling" heaven and earth so that the "not yet" of Christ's peace appears to be a possible "already" in some historical time. Instead, Ramsey insisted, "There is an *aeonic* discontinuity between the old and the new creation, which the Methodist Bishops have leveled to a linear worldview." Hauerwas agreed with most of what Ramsey had to say about the document, and added his doubts that the Methodist church is "ready to speak to the world about war," having urged the Bishops prior to the pastoral's completion, to challenge the Methodist people about basic Christian convictions rather than addressing other Christians and non-Christians.[45]

The issue of disarmament has continued to absorb the attention of the World Council of Churches (WCC) since the dawn of the atomic age. At its February 1946 meeting, the Provisional Committee of the WCC stated that "Man's triumph in the release of atomic energy threatens his destruction. Unless men's whole outlook is changed, our civilization will perish."[46]

In its five different Assembly Periods since 1948, the WCC has called at various times for multilateral reductions of conventional and nuclear arms, for the development of internationally accepted methods for peaceful settlement of disputes and change in order to rectify existing injustices, for the signing of the Limited Test Ban Treaty, and for the prohibition of all weapons of mass destruction.[53] In November 1981, the WCC Sub-Unit on Church and Society and the Commission of the Churches on International Affairs (CCIA) jointly organized the International Public Hearing on Nuclear Weapons and Disarmament, drawing particular attention to the following: "We believe that the time has come when the churches must unequivocally declare that the production, deployment and use of nuclear weapons is a crime against humanity and that such activities must be condemned on ethical and theological grounds."[47]

Most major Protestant denominations have now issued declarations condemning nuclear war (except for some of the fundamentalist sects). The Southern Baptists have shown a desire to balance concern for the nuclear debate with a reaffirmation of support for defense; the American Baptist Churches have passed a resolution calling nuclear weapons "a direct affront to our Christian beliefs and commitments;" The American Lutheran Church and the Lutheran Church of America have passed resolutions urging elimination of all nuclear weapons; the United Presbyterian Church General Assembly has backed the nuclear freeze and the policy of no first use.[48]

Anglican and Episcopal Denominations

As previously noted, the Christian churches other than the Roman Catholic Church largely identify their just war doctrine with that of international law. This is also evident in the Anglican Primates' Statement of 1981 in which the bishops identify with the final document of the 1978 United Nations General Assembly Special Session on Disarmament. This document and, therefore, the Anglican Primates' position, calls for a comprehensive nuclear test ban, a halt to conventional arms procurement and trade; the development of an alternative system of security to the accumulation of weaponry, and the mobilization of public opinion to counteract the armament race.[49]

In 1982 the Joint Commission on Peace, charged by the 66th General Convention of the American Episcopal Church, issued its report, "To Make Peace." The commision had been asked to present to the 67th General Convention, "a comprehensive program for implementing the 1968 House of Bishops' Pastoral Letter as it pertains to peace and war." The document stresses the role of peacemaking while rejecting a commitment to absolute pacifism. As with most of the other statements of the Protestant churches, its tone is more hortatory than doctrinal in character, urging Christians to engage actively in peacemaking efforts. It speaks of Christians' "dual citizenship," reminiscent of Augustine's "two cities," the City of God and the City of Man, and it emphasizes the need to face the real possibility of all-out nuclear war while pointing out the need to provide effectively for national security.[50]

In reaffirming the right of nations to provide for national security, the report admits a strategy of nuclear deterrence as "a necessary evil for the short term," and condemns the MAD policy and the intentional and indiscriminate destruction of population centers. Its task, however, as the Commission admits, remains unfinished and it recommends a three-year collaboration period with other groups to develop "greater awareness of the centrality of Christian peacemaking in their specific missions and responsibilities."[51]

The acceptance of nuclear deterrence as a "necessary evil" is presented largely without argument in this document, giving credence to van Voorst's criticism of the non-Roman churches in general: that is his contention that despite the statements made by conventional Protestant churches on nuclear war and deterrence, they have done "almost no wrestling with the ambiguities of deterrence or the justified use of nuclear weapons."[52] Ramsey, too, speaks of the modern Protestant movement to "renounce" war altogether as a tension pulling against the right they also admit as valid--the right to wage a just and limited war under certain circumstances. Ramsey states that Protestants (and it would seem Anglicans/Episcopalians as well) are in "substantial agreement" with traditional Catholic theory of just war on the "matter of limitation of war in principle by the immunity of noncombatants from direct attack." "The case is simply not argued as formally and as rigorously; and this may mean some loss in substantive understanding."[53]

Van Voorst concludes similarly that in contrast with Roman Catholic statements, the statements of the other churches reflect more divergence of opinion and weaker moral authority. He finds the Protestant statements are "earlier and occasionally even more sweeping, but at the same time--and with few exceptions--superficial and inadequately defined doctrinally,"[54] lacking especially an extended application of just war doctrine regarding the principles of proportionality and discrimination.

It will be extremely useful, then, to examine recent Roman Catholic statements on nuclear war and deterrence. Only a brief examination of them will be offered here, however, for, since these statements contain more detailed and nuanced moral arguments than their counterparts from the other churches, they will play a more active role in the current general moral debate on contemporary just war theory which absorbs most of the remainder of this study.

The Roman Catholic Church

As noted by James Johnson, the Roman Catholic Church has been for centuries the guardian of the classic just war tradition. The Roman Church began noticeably to curtail the right to resort to war during the nineteenth century, as Johnson sees it, and this largely because of the question as to whether "modern war" would be so intrinsically out of proportion to resultant evils as never to be justifiable. The First Vatican Council (1870) declared in fact that under conditions of large conventional forces, no *jus ad bellum* can exist. If evil effects outweigh the good, the fact that justice might sometimes *require* war, whether offensive or defensive, became a secondary considera-tion.[55] This position has sometimes helped preserve an unjust status quo, for as Johnson observes, "[resting] *jus ad bellum* so heavily on observance of the *jus in bello* would ... give the advantage to stronger forces generally and in particular to the forces of established order as over against revolutionaries, thus tending to support the status quo."[56]

In the nuclear age, the tension between an unjust situation and the judgment that nondefensive war is disproportionate suggests the need to move toward greater flexibility in finding other means of righting injustice than the use of military force and in moving toward limited wars without escalation when all efforts for nonmilitary solutions are exhausted.

Since World War II, there has been another noticeable shift in the Roman Catholic position and this can be traced through the statements of the popes, the Second Vatican Council, and the recent pastoral statements of the Roman Catholic hierarchy in various parts of the world.

Pius XII was the first pontiff who had to assess the meaning of nuclear weapons in the context of the just war theory. Throughout his pontificate, he continued to use just war theory as it has been articulated from the time of Augustine. However, his response to nuclear weapons contained three dominant characteristics, as identified by J. Bryan Hehir. These characteristics point toward a change in the church's direction. First, Pius XII emphasized the need for an international authority. The international system which had served until the 1940's had been powerless to prevent two world wars. Second, the pontiff attempted to incorporate nuclear weapons into the just war framework; he did not rule out their use and he assessed their moral significance in terms of the principle of proportionality: If their effects cannot be contained, they may not be used. Pius set limits to the use of some nuclear weapons, but left open the debate about the morality of limited nuclear war. Third, he ruled out a theoretical basis for a Catholic pacifist position and refused to provide moral justification for Catholic support of conscientious objection.

John XXIII's *Pacem in Terris* reveals a change in tone and theme. John recognized that nuclear weapons present Catholic theology with a new moral problem. The destructive capability and the more general conflict to which even the limited use of nuclear weapons may lead challenge the underlying premises of the just war tradition: i.e., that the limited use of force can be a legitimate extension of politics. "It is irrational to think that war is a proper way to obtain justice for violated rights." John accordingly called for the banning of nuclear weapons, for equal and simultaneous arms reduction, and for displacement of nuclear balance as the basis for peace.

Vatican II's *Pastoral Constitution on the Church in the Modern World* became the controlling text in Catholic moral theology on war and peace. The Constitution makes the following points: (1) The work of peace is tied to the establishment of justice within and among nations; (2) A new attitude and the responsibility of personal conscience regarding warfare is stressed; (3) Justification is given for a non-violent posture and for conscientious objection (although military service is recognized as a contributor to peace); for the first time, however, both the just war position and the option of Christian pacifism are recognized as acceptable alternatives for individuals.

(4) The just war position is reaffirmed allowing the right of states to legitimate defense and thereby leaving open the moral argument as to what constitutes an act of legitimate defense. (5) The right to use force is circumscribed; the Council reaffirms papal condemnations of total war and attacks on civilian populations. (6) No final judgment on deterrence is given; the moral dilemma posed by deterrence involves the *threat* to use nuclear weapons in order to *prevent* their use, but the declared *intention* to strike civilian centers is itself recognized as immoral.[57]

Paul VI issued no moral teaching document despite his well-known United Nations address of 1965: "No more war, war never again." He recognized a limited but real right of defense in a decentralized international system.

John Paul II reveals three themes in his teaching regarding nuclear war as noted by J. Bryan Hehir: (1) he acknowledges the right and duty of a nation to defend its "existence and freedom by proportionate means against an unjust aggressor," though this is severely limited because of the nature of modern warfare; (2) he endorses nonviolent solutions to problems; (3) his argument is cast in terms of the relationship between technology, ethics, and politics: the nuclear arms race is the most visible evidence of a larger issue, i.e., that modern technology can move beyond moral and political guidance submitting the human person to an impersonal power; and that there is therefore the need to reestabish the primacy of ethics and politics over technology. Thus, scientists, educators and religious leaders effect an atmosphere of choice by shaping the categories for choosing. Choosing effective action concerning the arms race would ultimately be carried out in the political arena.

The moral position on the possession and use of nuclear arms continues to evolve in the American Catholic Church as well as in the church at large. Many who once thought nuclear war between the two superpowers to be inevitable think so no longer, and some claim that one of the most important factors leading to this change was the statement of John Cardinal Krol when, as President of the U.S. Catholic Bishops Conference, he addressed the U.S. Senate Foreign Relations Committee in 1979 in support of SALT II. Within the context of the just war tradition, Cardinal Krol stated (1) that it is immoral to use strategic nuclear weapons under any circumstance even in self-defense; (2) that it is immoral to make explicit threats to use them; (3) in what Francis X. Winters calls one of the most incisive moral statements made until that time in the nuclear debate, possession of nuclear weapons is "morally neutral: as long as there is any hope of arms reduction and eventual elimination. Krol stated that 'Catholic moral reasoning is willing, while negotiations proceed, to tolerate the possession of nuclear weapons for deterrence as the lesser of two evils.'"[58]

This position is apparently either so startling or so misunderstood that many Catholics did not even learn of it until a year later. Yet the bishops arrived at their position beginning from the same point where they started on the right-to-life issue: the fragility of life and the need to shelter it. This position has not led to absolute pacifism, however. Self-defense remains a recognized right, but not an absolute right. It is qualified by the right of noncombatants not to be targeted and the right of people in the nations involved to believe that their leaders have determined that there is "reasonable hope of success" if war is waged.

In 1982 and 1983, Roman Catholic bishops throughout the world have issued pastoral letters on the topic of nuclear war. These included letters from the bishops of France, Germany, Holland, Belgium, Ireland, East Germany and Japan, as well as the United States. Geography has often played a role in the conclusions of various bishops when they address questions posed by nuclear weapons. Francis X. Winters points up one area of complexity the European bishops have had to face which the American bishops did not: the question of whether it is right for a country to abandon the nuclear deterrent while allowing nuclear weapons from other countries to be placed on its own territory.[59] The U.S. bishops, on the other hand, face nuclear questions from the vantage point of a superpower whose nuclear deterrent "umbrella" affects not only itself but the defense of the Western world.

In addition, Winters notes that there is a sharp divide betweeen statements made by bishops on the European Continent and those made by the English-speaking nations, i.e., those of Anglo-Saxon social and political culture. In general, he finds that the Continental bishops seem much more cautious in assessing the moral acceptability of deterrence. He attributes this to their geographical proximity to the Warsaw Pact nations and to the greater flexibility the U.S. and U.K. have with the capability to deploy both conventional and nuclear forces. France, for example, depends exclusively on its nuclear forces while West Germany has no nuclear forces but relies on those of the U.S. Winters points out that those on the Continent also tend to give greater deference to political authority.[59]

All the pastorals, regardless of origin, seem to overlap, according to Richard McCormick's comparative analysis, in placing the notion of a just defense within a "dominant imperative of peace, in accepting the legitimacy of just national self-defense, in being inspired by a condemnation of indiscriminate destruction and in John Paul II's conditioned acceptance of deterrence."[60] The most complex question the bishops face, and consequently the one on which one finds various shades of differences is the question of deterrence.

The German pastoral, "Out of Justice, Peace," accepts the papal judgment that deterrence can be judged morally acceptable at the present time. The German bishops, and those of Ireland and Belgium as well appeal to the same principle in reaching this conclusion: namely, choosing the lesser of two evils.[61] McCormick believes this approach evades the question of the conditioned intention to use nuclear weapons, for the evils include a morally evil intention and not merely two nonmoral evils. The Irish bishops stipulate three conditions: 1) that there be no intention to use the weapons against cities or population centers; 2) that the underlying philosophy not require superiority or equality but only deterrence; 3) that substantive efforts be made toward disarmament.[62] Threats, then, must be restricted to morally legitimate use. Like the Germans, the Irish consider the probablity of escalation ambiguous, and it is with this ambiguity that McCormick seems to think the moral problem lies. The ambiguity leaves one with "a small opening for the tolerance of a nuclear deterrent without that tolerance referring to one's own readiness (intention) to perform immoral action."[63]

The French pastoral distinguishes threat from actual use and adopts something like a "bluff" deterrent, a deterrent many judge to be neither credible nor moral. Unlike the French pastoral, which concentrates on the countercity threat, the American pastoral, as McCormick points out, recognizes the recent evolution in strategy and in nuclear technology, especially the movement from countercity to counterforce threat and the danger of preemptive or protective strikes presented by the presence of vulnerable nuclear forces.

The U.S. bishops' pastoral is perhaps the most complex of all those issued to date. McCormick calls it "more nuanced than any other official statement since World War II." The U.S. bishops accept a strictly conditioned deterrent based on the judgment that there may be some limited use of nuclear weapons that may be judged moral.[64] The "strictly conditioned deterrent" has been subjected to much recent criticism by moral theorists. John Langan, S.J. says that, at least in its first draft, the pastoral lacks a "morally satisfactory account of deterrence."[65] Charles Curran criticizes the bishops' final position as tolerating an "immoral (conditional) intent to perform moral evil." McCormick claims the pastoral offers no satisfactory justification for its position and is therefore subject to further ethical investigation.[66] Kenneth Himes, O.F.M. rejects the bishops' conditioned acceptance of deterrence, finding Bryan Hehir's "centimeter of ambiguity" unpersuasive. Mere possession, Himes says, still has "inbuilt intent" in the system. Because of the dangers of escalation, he rejects as unrealistic the notion that there may be some legitimate use of nuclear weapons. Himes discounts points made by Michael Novak and David Hollenbach on the difference between the intention to use and the intention to deter, calling the latter an immoral bluff.[67] Trying to justify deterrence is for Himes the "'significant flaw'" in the American bishops' statement, yet as McCormick notes, Himes does not offer unilateral disarmament as a solution.[68] He judges the policy to be morally wrong, but says it would be another matter to ask how one must act to reverse it.

William O'Brien finds the U.S. bishops' pastoral deficient in two main respects: (1) it fails to explain just cause adequately; (2) it accepts a "nominalist" concept of deterrence, i.e., an abstract concept which fails to take real world conditions into account. Regarding just cause, O'Brien particularly laments the lack of attention given to the nature of the Soviet threat, the character of the Soviet regime and the probable limits of reliable arms contral arrangements with the Soviets. O'Brien himself, as will be seen, argues for a "deterrence-plus" or a "deterrence/just-defense" posture: "a posture sufficient to deter based on credible capability and will to fight a nuclear war if deterrence failed," and he argues that this posture "must be reconciled with the constraints of just war doctrine."[69]

The American pastoral points up the various live issues still being debated among moral theorists. McCormick highlights the developing consensus that any use of nuclear weapons is morally unacceptable because of the almost unavoidable danger of escalation. If this is correct, appeal to the "lesser evil" principle cannot be sustained since one would have to tolerate *one's own* intention to do something immoral, and, as McCormick states bluntly, "The principle never meant that."[70]

O'Brien considers the U.S. bishops' pastoral, then, as a "starting point for the recent debate" on nuclear war and deterrence.[71] Returning once more to Johnson's schema, the pastoral assumes the most recent position in a long lineage that is the just war tradition. Where that tradition moves in the future will be determined in part by the questions this pastoral raises. The questioning and debate which the pastoral encourages will continue to push that living tradition to new limits. The focus of the present study will be to see whether three of the most outspoken contemporary theorists within that tradition move that debate forward by their own questioning and critique of what has gone before.

Three Contemporary Just War Theorists

The nuclear age presents a greater test of the application and adequacy of the just war tradition than has any previous age. The tradition is not only the province of the Churches, as has been seen, but it is also the work of academic moral theorists. The focus of this study now turns to three of the just war tradition's main contemporary academic proponents: Michael Walzer, Paul Ramsey and William V. O'Brien.

All three theorists have been or are presently engaged in univeristy teaching, and all have published widely on the topic of war, conventional and nuclear. Michael Walzer is a researcher at the Institute for Advanced Studies at Princeton University and a former professor of government at Harvard University. His major book on war, *Just and Unjust Wars* (1977), is an outgrowth of his involvement in the American antiwar movement during the late 1960s and early 1970s, during which time he carefully detailed the moral arguments of critics and defenders of the Vietnam War.

Paul Ramsey joined the faculty of Princeton University in 1944 and he remained as Harrington Spear Paine professor of religion until his retirement in 1983. His two chief books on war are *War and the Christian Conscience* (1961), and *The Just War* (1968). Prior to his death in 1988, Ramsey completed his last book on the topic of war, *Speak Up for Just War or Pacifism*. Of all Protestant theologians, Professor Ramsey is often cited as having the most carefully worked out position on just war. In addition to his writings on war and political ethics, he has written extensively in the field of medical ethics, from which he draws parallels to questions of nuclear war and deterrence.

William O'Brien is professor of government at Georgetown University. He has written more extensively on the particular problem of *nuclear* war than either of the other two theorists. His principal works in this area are *Nuclear War, Deterrence and Morality* (1967), *War and/or Survival* (1969), and *The Conduct of Just and Limited War* (1981). In addition to these, Professor O'Brien has written numerous articles in which he has interpreted Roman Catholic just war theory. His recent articles form a critique of the U.S. bishops' pastoral.

These three theorists approach questions on the morality of nuclear war and deterrence questions primarily from the disciplines of political theory, theology, and international law, respectively, and reflect the theoretical foundations upon which others in their fields structure their moral arguments on these same issues. In addition, the three are influenced by their Jewish, Protestant and Roman Catholic religious traditions. Thus they represent the major groups involved in the current nuclear debate. The chapters that follow focus on their arguments in order to determine how successfully their just war theories apply to the dilemmas raised by nuclear weapons.

Since the emphasis in contemporary just war theories is on *jus in bello* considerations, the two principles emphasized by twentieth century theorists may be expected to dominate the analysis of the theories of the three men. Therefore, chapters 2 and 3 are devoted to each of these principles in turn, giving first, a history of the principle and the role it has played in the just war tradition, and second, an analysis of the role it continues to play in each of the current theorists respectively. The possible uses of nuclear weapons have also highlighted the moral dilemmas involved in nuclear deterrence policy. Therefore, a separate chapter is devoted to the topic of use and deterrence, again with an analysis of the three respective theorists.

The final chapter focuses on the adequacy of the three positions to provide guidelines for nuclear war and deterrence as well as the consideration of a different perspective on the relevance of the just war tradition to the nuclear age. The analysis of these perspectives reveal an enlightened and yet practical direction for the just war tradition to take as the world prepares to enter the twenty-first century.

Chapter 2

The Principle of Proportionality
in Classic and Contemporary Just War Theories

Introduction

A comparison of the classic just war theorists' application of the principle of proportionality with contemporary just war theorists' application of the same principle reveals two major changes that have occurred. The first is a change of emphasis: more attention is being paid in contemporary thought to the use of proportionality in the *jus in bello* doctrine than to its use in the *jus ad bellum* doctrine, the primary emphasis of the classic just war theorists. The second change indicates a more substantive difference: in classic just war theories, the principle is applied only to so-called "nonmoral" evil consequences; in some contemporary just war theories, the range of nonmoral or "premoral" evils has been extended so that the principle of proportionality covers a wider range of consequences. Part of the reason for the second change may be the result of developments in weapons technology. Nuclear age theorists must ask to what extent morality has become a *function* of technological development and find answers to show how morality can continue to serve as a *guide* to such development instead.

In order to understand the significance of the changes between classic and contemporary thought, it will be helpful first to examine briefly the principle of proportionality as it is treated by several classic just war theorists, and then to analyze in more detail the contemporary positions of Ramsey, O'Brien, and Walzer on the principle of proportionality.

Classic Just War Theories and the Principle of Proportionality

In choosing the theorists who best represent the classic period, one may be guided by LeRoy Walters' choice of Aquinas (thirteenth century), Vitoria,

Suarez, Gentili and Grotius (all of the sixteenth and seventeenth centuries). The historians of the Roman Catholic tradition and historians of international law rank these as among the most "representative, creative, and influential just war theorists" and consider their theories to be "classic."[1] Since the classic just war theorists are not the focus of the present study, concern with them is limited to those areas where comparisons with contemporary theorists are most likely to be found. The first such area is their *jus ad bellum* doctrines.

The Role of Proportionality in Jus ad Bellum

Aquinas does not emphasize proportionality in his treatment of war, though he does emphasize it in his treatment of self-defense. In justifying self-defense, Aquinas appeals to the doctrine of double effect, and states, "[I]t is lawful to repel force by force provided one does not exceed the limits of a blameless defense."[2] Aquinas' reliance on proportionality is apparent in his later treatment of just cause for war when he states that a cause must be sufficiently grave to merit punishment especially in the form of lethal force. Aquinas insists that the common good may not be sought by *any* means; certain means such as lying, breaking promises, killing innocent persons are absolute prohibitions.[3]

The other four theorists take "two distinct but parallel standpoints," according to Walters. First, they apply the principle of proportionality to *jus ad bellum* in order to establish a "minimum limit" that determines whether the cause is indeed just: i.e., not trivial, but grave or weighty. Second, they apply the principle to the anticipatory comparison of the harm that would result from resisting the aggressor and the harm that would result from not resisting. Closely related to this second use of proportionality is "reasonable hope of success:" the theorists hold that justice suffers if a just war is lost. In this case, the evil effects would outweigh the good effects, and this would be considered disproportionate. It would be better not to go to war if it cannot be won. Grotius requires that even in defensive wars, the avenging side ought to be "much more powerful than the other party," while Suarez denies that proportionality applies to defensive wars at all since these are a matter of necessity, not choice.[4]

Range of Applicability

The theorists' "second standpoint," the application of the principle of proportionality to anticipatory harmful effects and good effects, begins to fill out the "content" of the principle of proportionality in classic just war theories. Proportionality is concerned with the calculus of both quantitative and qualitative effects. Grotius' "rules" to aid his calculus reveal this more clearly:

1. the essential goodness of two actions must be compared.
2. the goodness of the effects of two actions must be compared.
3. all four factors must then be related so that the higher proportion of good over evil always takes precedence.[5]

Walters' analysis of the classic just war theorists shows that they conceive of justice as being promoted if the side with the just cause wins, and frustrated if it does not. This immediately involves them in a "means-end" problem. Thus the strictly moral concern for promoting justice was considered to be contingent upon the utilitarian question of military success. In view of this fundamentally teleological orientation, it is not surprising that the four later theorists answered in unison: "Yes, in a war fought for a just cause, the end (promoting justice) does justify the use of all necessary military means.[6]

According to James Johnson, Vitoria's position is complex, since he allows for "simultaneous ostensible justice"; that is, that both sides may be fighting a just war--at least subjectively just. For example, one nation might be ignorant of its injustice while the other side is actually just and vice versa. On the other hand, there may be a case where both sides are equally just, as in the case where both sides have an equal right to property. The concern Vitoria voices over excessive injury or destruction seems to follow from the possibility of the belligerents being invincibly ignorant: "the one of the injustice of its cause, the other of the state of mind of the first." Johnson contends that at this state in its development, *jus in bello* is mostly concerned with noncombatants--who they are and what might be done to them--and, therefore, on means insofar as these relate to their effects on noncombatants.[7]

The theorists seem to include in "military means" any type of weapon that seems necessary to assure victory and any military strategy that officers deem necessary to defeat the enemy. Short of "last resort" cases, however, the theorists are concerned with limitation of means in their *jus in bello* doctrines.

The Role of Proportionality in <u>Jus in Bello</u>

For Aquinas, prudence is required in determining just cause, but he dwells less on proportionality dealing with means than the other theorists do. This is especially so since during his time some military actions were absolutely prohibited regardless of anticipatory consequences. The four later theorists operate from a basically teleological framework. In *jus ad bellum* they urge anticipatory calculation of the ratio between cause and probable damages: i.e., whether the cause is weighty enough to warrant the harm that would result from war. In *jus in bello*, as Walters suggests, they appear to reverse that ratio and ask whether the damages done in war fit the cause. Thus, for Vitoria the means should not "exceed the quality and nature of the wrong," result in "great evils for both sides," or cause the "'ruin' of the enemy." In Suarez, the key terms are "equality and mode," urging belligerents to "preserve the equality of justice." Gentili also warns against "excess in war," urging warriors to act "moderately" and to observe "justice and equity." Grotius is said to have given "the most central role to the concept of proportionality in war." He analyzes the means of warfare from the perspective of moral justice. His key term, "*temperamentum*," signifies "a mixture in due proportion" of "in proper measure" in the employment of military means.[8]

Range of Applicability

The qualitative and quantitative effects contained in the calculus of proportionality include the nature of the enemy's offensive power, the damage to one's own state, the enemy's state and the church, and harm to innocent persons.[9] The theorists appear to assign a relative value to each of the qualitative factors in order better to determine the balance between costs and benefits. Grotius even combines qualitative and quantitative factors in a general formula:

> Wherefore we must also beware of what happens, and what we foresee may happen, beyond our purpose, unless the good which our action has in view is much greater than the evil which is feared, or, unless, [when] the good and evil balance, the hope of the good is much greater than the fear of the evil. The decision in such matters must be left to a prudent judgment.[10]

In general, theorists do not dwell on the application of the proportionality-calculus but rather on the general principles. Proportionality involves more than a quantitative measurement in that political leaders also have to determine qualitative effects and assign relative values to them. This becomes an exercise in prudence. Walters summarizes their position as follows:

> An inescapable conclusion... is that proportionality was primarily a collective concept, a tool for macro-analysis. As applied to war during the course of hostilities, it required a predominance of *total* good effects over *total* evil effects, without requiring an exact correspondence of each person's fate--to his relative merit.[11]

James Johnson points out that from the time of Grotius onward, absolute limits begin to be eroded in the name of proportionality, the basis of moderation in natural law. After Grotius there is a de-emphasis on *jus ad bellum* and greater emphasis on *jus in bello*. More will be said of the possible reasons for this change in Chapter 5. It is sufficient for now to note that the right to wage war is more easily assumed when there is a de-emphasis of *jus ad bellum* and, consequently, a deemphasis of just cause. This, along with other political and historical factors sets the stage for what Johnson calls a rebirth of "total war," a concept that contains "a powerful notion," in Johnson's words: "This is the idea that there exist certain values, perceived as ultimate, in defense of which individuals and nations must be prepared to fight with no observance of restraints."[12]

Total wars may take the form of "holy wars," national wars and ideological wars.

Johnson suggests four factors that tend to produce total wars, factors that the late medieval world began to experience: "1) a goal able to justify totalistic means, 2) a high degree of psychological motivation on the part of the belligerent populace, 3) the capability to wage such war, and 4) an opponent of similar or greater military capacity."[13]

These factors were all present to some degree by the seventeenth and eighteenth centuries. They are even more prevalent in the twentieth century. The necessity to emphasize limited war is, therefore, all the more urgent in the minds of contemporary just war theorists.

Comparison with Contemporary Just War Theories

Change in Emphasis: Jus ad Bellum to Jus in Bello

It has already been noted that there has been a change in emphasis in modern just war theories: from a concentration on *jus ad bellum* to *jus in bello*. In the nuclear age, *jus ad bellum* has been greatly affected by growing concern regarding the ability of nations to observe the principle of proportionality in *jus in bello* conditions. The change begins with Grotius. An examination of each of the three contemporary theorists gives further evidence of it. Before beginning a closer study of them, however, more should be said of the second major difference between the two sets of theorists. This is the change in what might be called the "range of consequences" to which the principle of proportionality applies. This change is linked to a difference in what is meant by "good" and "evil" effects of given military actions.

For Aquinas, proportionality is only called into play when a choice must be made between acts that are not morally evil in themselves (*non mala in se*). The choice resulting in *fewer* physical or "nonmoral" evil consequences is the moral choice. In contrast to this position, many contemporary "proportionalists" are "consequentialists," who choose the action to be performed on the basis of all the anticipatory consequences. The consequences become the end or reason for acting. For Aquinas, there are things that may not be done *regardless* of the consequences: moral goods and evils are not commensurate with nonmoral goods and evils; they may not be weighed on the same single scale. He maintains that in war, killing the innocent (a moral evil) may not be overridden by the nonmoral good of, say, destroying a military supply depot. For contemporary consequentialists, killing the innocent may be permitted if the "total good" resulting from destroying the supply depot outweighs the "total evil."

John Connery offers some insight into the traditional view of proportionality when he says it was not used with negative obligation but only with affirmative obligation or with positive legislation.[14] The more modern concept of proportionality, he contends, makes some acts previously considered morally evil to be only "premorally" evil: i.e., the acts only become evil in light of the consequences surrounding them. "The implication contained... seems to be that these acts are wrong *when* they are against [a] good... and not *because* they are against [a] good."[15]

While admitting that one may make a moral judgment only after considering the object and circumstances of the act, Connery says that the position more in keeping with tradition is that some moral judgments can be made by considering merely the object of the act. Such acts are "morally definable" and no further calculation is necessary. This is the case with Aquinas who forbids the killing of the innocent no matter what the consequences.

However, as has become evident, the four later just war theorists are willing to make exceptions in matters of "last resort." They attempt to place limitations on the means of warfare; however, because they include the *total* consequences of a military action, quantitative and qualitative, and because they operate in a teleological framework, ultimately the principle of proportionality outranks all other principles.

One contemporary theorist, Paul Ramsey, seems to want it both ways. He wants the absolutism of Aquinas and the flexibility of the four later classic theorists. He tries to do this by separating all the "morally relevant circumstances" of an action into qualitative and quantitative effects. The former he places under the principle of discrimination; the latter he places under the principle of proportionality.[16] It remains to be seen how effectively Ramsey is able to combine these two approaches.

Three Contemporary Theorists and the Principle of Proportionality

PAUL RAMSEY

Definition

In *War and the Christian Conscience* (1961), Ramsey does not expand his definition of the principle of proportionality much beyond saying it is a "calculation of consequences, or the weighing of anticipated greater goods or lesser evils."[17] Later he identifies it with "prudence."[18] The principle of proportionality includes, he says, "[A]ll that Reinhold Niebuhr ever said about politics and war..., that nations, statesmen and citizens are acting responsibly when they choose and vigorously support policies and decisions which are likely to secure the lesser evil (or the greater good) among their mixed consequences."[19]

In a later article (1973), Ramsey concentrates entirely on the use of proportionality in *jus in bello*, which, he says, is governed by two principles: the principle of discrimination, or the moral immunity of noncombatants from intended direct attack (the topic of the next chapter), and the principle of proportionality "or prudence, or the requirement that costs in destruction accepted and exacted be warranted by benefits there is reasonable expectation of gaining"[20] (thus incorporating into his definition the classic theorists' "reasonable hope of success").

David Little's analysis of Ramsey's moral reasoning about political matters may be helpful.[21] Little suggests that thinking morally involves eventually having to justify prescriptions or action guides; this is the process of "validation." The process of validating a particular moral norm entails appealing to a hierarchy of increasingly general principles and arriving finally at an ultimate or basic principle. This ultimate norm will be the basic validating norm. Ramsey's process of validation is the first topic addressed in the analysis that follows.

An examination of the "range of applicability" follows the analysis of Ramsey's validation of the principle of proportionality. This examination includes those particular effects or consequences proper to the principle of proportionality that enable one to form a moral judgment about the contemplated act. In the course of this examination, it is evident that the principle of proportionality is related to the principle of discrimination in a number of complex ways. However, a more complete analysis of this interaction is postponed until the following chapter where the focus is on the principle of discrimination.

Validation

The Ultimate Norm

Ramsey himself describes his process of validation in "The Case of the Curious Exception" (1968).[22] In this article, he outlines his deductive approach to morality: he first identifies the ultimate norm, then the general or abstract principles that are derived from it. From these principles he derives the definite action principles and then the definite "rules" which guide one's actions. Finally, he determines the "subsumption of cases" (finds what is common in each type of case) to which rules and principles apply. This process enables him to determine what ought to be done in specific instances.

Ramsey is consistent in taking as his ultimate norm Christian love or agape. From Basic Christian Ethics in 1950 through *Speak Up for Just War or Pacifism* in 1988, it is and has been his "ultimate logical justification for his lower-order principles."[23] Agape is defined as that "love which for itself claims nothing may yet for the sake of another claim everything."[24]

This love or agape has two sources: God's own righteousness and love and the reign of this righteousness in the kingdom of God. The 'righteousness' of which Ramsey speaks is characterized by God's convenantal love with humankind and this love becomes the measure for the fidelity humans are to give to the covenant between God and human beings. Jesus Christ is the perfect exemplar of this fidelity and his divine justice completes "the tendency of justice to topple over into benevolence." Thus, Ramsey demands that "Christian ethics and Christian political theory... be decisively and entirely Christocentric."[25]

Some have asked whether agape is a deontological or a teleological validating norm. Frankena has suggested that it is teleological in that it can be construed as a form of utilitarianism: loving God's creatures is equivalent to promoting for them the greatest balance of good over evil.[26] Thus one may be an "act-agapist," one who does the most loving thing in each situation; or a "rule-agapist," one who acts according to rules of action that seem most love-embodying. Don Thomas O'Connor seems to agree with Frankena in recognizing in Ramsey a combination of rule-agapism and act-agapism. He also agrees with Frankena that when basic principles conflict, decisions must be made on the basis of consequences, that is, on the basis of proportionality.[27]

Charles Curran, on the other hand, claims that Ramsey changes his position--that he seems in *Basic Christian Ethics* to reject universal norms,[28] but later rejects any kind of situation ethics and begins to *defend* universal norms. Ramsey, he says, grounds these in agape and later in "canons of loyalty."[29]

Ramsey replies, however, that Christian escatology implies that reliance on doing good consequences has been set aside. Righteousness entails rather obedience to God's will, and living together in convenant-love, no matter what the consequences. "A teleological calculus... can be included in Christian ethics *only* in the service of its definition of righteousness, and subordinate to its view of obedient love."[30]

Ramsey believes Frankena's typology is too abstract and not suitable for an analysis of Christian ethics. He speaks of act-agapism and "summary rule-agapism." According to summary-rule agapism one takes the circumstances of the act into account so that the rules of conduct are only "summaries of experience, records of past acts of loving obedience"; these rules may be violated whenever love dictates. Both, Ramsey says, lead to agapism and all have their place in Christian ethics.[31]

If this is so, it is difficult to see how Ramsey can sustain a claim that agape is not teleological. In fact, however, he does not claim quite that; he seems to want to combine deontology and teleology into a new "mixed" type of norm. Little's analysis is again helpful here.

Little identifies two sides or dimensions in agape as Ramsey describes it: the discretionary side, indeterminate and mathematically incalculable--even inexpressible in terms of abstract principles; and the formalistic or rational side, which *can* be expressed in principles. In relation to the discretionary side, Ramsey is an "act-agapist," a person filled with agape, who "has discretion to make creative, unpredictable and 'unmeasurable' decisions. On this side, Ramsey looks like a "situation ethicist."[32]

But one can hardly call Ramsey a situation ethicist if one examines his moral conclusions more carefully.[33] This is because situationism does not obtain on the formalistic side of agape. The formalistic aspect of agape determines the limits within which discretion takes place. It is revealed by covenantal fidelity and excludes the calculation of consequences. "Fidelity obligations determine the rightness of actions, not according to some standard for evaluating good or bad ends and consequences, but according to the qualities and characteristcs of actions themselves; that is, according to the *form* the acts take."[34] Ramsey gives special emphasis to this formalistic side of agape:

> Agape defines for the Christian what is right, righteous, obligatory to be done among men; it is not a Christian's definition of the good that better be done and much less is it a definition of the right way to the good... the Christian understanding of righteousness is therefore radically nonteleological.[35]

The formalistic side reveals the "outer limits" where specifications for right and wrong actions are determined by reason and are exceptionless, according to Ramsey. Little says it is "covenantal fidelity" which most clearly illumines the formalistic side of agape. It *requires* certain kinds of actions, "definite action-rules" and explains the "rule-agapist" aspect of Ramsey's position.

The formalistic side of agape is the deontological dimension. Because it sets the limits for the discretionary or teleological side, it holds the teleological dimension in a subordinate position: "in the matter of teleological judgments, rational certitude must give way to some other kind of intuitive or possibly religiously inspired certitude."[36]

The formalistic side of agape reaches beyond calculation and is not subject to judgments involving the calculation of consequences alone. It also yields certain principles that delineate the "outer limits" beyond which teleological calculations cannot reach. This has implications for the principle of proportionality as will become evident.

General Principles

Applying Ramsey's way of validation to his just war theory, one finds that the formalistic side of agape yields three political ethical principles which also figure into Ramsey's overall just war doctrine. These are *ordo* (the order of power), *justitia* (the regulative ideal of all political action) and *lex* (the legal order).[37] These principles are interrelated so that any political decision maker must take all three into account; for example, in the case of war, the use of power (or military force) must also be legal and just.

Not all that is just and licit is to be done, however. Ramsey must then appeal to another principle; and it is here that the principle of proportionality comes into play.

Ramsey does not derive the principle of proportionality from any of the three: order, justice or law. Rather, he bypasses these as well as natural law and derives the principle of proportionality directly from agape.

The limitation placed upon conduct in the just war theory arose not from autonomous natural reason asserting its sovereignty over determinations of right and wrong (and threatening to lead Christian faith and love which are and should be free, into bondage to alien principles), but from a quite humble moral reason subjecting itself to the sovereignty of God and the lordship of Christ, as Christian men felt themselves impelled out of love to justify war and by love severely to limit war.[38] Elsewhere Ramsey says, "Love for neighbors... required the grounds for admitting the legitimacy of the use of military force. Love for neighbors at the same time required that such force be limited."[39]

Having identified agape as the ultimate validating norm for Ramsey's principle of proportionality, one may now move on to the range of applicability Ramsey gives to the principle.

Range of Applicability

Jus ad Bellum

The first area where Ramsey applies the principle of proportionality in his just war doctrine is in *jus ad bellum* decisions. Thus the determination of just cause is subject to the test of prudence and proportionality. This means that within the limits set by *ordo, justitia* and *lex*, the cause for resorting to the use of military force must be sufficiently grave and the hope of success reasonably certain to warrant the amount of damage which will result from the war. This requirement of proportionality is inherent in social order, Ramsey claims, and is not a unique requirement superimposed on just war theories by Christian or Western ideology. Thus in Marxist-Leninist doctrine, any nonpredatory or liberating class struggle is a "just cause" for war. Even though such a war is justified according to communist standards, however, it is still subject to the test of prudence and proportionality, since there are multiple consequences to the use of force. There may, after all, be other ways of achieving "justice" and "peace" as Communism defines these. The consequences of war may include what Edvard Kardelj in *Socialism and War* calls "reactionary consequences on a world scale." What Karkelj and others who espouse the Marxist-Leninist doctrine seem to be saying is that although any class struggle leading to war is sufficient to make a war "just," some such "wars of liberation" cannot succeed for various reasons, and will result instead in greater opposition to the communist cause. If this is the case, it is better not to fight such a war because the war would lead to greater "evil": reactionary opposition to the communist cause.[40]

Ramsey calls the judgment not to go to war in these circumstances, *jus contra bellum.*[41] It applies not only to conditions that make a communist "just cause" unattainable, but also to conditions that seem to obviate the winning of a "just war" as understood in traditional Western democracies. Because nuclear wars seem unwinnable, Ramsey finds *jus contra bellum* particularly applicable as a basis for establishing new forms of governance in the nuclear age.

Ramsey, then, is more concerned with providing guidance on how to limit wars rather than on how to decide if one should go to war in the first place. He is interested in providing "moral tools" that political and military leaders can use in making *jus in bello* decisions. The key tools of all political decision-makers are what Ramsey calls "those summaries of political wisdom known as 'the principle of proportion' and 'the rule of double effect'." These tell the decision-makers not *what* to think but *how* to think.[42]

Ramsey's *jus ad bellum* doctrine thus reveals the discretionary side of proportionality. In *jus ad bellum* Ramsey does not have an external absolute abstract standard one may use to evaluate objectively the balance of good and evil, nor does he specify any hierarchy of goods to be sought. The *ends* of war are left to the discretion of the political decision-makers. "Outsiders," as Little calls nonmagistrates, are not able to evaluate ends of political action with as much certitude as they can evaluate means. Decisions on ends are subject to the specific value judgments of magistrates and these are discretionary. This helps to explain why Ramsey devotes less attention to *jus ad bellum* and the role proportionality plays than he does to *jus in bello* and the role of discrimination, which concerns means. In *Speak Up for Just War or Pacifism*, Ramsey expands on the principle of proportionality, calling it "more than a *formal* principle," therefore, not derived from agape in quite the same way as the principle of discrimination. He points out that the number of nuclear weapons the superpowers now possess makes it evident that there are too many weapons, that both sides would soon *run out of targets* if the weapons were ever used. Thus, he concludes, nuclear deterrence has become "inherently disproportionate."[43]

One may expect a greater range of applicability for proportionality in Ramsey's treatment of *jus in bello*, however, since Ramsey claims that everyone can subject the evaluation of means to rational analysis. Therefore, *jus in bello* proportionality is a more proper subject for universal judgment. The discretionary dimension of agape dominates Ramsey's treatment of *jus ad bellum* proportionality. In Ramsey's treatment of *jus in bello* proportionality, however, the formalistic dimension of agape dominates.

Jus in Bello

Indeterminacy and Incommensurability

Since this examination concerns the "range of applicability" of the principle of proportionality in Ramsey's just war theory, identification must be made of the particular kinds of consequences which the principle governs. Are *all* consequences to enter the moral calculus or are only some particular types to be included?

Walters maintains that Ramsey makes a distinction between qualitative and quantitative consequences: those that can be measured on a single scale of values and those that cannot. The quantitative consequences become the proper objects for evaluation by means of the principle of proportionality; qualitative effects are to be considered within the domain of the principle of discrimination. Thus, Ramsey is critical of those who "mix" together all consequences, quantitative and qualitative, measure the anticipatory "net" results, and base their decision regarding the morality of an action *solely* on their calculation. Such "proportionalism" is really a form of "consequentialism," which Richard McCormick defines as "[a]n act is wrong because of the bad consequences it *will have*, because of what is *likely to follow* upon it, both in the short and long run... if it is these considerations alone that determine rightness or wrongness.[44]

Ramsey criticizes this method of determining the morality of actions for two reasons: first, all the consequences of an act, both in the long and short runs cannot possibly be foreseen; second, all "goods" and "evils" cannot be measured on a common scale. Choices dependent on consequences that are doubtful, unknown and/or incommensurable are "indeterminate" and cannot be considered within the domain governed by the principle of proportionality.

Ramsey finds only one type of case where the proportionality principle can determine the morality of a given action: that is, one type which has commensurable consequences. An example of this type would be a case in which one must act to protect a certain value such as the value of life. There may be an abortion case, for example, in which, rather than lose two lives, one life must be taken in order to save the only one that can be saved. Another example occurs when it is necessary to kill fewer rather than more noncombatants in legitimately targeted acts of war. "Such body counts are the only instances I can think of in which there is clear commensurate meaning in the final judgment of proportion under the rule of twofold effect."[45]

More needs to be said about "the rule of twofold effect," in which Ramsey finds it necessary to introduce the distinction between direct and indirect intentionality. This rule is chiefly called into play by Ramsey where the principle of proportionality and the principle of discrimination intersect. Therefore, treatment of Ramsey's direct/indirect distinction will be postponed until after a more thorough analysis of the principle of discrimination is made in chapter 3.

A similar problem occurs in areas that Ramsey calls "incommensurable." When confronted with moral dilemmas in which there are incommensurable conflicting values at stake, proportionality offers no way to determine the greater or lesser good or evil according to Ramsey. In addition, "values may be comparable qualitatively, yet there may be no way to measure addition to the one against subtraction from the other."[46]

Thus, as Ramsey views the problem of indeterminacy, there may be "gaps" which cannot be measured even on a single scale of values; and there may also be an incommensurability of good and evil effects which cannot be measured on the same scale at all. Such situations lie beyond the scope of mathematical calculation and are more properly the objects of the formalistic dimension of agape.

The relation of the discretionary and the formalistic aspects of Ramsey's *jus in bello* doctrine will be expanded in the next chapter. Let it suffice for now to say that in *jus in bello* Ramsey gives the principle of discrimination higher lexical priority than the principle of proportionality.[47] If the principle of discrimination is violated, the contemplated action never reaches the test of proportionality. However, a situation where a military target could be attacked without violating the principle of discrimination, and yet would result in widespread death of noncombatants and collateral damage, may still be judged morally evil because it violates the principle of proportionality. In such a situation, "the principle of proportionality is controlling over the principle of discrimination in determining whether it is finally *just to do* even those actions in war that can be shown to be discriminate."[48]

In other words, the two *jus in bello* criteria of discrimination and proportionality are individually necessary and jointly sufficient to justify military actions, Ramsey asserts. He claims that because wars in which weapons of mass destruction are used cannot effect their political purpose, many instances of modern warfare become disproportionate sooner than they become indiscriminate.[49] For example, the destruction of a legitimate military target by means of nuclear weapons or conventional weapons of equal strength may violate the principle of proportionality if the plant is located close to urban centers. It may not violate the principle of discrimination, however, since the urban center is not targeted directly. The political purpose of such targeting may be to stop the enemy from continuing its own attacks, but the effect may be a nuclear exchange that results in as much devastation for the "retaliator" as for the aggressor. The way contemporary wars are fought is, then, a function of both military technology and the way nations are organized for war. This fact will have implications for judgments of proportionality in wars in the nuclear age.

WILLIAM V. O'BRIEN

Definition

Like Ramsey, O'Brien often equates proportionality with prudence, although he uses the term, "reasonableness."[50] Beyond this similarity, however, the definitions offered by the two theorists diverge, indicating significant differences which begin to emerge in their respective just war theories. In his earliest writings on war in 1960, O'Brien claimed it would be difficult to define proportionality.[51] In many ways the standard of proportionality resembles the standard of reasonableness. One learns what it is in the same way that the civil jurist learns what the "reasonable man" or the "reasonable rate" is: by studying case after case. Often it is determined *post facto* by the judge in a civil court in the first case, or a military tribunal in the second. A civil judge learns through "case law" what the "reasonable man" would do in a given instance. The military judge must learn through case studies what the "reasonable colonel" would do; that is, "the judge on a military tribunal must decide time after time whether a military measure was proportionate to a legitimate military end."[52]

In that same year, 1960, O'Brien says, "Proportionality means not doing more than is necessary."[53] Here he seems to be reflecting what McDougal and Feliciano say of "necessity" in *Law and Minimum World Public Order*. These authors claim that the requirement of proportionality is really another application of the "economy in coercion"; it is often stated abstractly, but ultimately they claim that the principle of proportionality is subject to "that most comprehensive and fundamental test of law, reasonableness in particular context."[54]

"Necessity" corresponds to "utility." In later works, however, O'Brien begins to draw distinctions between utility and proportionality, and between "military necessity" and "legitimate military necessity." In *legitimate* military necessity, "utility is subject to normative restriction."[72] It is not yet clear whether O'Brien means that "proportionality" is also subject to some other normative restriction. It is, after all, a normative restriction itself. Utility is restricted by proportionality and may be subject to other restrictive principles as well. O'Brien implies this as he describes the military use of various chemical-biological agents and restrictions of their use by international law, the danger of escalation, and the principle of discrimination.

In his recent major work in just war theory (*The Conduct of Just and Unjust Wars*, 1981), O'Brien states,

> The principle of proportion implies that there is a standard whereby proportionate means may be distinguished from disproportionate means, by the belligerents as well as by third party observers. This is perhaps the most important application of the principle of responsibility to meet an international standard in the conduct of war.[73]

O'Brien continues to find proportionality difficult to define, speaking of the "elusive character of the principle of proportion," yet maintaining its "central importance." Thus one never finds in his works a precise definition of proportionality. It is a principle, nevertheless, which assumes a higher priority ranking in his total just war theory than it does in Ramsey's. One might expect that imprecision in the definition of such an important concept would weaken O'Brien's entire theory. However, one must be mindful of O'Brien's method of moral reasoning: he does not proceed in a deductive fashion from well-defined first principles as Ramsey does. Ramsey speaks first of what "ought" to be and proceeds to "what is"--a progression from the more clear to the less clear. O'Brien, on the other hand, uses the inductive method: he begins with "what is" and proceeds to discover "what ought to be." Ramsey begins with principles and applies tham to cases. O'Brien begins with cases and reasons back to principles. Each "case" offers different facets for analysis, and it may often be difficult to distinguish sharply among the aspects of various principles as they overlap and interact. It will be helpful, then, to examine O'Brien's method of validating the principle of proportionality.

Validation

Since O'Brien's approach to studying the morality of military action is inductive, it begins with what can be experientially observed: i.e., his analysis begins with the reasons nations go to war (*raison d'état*) and the ways in which they conduct wars already underway (*raison de guerre*).

As he examines the reasons for which wars are fought and the methods used (the "war-conduct"), O'Brien finds that certain similarities emerge: states distinguish between situations that justify going to war and those that do not; once they become belligerents, they concern themselves with limitations of the means of warfare and proscribe certain acts. These various concrete cases become the subjects of review by military commanders and statesmen and many become the topics of international law. Once situations reach this stage of abstraction, the moralist may analyze the law for general principles which seem to be at work influencing decision-makers' judgments. This is the process O'Brien uses in identifying the general principles behind limitations of force in war situations.

General Principles

Utility and Military Necessity

Judgments made by political decision-makers and military commanders suggest that one of the principles operative in war is "utility," or what O'Brien understands by "military necessity." In international law terminology, military necessity connotes either of two extremes: an excuse for the excesses of war, i.e., nonobservance of the customary rules or laws of war (*Kriegsraison*, advanced by German writers of the late nineteenth and early twentieth centuries); or the prerequisite for any law of war at all. The latter connotation is what is meant by Francis Lieber in his limited war theory, which was adopted in essence by the Hague Conferences of 1899 and 1907. The first connotation is an extreme form of military utility based on the thought of such philosophers as Machiavelli, Hobbes, Fichte, and Hegel. Von Hartman, speaking in a similar vein, expresses this view as a negative role of military necessity in the application to the laws of war: "the greatest kindness in war is deadly efficiency which ends the whole affair quickly and decisively. Acts of cruelty, terrorism, deliberate devastation and impoverishment, directed against an entire nation's 'personal and material resources of war' are necessary."[57]

In Lieber's definition, on the other hand, military necessity plays a positive role: "Military necessity... consists in the necessity of those measures which are indispensable for securing the ends of war, and which are lawful according to the modern law and usages of war."[58]

According to Lieber, the only *legitimate* military necessity is that which is contained in and limited by the laws of war. O'Brien maintains that Lieber's interpretation continues to have greater significance today, and he defines the principle of military necessity as follows: "*Military necessity consists in all measures immediately indispensable and proportionate to a legitimate military end, provided they are not prohibited by the laws of war or the natural law, when taken on the decision of a responsible commander, subject to judicial review.* (O'Brien's emphasis)[59]

O'Brien, like James Johnson, sees a continuum in the relation between legal principles regarding just war, which are not necessarily *moral* principles, and principles of the just war tradition which are more properly called "moral." Therefore it is not surprising that he turns not only to positive international law but also to the more abstract "law of nations" and "natural law" in his search for the principles which set limits to military necessity.

Legitimate Military Necessity

O'Brien defines the principle of *legitimate* military necessity as follows: "Military necessity... means controlled violence... which is proportionate to legitimate ends and which is permitted by the law of nations and the natural law. To distinguish this fundamental concept from the other uses and abuses of the term "military necessity," I call it *legitimate* military necessity."[60]

He identifies three essential elements in this definition: (1) the necessity is immediately indispensable and proportionate to a legitimate military end; (2) the necessity is limited by the laws of war and natural law; (3) it is determined by the decision of a responsible commander and subject to judicial review.[61]

The first element grants nothing extraordinary, says O'Brien; it merely cites the right to perform the normal, legitimate acts the law terms "permissible violence." An act that is necessary is not simply an act that has some military utility, but only one without which a legitimate military object cannot be obtained. O'Brien must use "legitimate" here in a "nonmoral" sense. Otherwise, he could be accused of "begging the question" in assuming morality wherever there is legality instead of trying to discover whether what is legal (legitimate) is moral. By the "immediateness" of the necessity, O'Brien interprets a *directness* in the relationship between military means and ends, not necessarily an immediateness in the temporal sense. O'Brien claims that both the immediacy and the imperative necessity are conditions necessary to satisfy the requirements of proportionality. The principle of proportionality, in other words, cannot be applied until these two conditions are met. O'Brien concludes that "[a]ll acts of war must be proportionate to a legitimate military end."[62]

A second element in O'Brien's definition of legitimate military necessity, command responsibility and judicial review, is a post-World War II phenomenon. O'Brien cites an an example the Hague Convention on the Protection of Cultural Property in the Event of Armed Conflict of May 14, 1954. This convention determined that an officer commanding a force the size of a division or larger is the responsible decision maker. As an example of judicial review, O'Brien refers to the UN police action in Korea for which the UN General Assembly served as a reviewing body. (O'Brien admits that the term, "judicial review," is not quite accurate in this case.) Such proceedings show that a previously thought "uncontrollable" element in the law of war has been made subject to review as one of the requirements for legitimate military necessity.

The third element in legitimate military necessity, and one unique to O'Brien's formulation, is the inclusion of natural law and the law of nations. More will be said in the section of this chapter on *jus gentium-jus naturale* about these interrelated sources of moral principles. When they are added to the other two elements of legitimate necessity--immediate necessity proportionate to a legitimate military end and determination by a responsible commander subject to judicial review--O'Brien concludes that "the principle of legitimate military necessity provides a normative basis for the law of war and a standard for measuring the limits of permissible violence. This standard remains constant regardless of the circumstances of the belligerent."[63]

In actual experience, O'Brien found when he did a comprehensive study of the historical evolution of the concepts of military necessity that most of the authorities studied do not recognize the positive principle of legitimate military necessity but emphasize its negative connotation as granting exceptions to the positive laws of war. He cites the treatment of the positive connotation by Dunbar, Tucker, McDougal and Feliciano as evidence that the principle has been "rediscovered" and is receiving increased recognition.[64]

O'Brien thus claims that the principle of legitimate military necessity contains a "normative basis" for the law of war. Examination of positive international law reveals three underlying principles. In addition to military necessity (not simply the "utility" discussed at the beginning of this chapter but the utility limited by considerations of proportionality), humanity and chivalry.

Humanity

Humanity, the second general principle, forbids the infliction of suffering, injury or destruction not actually necessary for the accomplishment of legitimate military purposes. The principle of proportionality is central to the judgment of how much suffering is permissible. The humanity principle is also closely related to the principle of discrimination, which protects innocents from direct attack. The principle of humanity and the principle of discrimination do not, however, "preclude unavoidable incidental civilian casualties which may occur during the course of attacks against military objectives, and which are not excessive in relation to the concrete and direct military advantages anticipated."[65]

Evidence for the principle of humanity is found in the Hague Convention IV of 1907, article 22, which states that "the right of belligerents to adopt means of injuring the enemy is not unlimited," and also in the Geneva Conventions of 1949: "usages established among civilized peoples from the laws of humanity and the dictates of the public conscience." The Nuremburg trials also label certain acts "crimes against humanity."[66]

Chivalry

Evidence for the third principle, chivalry, is reflected in various codes of military practice. One such code is the Air Force Manual (AFP 110-31, 1-6) which states that "the conduct of armed conflict in accord with well-recognized formalities and courtesies... recognized today in specific prohibitions such as those against poison, dishonorable or treacherous misconduct, misuse of enemy flags, uniforms and flags of truce."[67]

The three principles taken together reflect a mixed character: moral and non-moral. They indicate to O'Brien that he has not yet uncovered the deeper principles underlying positive law. Disagreements as to how much suffering is superfluous, how many noncombatant casualties are too many even in an "indirect" attack, all point to "gaps" in positive law related to proportionality. Proportionality is controlled by a deeper law at work, the law of nations or *jus gentium*.

More General Principles: <u>Jus Gentium</u> and <u>Jus Naturale</u>

Jus Gentium

Critics claim that the old legal order governing international force has collapsed under the impact of total war. O'Brien's view, however, is that the legal order reveals principles that are more general and, at the same time, more readily applicable to new situations. He also believes that the legal order must be constantly measured against this broader view in order that it may more adequately reflect these principles. Noting where international consensus lies, he induces the principles which give rise to such an agreement. These principles form the *jus gentium*, the law of peoples or nations. O'Brien finds evidence of its influence under various titles in international law documents in phrases such as the "laws of humanity" and the "dictates of the public conscience" in the Preamble to the Hague Convention IV of 1907, and in phrases like "crimes against humanity" in the Nuremburg Code.

O'Brien then turns his attention to the *jus gentium* to search for the principles underlying legitimate military necessity: "No comprehensive definition of the principle of legitimate necessity can avoid recognition of some higher law normative element which restrains belligerents no matter what their subjective predicament and no matter what the state of positive law of war."[68]

The "subjective predicament" changes, obviously, according to developments in weapons technology. No positive international law has specifically dealt with nuclear warfare, for example; but it is O'Brien's position that positive law will reveal concepts which may serve as guidelines for drawing up a more comprehensive law to deal with nuclear warfare in the future.

In keeping with his inductive approach, O'Brien, like a "twentieth century Grotian," tries to analyze the pattern of behavior in society to arrive at the ethical consensus or "common sense of mankind which would serve as a normative basis for international law.[69]

Natural Law Principles

In the Scholastic tradition the principles of the law of nations are recognized as secondary principles of natural law. O'Brien blends them, as Grotius does, with natural law principles to form what he calls a "state of nature-natural law."

O'Brien finds it necessary to appeal to this state of nature-natural law when he searches for principles to guide moral conduct in the nuclear age, for when he enters the nuclear war arena, he enters an uncharted area of international law. It is necessary, therefore, to establish "working hypotheses about the universal conscience of mankind with respect to nuclear war."[70]

Reactions to the bombings of Hiroshima and Nagasaki and nuclear testing may, however, give some moral direction. O'Brien's approach is further hampered by the difficulty of focusing on what he identifies as the real question to be addressed by the "universal conscience of mankind:" not, "Is nuclear warfare permissible?", a question of means, but, "Is nuclear warfare against communist armed attack a legitimate military necessity?", a question of ends *and* means.

Human Dignity

Because he cannot appeal to positive law and actual experience, O'Brien departs from his inductive approach and turns to the Thomistic-Suarezian deductive natural law to supplement his state of nature-natural law approach. He begins to probe *jus naturale* for principles from which to deduce answers to his question on ends and means of nuclear war, and identifies the principle of "human dignity." This principle, he says, accounts for the limits of military necessity and *raison d'état*.

The limits of military necessity and *raison d'état* are discovered, O'Brien argues, through acknowledgment of a hierarchy of values which subordinates the value of the state to that of the individual person. The principles which give rise to this conclusion concern the threefold relationship between the human person, the state, and international society, each with rights, and duties and "necessities," and each limited by the hierarchy of values established by natural law. *Jus gentium* has generally recognized that the state is a means to achieve the ends of its human subjects through positive international law to some extent. So, too, the limits of the state's military necessity are set by the minimum requirements of human dignity, which becomes what O'Brien terms an "internal immanent limitation" on military necessity.[71]

Interdependence of Peoples

The external immanent limitation on military necessity lies in Suarez's concept of international society--the interdependence of peoples. Notions of international common good and the "higher necessities" are derived from this truth. The subordinate place of the state in the natural law hierarchy of values means that the use of weapons which would result in disproportionate injury to the earth, its resources, and humankind is immoral.

Ultimate Norm

The ultimate norm which seems to be the source of the principle of proportionality, according to O'Brien is, then, "respect for the human person."

"Respect for the human person" also underlies the principle of "the interdependence of peoples." Nevertheless, "the interdependence of peoples" functions as a *necessary condition* for "respect for the human person," since no individuals can satisfy their own needs without relying on others, and by the same token, without being relied upon by others. For O'Brien, this implies that individuals need particular forms of community, especially political community. He gives special emphasis to the needs of this particular type of community, and is criticized by Grisez and Boyle, who claim that "human community may take many forms, of which political society is only one."[72]

In summary, O'Brien has traced the principle of proportionality back through "legitimate military necessity," which reveals the principles particularly relevant to proportionality, military necessity, and humanity. These principles of a somewhat "mixed" character point to deeper principles of *jus gentium-jus naturale*, namely, the principles of respect for human dignity and the interdependence of peoples. The latter principle has special significance relating to *nuclear* conflict, as will be seen in chapter 4.

Having examined how O'Brien grounds the principle of proportionality in human respect and the interdependence of peoples, one can better examine the areas where he applies the principle in his just war doctrine.

Range of Applicability: The Proportionality Calculus

Jus ad Bellum

O'Brien recognizes three major categories of *jus ad bellum* guidelines currently at work influencing political decision-makers: (1) competent authority orders the war for a public purpose; (2) just cause; and (3) right intention. He admits of no hierarchy here except that "just cause" must be determined prior to any decision to initiate war. The just cause also sets the central and "underlying referent" for the determination of proportionality in the use of means. A second set of "subordinate criteria" includes the following: (4) proportionality of means; (5) the exhaustion of all peaceful alternatives; and (6) having a right intention both in the decision to wage war and in the choice of the particular means used to wage war.

O'Brien refers to the principle of proportionality as the "heart of the just cause," balancing *raison d'état*, the high interests of the state, and *raison de guerre*, the military means used to achieve those interests. At the level of *raison d'état*, the principle of proportionality is "multidimensional": (1) the ends offered as just cause must be good enough to warrant the extreme measures of armed coercion; (2) the projected outcome must show that the probable good resulting from the war will outweigh the probable evil which the war will cause; (3) the weighing of good and evil is made difficult since wars affect not only the belligerents but third parties as well, and all this must be weighed against the international common good, which is, in turn, necessarily affected by war; (4) the just party must also calculate to see what its probability of success is. All these must be met to satisfy the multidimensional requirement of just cause. In addition, this calculation must be reviewed at critical points during the conflict as well as at its initiation.[73]

O'Brien defines the calculus of proportionality as "the total good to be expected if the war is successful balanced against the total evil the war is likely to cause";[74] and elsewhere, in relation to nuclear war: "The calculation of proportionality of deterrence and defense means to the values defended must be made in the light of the probability of success."[75]

Thus the "goods" and "evils" in O'Brien's calculus include both quantitative and qualitative values, and at least some of these have been specified.

Ramsey has no objective external standard by which to determine the proportionality of good to evil results in his *jus ad bellum* doctrine. O'Brien, on the other hand, has such a standard: international law--though admittedly, he recognizes certain "gaps" in that law. This implies that in some cases one must look to *jus gentium-jus naturale* for guidance. There are also instances in international law that O'Brien criticizes. For example, he criticizes the UN Charter for stipulating that legally permissible offensive war be limited to a Security Council enforcement action. This development in international law, he says, elevates peace, security and stability above justice in the international hierarchy of values.[76]

Except for the added emphasis on the international community made necessary by a changed global environment and modern technological changes in weaponry, O'Brien's *jus ad bellum* doctrine closely resembles that of the classic just war theorists. But O'Brien must apply his just war theory in a new way to the war that has not yet been fought: nuclear war. In classic just war theories, the "dual character" of proportionality in most facets of conventional war is emphasized: the effects on the enemy and on one's own side. The use of nuclear weapons increases the likelihood of producing more devastating effects on third parties than has ever been possible before. Thus in the nuclear age, "the proportionality calculus must include an assessment of effects on the enemy, military and civilian; one's own side, military and civilian, one's allies, neutrals, the earth and the human race in general. The introduction of nuclear weapons introduces third parties which include all humanity."[77]

Jus in Bello

O'Brien emphasizes that the central referent for proportionality even at the level of *jus in bello* is "just cause." This is "the ultimate justification for all means of war..."[78] But just cause is not the sole referent; if it were, one might put together an entire "war package" containing means designed to achieve the war's end, yet bypassing any need to examine the discrete means proposed against alternative means which might accomplish the same ends at lower costs. Once again, judgments of reasonableness or proportionality are called into play.

Proportionality in *jus in bello* plays a twofold role: it governs military means as they relate to the legitimate end of war, the just cause; and it governs means as they relate to discrete or limited legitimate military ends within war. The determination of proportionality in the first sense is primarily the responsibility of the political decision-makers; in the second sense, it is primarily determined by the discretion of the military commanders.

Authorities in recent wars have almost universally accepted the distinction O'Brien describes. They have thus accepted a separation of the proximate military end from the final political end of war. Thus, Rommel was judged in light of the limited military objective of driving the English from Egypt and not in light of Hitler's ultimate aim of illegal conquest. "'[N]ecessity' is of the proximate military order of *raison de guerre* rather than of the final political order of *raison d'état*."[79]

O'Brien points out that the two levels often overlap in such a way that certain tactical decisions,[80] such as the firebombing of German cities, establish a strategic pattern which affects the total calculus of proportionality. And in a kind of reverse relation, strategic decisions also have tactical implications. The example O'Brien offers is the strategic choice to defeat Japan by strategic bombing of cities rather than ground conquest, thereby saving "costs."

The standards of reasonableness are primarily found in "general, conventional and customary international-law prescriptions."[81] Even some apparently lawful means may become unlawful when their use is superfluous (disproportionate).

Consistent with his derivation of proportionality from the ultimate norm of "respect for human dignity," O'Brien has stated that "use of cruel means without any commensurate military advantages is proscribed." It is not clear whether O'Brien is limiting the "proscriptions," in this instance, to what is limited by moral principle, or by positive law alone, for he continues, "but as far as outright destruction of active military personnel and clearly military installations are concerned, mere quantitative exaggerations are perfectly permissible."[82]

Thus, what O'Brien seems to be implying is that the kinds of effects or consequences governed by the *jus in bello* principle of proportionality are the qualitative effects related to respect for human dignity on both combatants and noncombatants. Merely quantitative effects on combatants are not included in the proportionality calculus. In making such a sharp distinction between combatants and noncombatants, O'Brien seems to be violating his ultimate norm, respect for human dignity. It is necessary to see if he makes other distinctions within the category of combatancy in order to meet the requirements of respect for human dignity, but discussion of this subject must be delayed until the next chapter, which deals with noncombatant immunity.

According to the principle of the interdependence of peoples, the proportionality calculus must include effects on the earth and the human race in general. However, in excluding "legitimate" military targets from the range of applicability of the principle of proportionality, it is difficult to see how O'Brien can avoid justifying too much damage and harm to "the earth and the human race in general." If, for example, there is a choice to be made on whether to drop a ten-megaton bomb or a twenty-megaton bomb on a legitimate military target, one may ask on what basis O'Brien would choose either weapon. Legitimate military targets are beyond the bounds of the boundaries of proportionality, and so either weapon would be acceptable, considering the principle of proportionality alone. O'Brien could respond to this criticism, however, by appealing to the principle of humanity and the interdependence of peoples, for the larger bomb may have greater collateral effects on the civilian population and cause greater suffering.

O'Brien does recognize the principle of discrimination as another limiting principle of *jus in bello* but he gives it a decidedly subordinate role to the principle of proportionality. In this way, he is subject to the criticism that he is justifying too much harm. More will be said later of the interaction of the two principles. It is worth mentioning here, however, that O'Brien does not try to get around this problem by means of the principle of double effect nor by the direct/indirect distinction Ramsey makes.

This is Ramsey's criticism of O'Brien. Ramsey believes O'Brien does not see that noncombatant immunity means that only counterforce warfare is just.Ramsey says that O'Brien makes a mistake in saying proportionality is the *essence* of legitimate military necessity. O'Brien, he maintains, errs in giving primacy to the principle of proportionality, which is presently giving rise to a "no greater evil" *pacifism* instead of a just war conscientious objection. If the essence of "legitimate military necessity" were proportionality, Ramsey says,

> it would be morally permissible for nations to inflict a *barely-intolerable* damage without distinction between counter-*force* and counter-*people* warfare. If he does not give greater attention to other just war criteria, he will be bound to move toward endorsing any conduct that has military decisiveness in gaining the end of victory.[83]

Ramsey recognizes, however, that Catholic ethics is committed to some kind of "ethics of means" as well as to "morality proportioned to ends," even to a greater extent than Protestantism. What Ramsey is urging is that O'Brien move more toward looking at this ethic of means and less toward considering the ends of actions as he defines legitimate military necessity.

O'Brien has maintained that the principle of legitimate military necessity embraces all the elements of the just war and international-law *jus in bello*[84] and that the essence of legitimate necessity is proportionality.[85] His thesis has been that there is a moral imperative at work in the *jus gentium* to develop the institution of limited war in every age, including the nuclear age. An important corollary of this thesis, as he sees it, is to develop realistic principles and rules for the regulation and limitation of modern warfare. From the historical development of the law of war, he sees the central problem of this task to be defining "proportionality" in concrete belligerent situations."[86] It remains to be seen whether O'Brien can overcome Ramsey's criticism; i.e., whether giving proportionality the central role in determining legitimate military necessity can provide a just war theory consistent with the general moral principles of the just war tradition.

MICHAEL WALZER

Definition

Like O'Brien, Walzer uses an inductive approach to try to discover the principles of morality underlying judgments about war. Accordingly, he examines "what is" before deciding "what ought to be." The "what is" is the "war convention:" that "set of articulated norms, customs, professional codes, legal precepts, religious and philosophical principles, and reciprocal arrangements that shape our judgments of military conduct."[87] The principle of proportionality is part of that convention, and just as the convention itself is the product of centuries of debate, criticism, and revision, so one can expect that proportionality will be subject to criticism and revision. This is what Walzer attempts to do. His chief criticism of proportionality as it is understood in recent times, is that it has become too weak a constraint on military necessity.[88]

As O'Brien had difficulty defining proportionality, so Walzer also never gives a precise definition. At one point he says simply that the principle of proportionality is a calculation of costs and benefits.[89] Walzer sometimes calls proportionality a "rule," sometimes a "principle," but he does so interchangeably and seems to mean by both "a precept that ought to be followed,"[90] and not simply a rule of thumb or utilitarian "summary rule." In fact, Walzer explicitly rejects the summary rule notion of proportionality found in Sidgwick's view of the war convention. In Sidgwick's utilitarian schema, a twofold rule sums up the war convention and at the same time imposes an "economy of force" doctrine on belligerents. The twofold rule actually gives two criteria which must be met before military action is taken. These criteria are meant to determine excess harm in war; they are (1) that the action lead to victory (understood as "military necessity"); (2) that the action meet the requirements of proportionality defined as "[weighing] 'the mischief done,' which presumably means not only the immediate harm to individuals but also any injury to the permanent interests of mankind, against the contribution that mischief makes to the end of victory."[91]

Sidgwick maintains that proportionality operates as the measure of utility and ranks highest in a lexical ordering of the rules and customs of war. But Walzer insists this is not actually the case--that "the limits of utility and proportionality do not exhaust the war convention. [Rather] the war convention invites soldiers to calculate costs and benefits only up to a point and at that point it establishes a series of clearcut rules--moral fortifications, so to speak, that can be stormed only at great moral cost."[92]

Elsewhere Walzer speaks of proportionality as a "doctrine," one which fixes firm limits to the length of wars and how they are settled: "Proportionality is a matter of adjusting means to ends... [In wartime] there is an overwhelming tendency... to adjust ends to means instead, that is, to redefine initially narrow goals in order to fit the available military forces and technologies."[93]

Because of the tendency to use what Walzer later calls a "sliding scale," he severely limits his own use of proportionality. He finds in the war convention evidence of other principles that impose limits on the waging and fighting of wars. Proportionality is useful insofar as it limits the cruelty of war, but for Walzer, it does not go far enough. Utility or military victory is not the proper standard against which to measure the proportionality of the values at stake in war.

Validation

Walzer does not begin with the foundations of morality but with the "superstructure," the world--or in this case, the "war convention"--as he finds it. Walzer is a practical moralist and his method, like O'Brien's, is inductive and casuistic. Therefore he probes actual events, current practices and customs, and positive international law in his search for an ultimate norm.

The moral life for Walzer is a "social phenomenon... constituted at least in part by rules, the knowledge of which (and perhaps the making of which) we share with our fellows."[94] War itself is a social phenomenon that cuts across all society, and so, some of the rules "we share with our fellows" will be spelled out in positive international law. Yet Walzer holds, as O'Brien did, that positive international law will be only partially complete--it will contain "gaps" since it does not fully express the principles and values shared by the peoples of the world. The "legalist paradigm," a phrase James Dixon describes as capturing "the most contemporary formulation of the right to make war,"[95] is, nevertheless, useful to Walzer as an indicator of where our shared principles lie. Walzer proposes five revisions to this paradigm in the face of actual international practices and people's concept of justice in contemporary society.

None of the limits Walzer finds in either the unrevised or his revised legalist paradigm is accepted simply because it is considered useful. Walzer examines utility in the concept of "military necessity" in his search for basic moral principles underlying the war conventions. The four different meanings he finds for "necessity" will be examined in the section on the range of applicability of proportionality. Though he recognizes the role utility plays in both law and military necessity, Walzer finally rejects the primacy of utility as the foundation that society uses to justify acts of war. "Belligerent armies are entitled to try to win their wars, but... [t]hey are subject to a set of restrictions that rest in part on the agreement of states but that also have an independent foundation in moral principle."[96] Elsewhere Walzer states,

> Beyond the minimal limits of "conduciveness" and proportionality, [utilitarianism] simply confirms our customs and conventions, whatever they are, or it suggests that they be overridden; but it does not provide us with customs and conventions. For that, we must turn... to a theory of rights.[97]

The Ultimate Norm: Right to Life and Liberty

Walzer declares at the outset of *Just and Unjust Wars*: "The morality I shall expound is in its philosophical form a doctrine of human rights."[98] Walzer makes use of a social contract metaphor in reaching this conclusion. He has found that where contemporary arguments are made for just war, nations claim that they must protect their individual citizens' rights to life and liberty, or their own rights as nations to survive. This is an indication to Walzer that his ultimate norm of the war convention lies in the notion of rights.

Hauerwas calls Walzer's abandonment of historical method "one of the weakest aspects" of his just war theory. He thinks Walzer is trying to do the impossible in offering his account of "rights" as a foundation for his just war principles. Walzer makes a "Kantian" attempt to avoid the kind of close attention to history that he finds necessary to examine the morality of war and ultimately fails to do so, according to Hauerwas.[99] In taking the position he does, Walzer intends to reject a utilitarian approach to just war theory. Instead, he attempts to treat rights as absolute values. Whether he can sustain this position against the demands utility makes in warfare remains to be seen. The rights with which Walzer is concerned in warfare, and more specifically in aggressive acts of war, are the individual's rights to life and liberty. He makes no attempt to explain how these rights are founded, although in an article on World War II, he speaks of the "intrinsic value attached to the human personality."[100] More about that in the next chapter. "Somehow," Walzer says, "[rights are] entailed by our sense of what it means to be a human being."[101] Later he describes them as being "in an important sense distributive principles. They distribute decision-making authority."[102]

In war, both the nation's right to survive and the individual's rights to life and liberty are at stake. Persons cannot be forced to fight and risk their lives nor ought they to be threatened with war or warred against unless those persons have surrendered or lost those rights. The individual's rights to life and liberty are for Walzer the "fundamental principle" underlying judgments regarding wartime conduct. (The question of whether he considers them a "single" right or two separate rights is dealt with in the next chapter.) Walzer concludes, "It is only inadequately expressed in positive international law, but the prohibitions established there have this principle as their source."[103]

Individuals need to act collectively to guarantee and secure their rights, according to Walzer, and the state is the instrument they use to act collectively. The state, then, is composed of the people and its government. The government is, in turn, bound to defend the rights of its people, its principal duty being to protect the right of the people to territorial integrity and political sovereignty. This also presents a paradox for Walzer.

Walzer recognizes the difficulty resulting from the state's need to defend its citizens' rights to life and liberty; for in so doing, the state seems to violate the very rights it sets out to defend. Using the social contract model, Walzer holds that the people forming such a collectivity would agree on the need to defend their collective existence in the state in order to preserve their fundamental rights to life and liberty. Thus even the state's right to defend its collectivity's life and liberty--that is, its political sovereignty and territorial integrity--proceeds from the individual's rights to life and liberty. Therefore, in addition to basing its right to wage war on its need to maintain its independence and sovereignty, the right of the state to wage war is also based first and foremost on the rights of the individual to life and liberty.

This "right of the state" also presents Walzer with a paradox in his theory. Many states violate the rights of their citizens and some argue, as Charles Beitz points out, that "the protection of human rights... is ill-served by the nearly blanket protection of political sovereignty and territorial integrity that Walzer advocates." Walzer will allow intervention by outside forces under certain conditions but, for the most part, he subscribes to the idea that peoples are more likely to preserve their freedom, to develop the virtues needed to maintain their freedom, if they struggle to achieve their own freedom. Walzer's "morality of states" concept, is thus a contrast with the "cosmopolitan" view of natural law theorists like Vitoria and Suarez. He holds that the state's moral character is such that it acts as a "social agent" and is not changed by any degree of corruption or injustice within it. This Beitz calls misleading. States are affected by external forces for good or ill; they are not self-enclosed entities and, therefore, Beitz claims that other states can be expected to redress the wrongs inflicted on them by their own governments.[104]

Proportionality

As a principle of the war convention, proportionality, too, ought to be traceable to the individual's rights to life and liberty. Walzer, however, seems to trace it back indirectly, through the general principle of utility. Utility, in turn, is subject to the restrictions set by the rights to life and liberty. These rights act as a boundary beyond which utility and, consequently, proportionality, do not apply. Because of the restrictions under which proportionality must function in Walzer's theory, it plays more of a negative than a positive role: it does not make further rules. Its purpose, rather, is to determine when other rules may be broken.

If their source is in individual rights, the rules and customs of warfare have been drawn up to maximize respect for the individual's rights to life and liberty. Thus, proportionality must function in such a way that it maximizes respect for these rights. If it operates in this way, there are certain consequences that cannot be measured by the proportionality calculus.

Range of Applicability: The Proportionality Calculus

<u>How</u> binding is the principle?

Before considering *where* the rule of proportionality is appropriate, that is, the actual range of its applicability in warfare, it will be helpful to consider a prior question--one that Walzer himself addresses. That is the question of <u>how</u> binding the rules of war are in the first place. This will give some idea of the nature of the conflicts the rule of proportionality is meant to help resolve.

Walzer has examined four choices which theorists make in judging the morality of the rules of war. These choices differ from one another in the importance they give to the principle of proportionality and may be set in priority order with the one giving highest importance to proportionality ranked first, as follows.

First, the rules of war are to be ignored when they conflict with proportionality. They may not be broken for military necessity alone, but they may be broken for the sake of the just cause. This is the realist's view, according to Walzer, and it is often attributed to American military policy, though he maintains it is actually more universal. This attitude is especially apparent in Mao Tse-tung's policy of the "Eight Points," which are to govern the conduct of war but which are to be set aside when victory demands. They are the "rules of thumb" that can be broken for the sake of the cause--general precepts of honor and utility to be observed only until observing them comes into conflict with the requirements of victory. Walzer dismisses this option as a misunderstanding of the status of the war convention.[105]

Second, the rules are to be observed on a "sliding scale" basis: "the greater the justice of one's cause, the more rights one has in battle."[106] As the moral urgency of a just war increases, then, the moral necessity to observe the rules of engagement decreases. Walzer attributes this view to John Rawls. It is also expressed in terms of outcomes: the greater the injustice likely to result from defeat, the greater the allowance to violate the rules. According to Walzer, such a position does not morally "fit" since the war convention as he describes it does not give a *range* of actions over which a sliding scale may move. Rather, the actions it prescribes are distinct one from the other with certain inadmissable acts being barred. A sliding scale would act like a utilitarian ruler directly contrary to the reason why the rules were set up in the first place: to limit the destructiveness of war.

Third, an alternative to the sliding scale argument is a position of moral absolutism: the rules are inviolable no matter what. Ramsey tries to take this position regarding discrimination. Walzer calls it a "hard line to take, one which is not for most people a plausible moral doctrine,"[107] especially in modern times when so much is at stake.

Fourth, another alternative to the sliding scale argument is summed up by Walzer in the maxim: "[D]o justice unless the heavens are (really) about to fall."[108] This is the option Walzer chooses to defend. It is also the option which opens his entire just war theory to criticism. Attention must be given to the range of consequences implied by such an approach to the rule of proportionality.

Where does the rule apply?

According to Walzer, the rule of proportionality can be applied wherever the principle of utility is morally applicable: i.e., in the area of military necessity. In every other area, utility is subject to the constraints of the individual's rights to life and liberty. "The world of necessity," he says, "is generated by a conflict between collective survival and human rights."[109] As Walzer recognizes in actual practice, however, "the values against which destruction and suffering are to be measured are... readily inflated."[110] Political and military decision-makers have often expanded the area of military necessity beyond its legitimate bounds.

Difficulties in keeping the area actually governed by military necessity within its proper moral bounds are encountered especially where there is conflict between *jus ad bellum* and *jus in bello*. Walzer does not discuss these difficulties systematically. At various places in *Just and Unjust Wars*, however he does address four different concepts of necessity. Political and military decision makers make various "pleas of necessity" in order to justify certain acts of war. In doing this they use the principle of proportionality to show that the benefits resulting from a given military action outweigh the harms, and that the resultant benefits are "necessary." The four concepts of "necessity" help to clarify Walzer's moral limits of the range of applicability of both utility and proportionality. It will be helpful, then, to examine each of them in turn.

Necessity$_1$[111]

The first "plea of necessity" Walzer discusses is the necessity that lies at the core of the *Kriegsraison*. This doctrine justifies any action that results in military victory, that is, in winning a war. Proportionality in *Kriegsraison* is used to justify whatever will reduce losses or will result in victory. The plea of necessity$_1$ is to undertake that course of action "necessary to compel the submission of the enemy with the least possible expenditure of time, life and money."[112]

If the war convention simply contained summary rules, the war convention might be set aside during such times of necessity$_1$ and be overridden by utility and proportionality. In actual fact, however, Walzer sees that this is not the case. Thus, according to rules and customs of war, belligerents are bound to respect certain people who are regarded as noncombatants. Even soldiers who are not engaged in combat sometimes enjoy a kind of "partial" combatant status when they are not actually engaged in military action. Walzer concludes that what is involved in limiting *Kriegsraison* is "not so much a calculation of proportionality and risk as a reflection on the status of the men and women whose lives are at stake."

Conflicts between utility and respect for persons' lives arise in Walzer's discussions of the principle of double effect. He attempts to revise this principle and the implications of this are examined in the next chapter on noncombatant immunity.

Necessity$_2$[113]

The second plea of necessity is discussed in the context of Walzer's treatment of neutrality and violations of neutrality. Violating a neutral state's right to neutrality in wartime will almost certainly result in the deaths of innocent people. Unless this can be proved to be really necessary, therefore, the principle of proportionality cannot be allowed to play a part in balancing good and evil effects of a violation. In Walzer's example Germany attacked Belgium, a neutral state, in August 1914. Chancellor von Bethman Hollweg justified this action on the grounds of military necessity: that France was about to invade Germany and that on the strategic level, such an attack would be "disastrous" to Germany: i.e., Germany would be defeated. In actual fact, however, Germany's survival was not at stake; rather, Germany's attack on Belgium was a matter of expediency in striking a blow against the French and winning a quick victory on the western front before engaging the Russians on the eastern front. On the moral level, Walzer believes that what was at stake was not Germany's survival as an independent nation, but rather Alsace-Lorraine and Germany's African colonies. Walzer concludes that the argument is invalid on both the strategic and moral levels as not representing a true "necessity."

Necessity$_3$[114]

The third plea of necessity was made by Churchill and other British leaders to justify the terror bombing of German cities, in which 300,000

Germans, mostly civilians, were killed and 780,000 seriously injured. At the military level, the purpose of the bombings was to destroy civilian morale. Churchill believed that tactical use of the bombers could not stop Hitler and that "the bombers alone... provide[d] the means of victory." Walzer asks whether proportionality can be applied in this case: i.e., "should I wager this determinate crime (the killing of innocent people) against that immeasurable evil (a Nazi triumph)?" He concludes it cannot; for in actuality, Churchill in 1942 admitted that the U.S. and Russia had inflicted such injuries on the German army that they opened up other possibilities besides the bombing of cities. The bombing was, nevertheless, continued in order to cripple the German war effort. Therefore the argument used between 1942 and 1945 was utilitarian in character: "its emphasis was not on victory itself, but on the time and price of victory."

Even on a utilitarian calculation, Walzer concludes the bombing was not justified: "the deliberate slaughter of innocent men and women cannot be justified simply because it saves the lives of other men and women." Such a bizarre accounting is encouraged by utilitarianism, according to Walzer. "Acknowledgment of rights" puts a stop to this kind of calculation.

The decision to use the atomic bomb on Hiroshima was also the result of this type of plea of necessity. It differed from the British bombings in Europe in that the British argument against Germany was, "If we don't do X (bomb their cities), they will do Y (win the war, establish tyrannical rule, etc.)." The U.S. argument was, "If we don't do X (use the A-bomb), *we* will do Y (kill more people in prolonged fighting)." Walzer argues that the United States went ahead with the decision to use the atomic bomb because its war aims included Japan's unconditional surrender. Because Japan's own war aims did not include the extraordinary sort of subjugation of its opponents that Nazi Germany's aims did, Walzer maintains Japan needed only to be defeated, not overthrown. Proportionality , then, was wrongly applied since this was not a true case of "necessity." Walzer concludes, "The only possible defense of the Hiroshima attack is a utilitarian calculation made without the sliding scale... a calculation made, then, where there was no room for it, a claim to override the rules of war and the rights of Japanese civilians."[114]

But the U.S. did use a "sliding scale" against the Japanese as retaliation for Pearl Harbor, for cruelties to U.S. prisoners, and to shorten the agony of war.

Walzer concedes, however, that some situation may demand breaking the war convention. What is the nature of this situation that merits such a reversal of his thinking? One must turn to "necessity$_4$" to find the answer.

Necessity$_4$[115]

The alternative Walzer offers for the sliding scale argument is summed up in his maxim: "[D]o justice unless the heavens are (really) about to fall."

Childress says that Walzer argues against utilitarianism throughout his theory, but that he finally surrenders to one form of it here.[116]

Walzer concedes that this fourth concept of necessity is a kind of utilitarianism, "a utilitarianism of extremity... in which the only restraints upon military action are those of utility and proportionality. Acknowledging that critics may accuse him of using the "sliding scale" argument, Walzer tries to make clear the distinctions between the two. Ordinarily, when combatants are confronted by the rights which the rules of war were drawn up to protect, the noncombatants' rights to life and liberty, they must "stop short" and turn aside without calculating consequences. If they use a sliding scale argument, they will try to justify breaking the rules much sooner than when extremity demands such action. Thus, Walzer claims that the sliding scale argument erodes the war convention bit by bit, while his argument from extremity does not erode it but severs it suddenly and only at the last moment. The reason for holding onto this rule to the end is respect for individuals' rights and the "status" of persons as rights-bearers. These rights, he says, are still standing even as they are being overridden. The person who overrides them must bear the guilt for taking such action. It is this fourth argument of Walzer that provides the best account of the conflict between *jus ad bellum* and *jus in bello* and most fully recognizes the force of each.[117]

Necessity, then, can rightly be claimed only at the point of "supreme emergency." There are two criteria that determine when this situation has been reached: the first is that the danger must be imminent; the second, that the nature of the danger must be of an unusual and horrifying kind. This means that the danger must be interpreted as threatening disaster for a political community, since, as Walzer argues, "the survival and freedom of political communities... are the highest values in international society."[118]

According to Walzer, Nazism posed such a threat. Thus Nazism satisfied the second criterion of a supreme emergency. When the Nazis began to carry out their threat, they satisfied the first criterion, "imminence," as well, thereby justifying the *jus ad bellum* conditions.

The same criteria must be invoked before violating the *jus in bello* conditions. When Walzer examines certain actions during World War II, an otherwise "just war," he finds that both criteria were not always met; for example, it has already been seen that the British "terror bombing" of German cities reached its height long after the supreme emergency had passed. Likewise, the decision to use the atomic bomb on Hiroshima was the result of a strategy to achieve victory in a shorter period of time.

Overriding the rights of the innocent to life and liberty is ultimately a matter of utilitarian calculation, even in supreme emergencies. The principle of proportionality is used to weigh the consequences, and utility is the norm to which the appeal is made. Thus Walzer, who has struggled to avoid the utilitarian calculus throughout his just war theory does seem to surrender to it here. His position leaves him with a paradox: he justifies the actions undertaken in supreme emergencies, but even after justifying them, he calls the agents who perform them "guilty." In supreme emergencies, Walzer concludes, "there is no honorable or moral course for a man to take, no course free of guilt and responsibility for evil."[119] It is possible that Walzer can avoid this paradox if he uses Richard McCormick's concept of "proportionate reason" and the inherent relation between the contemplated action and the value being sought. This possibility will be explored, but only after a more thorough investigation of "the value being sought," the rights to life and liberty. This consideration leads directly to the issue of noncombatant immunity.

Chapter 3

The Principle of Noncombatant Immunity
and Contemporary Just War Theories

Introduction

The change in emphasis from *jus ad bellum* conditions to *jus in bello* conditions between classic and contemporary just war is especially evident in the development of the concept of noncombatant immunity. As with the principle of proportionality, so with the principle of noncombatant immunity there is a correlation with the technological development of weapons and the ways in which nations wage war. In addition, theorists have differed in their understanding of the relative or absolute binding power of this principle. It seems that this, too, may be a function of the destructive capacity of weapons rather than a guide to their development. Weaponry has had a tendency to become more indiscriminate in its destructive power, though there are some signs in the nuclear era that this trend may be changing. In 1954, for example, the U.S. tested thermonuclear weapons with a fifteen megaton explosive capacity. By 1956, however, President Eisenhower issued a directive stating, "Bombs with yields greater than two megatons should be used only for very special purposes... [and targeting should be tailored so as not to cause] unnecessarily high population losses."[1]

There has also been increased emphasis on precision targeting. For example, Martin Marietta Aerospace is developing precision-guided "submissiles" for the Army's Tactical Missile System. These "follow-on warheads" will seek out and destroy moving armored units.[2] Likewise, the Strategic Defense Initiative Organization continues its "maturing directed-energy technology," anticipating a decision on whether the weapons concepts and system-level tests are warranted. SDI is conducting experiments to ensure that multiple targets can be distinguished against varied backgrounds.[3] Whether such weapons will lead to greater likelihood of war than weapons of massive destruction is, of course, another question.

While the principle of proportionality is generally considered relevant in limited war theories of the twentieth century, the principle of noncombatant immunity has tended to be ignored to the extent that some international law experts claim international law should no longer even pay lip service to it.[4] Yet Richard Hartigan notes in his dissertation on noncombatant immunity that the post-World War II period has witnessed a "renaissance" in just war theorizing; and, at a time when actual practice seems to indicate otherwise, post-World War II just war theories have focused on the principle of noncombatant immunity. Hartigan attributes this "solely to the fact of the nature of modern warfare. [N]ot until the twentieth century could so many nations mobilize such a totality of their human and material resources and employ them so effectively to wage war. The phenomenon of 'total war' in the fullest sense of the term is, therefore, a fact which is unique to this century."[5]

The future also seems to hold the prospect of weapons capable of greater indiscriminate destruction than at any time in history. While some weapons are being designed to be more precise in their targeting, if there is to be any hope that future warfare is to be limited, consideration must be given to the morality of the means and methods of conducting war, i.e., to the *jus in bello* conditions. Understanding the principle of noncombatant immunity and determining the extent of its binding power is key to determining the applicability of just war theories to nuclear war and deterrence policies. In an analysis of this important just war principle, it will be helpful to look first into the historical development of the concept of noncombatant immunity. As James Johnson's work in this area has shown, tracing the roots of the *jus in bello* principle of noncombatant immunity is of more than merely historical interest. The consensus on the principle reached during the fourteenth century has "defined the terms of discourse for subsequent treatment of this aspect of the limitation of war."[6]

Some contemporary theorists reflect the thinking of earlier theorists to a greater degree than others: Ramsey, for example, depends on Augustine for the foundation of his just war doctrine and on Aquinas for further development of particular moral categories such as "indirect action" and "double effect." It would be well, then, to dwell briefly on the sources of the classic just war tradition before turning to the classic just war theorists themselves.

Classic Just War Theories and the Principle of Noncombatant Immunity

Historical Development

James Johnson maintains that "'a just war doctrine' *does not exist* prior to the end of the Middle Ages," but that prior to about the year 1500 there were two doctrines: one religious, dealing with *jus ad bellum*, and one secular, dealing primarily with *jus in bello*.[7] He gives four sources of the classic just war tradition: two religious and two secular. The religious sources are (1) the canon law tradition which is built upon the work of Gratian, the Decretists and the Decretalists; and (2) the theological tradition, including but not limited to Aquinas. The secular sources are (1) civil law, which updated Roman law, and (2) the chivalric code, a curious blending of secular and religious elements in the culture of the day. The focus here will be upon the religious sources as being more concerned with the *moral* reasoning behind *jus in bello* conditions and on the chivalric sources which also reveal strong religious influence. As will become evident, however, neither the Church nor the secular sources were *exclusively* concerned with the *morality* of war.

Religious Sources

Canon Law Tradition

The Peace of God, The Truce of God and The Ban on Weapons

Of the three attempts of the canonists to limit war (the "Peace of God," the "Truce of God" and the ban on weapons), the Peace of God seems to contain the roots of noncombatant immunity, according to Johnson. The Peace of God was an attempt by the Church to draw combatant/noncombatant distinction according to people's social functions: i.e., it exempted those involved in religious duties from the violence of war. By Gratian's time, the list had expanded to include eight classes of persons, listed two centuries later by Gregory IX in *De Treuga et Pace*: clerics, monks, friars, other religious, pilgrims, travelers, merchants and peasants cultivating the soil--all these were to be spared the ravages of war. Gratian even mentions these persons' animals and goods and peasants' lands as well.[8] The Truce of God, promulgated by the Council of Narbonne in 1054 and again by the Third Lateran Council in 1179, provided that certain days would be days of peace when no fighting should take place. These days included Christian festivals and the period from Wednesday sunset to Monday dawn.[9] The ban on weapons occurred later than the Truce of God or the Peace of God. In 1139, the Second Lateran Council banned the crossbow, bows and arrows generally and siege machines in wars among Christians.

Johnson identifies two ways of defining noncombatants: by social function, and by the individual's inability to bear arms. The Peace of God, which contains the origins of noncombatant immunity, focused on the first. It did not mention women, children, the ill or any others unable to bear arms, although the reason for this omission may have been that these groups were already presumed exempt. Johnson suggests that the list reveals a certain bias of the church--one which found her understandably "preoccupied with her own."[10] Gratian's list was more inclusive; he denied clerics the right to participate in war, and added women and the unarmed poor to the list of noncombatants, a distinction made on the basis of an inability to bear arms. Gratian's additions reveal a developing synthesis between Church and secular sources.

Johnson attributes the reasoning behind Gratian's list of noncombatants and Gregory IX's list in *De Treuga et Pace* to a simple form of justice: those not having the occupation or social function of making war should not have war made against them. However, as women, children, and others unable to bear arms are not mentioned on the original lists, one might question whether Johnson's explanation is correct. It is possible, however, as Johnson notes, that the immunity of those unable to bear arms was already presumed.

Gratian, the Decretists and the Decretalists

Johnson claims that even though Ramsey bases his contemporary just war theory on Augustine, the best place to begin a study of the moral and legal *jus in bello* doctrines is in the Middle Ages with Gratian's *Decretum* and not with Augustine himself. According to Johnson, even Aquinas' references to Augustine do not go beyond Gratian, who cites Augustine.[11]

Gratian's *Decretum*, the *Concordia Discordantium Canonum*, "climaxed the development of early medieval canon law collections and inaugurated the period of systematic canonical jurisprudence," says Frederick Russell. It is also a point of departure for theologians as Aquinas' use of the *Decretum* shows. Causam 23 of the *Decretum* poses the basic problems of warfare to be resolved and gives a framework wherein the just war debate may take place. Russell calls Causam 23, the "locus classicus of texts concerning warfare." In it are found comprehensive Augustinian texts, the teachings of the Fathers of the church, papal teachings and Roman law: material which has provided for the future growth of international law.

The canonists of the twelfth century who used Gratian's *Decretum* and commented on it are called the "Decretists." Russell gives as their heyday the period from 1140-1190. Those commentators who wrote after 1190 and throughout the thirteenth century and who made extensive use of the new decretals are called "Decretalists." These canonists begin to shift their primary attention from the *Decretum* to contemporary papal legislation and gave more detailed descriptions of how just wars should be fought. The Decretalists offered few innovations but, as Russell points out, they gave more systematic expression to just war principles. Recognizing that the *jus in bello* conditions, whether inspired by custom or canon law, were based more on expediency and military necessity than on the rights of bystanders, the Decretalists give increasing concern to the legal limits of war. Nevertheless, perhaps because wars were most often feudal wars fought between knights for booty, Russell points out that the Decretalists hardly ever mentioned death as a consequence of war. They seemed more interested in treating war as "a mercantile profession," and in showing that in war, too, "crime [does] not pay." The Decretalists treated war as an "extraordinary form of a lawsuit," emphasizing authorities and jurisdictions rather than just cause or divine intervention and making extensive use of Roman law procedures.[12]

During the time of Gratian and the Decretists, the disciplines of canon law and theology merged. After 1200, however, each began to develop its own sphere of competence. The theologians elaborated their doctrine along different but parallel lines, their most distinctive contribution being, according to Russell, "the naturalness of the just war based on the naturalness of human societies and the pursuit of the common good."[13] Russell says that the theologians placed more stress on the moral dimensions of warfare and showed more suspicion of warfare than the canonists did. However, the theologians were less able to discuss certain aspects of the just war tradition, such as the problem of "proper authority," because they lacked the canonists' expertise in matters of conflicting jurisdictions. Russell contends that in time, the canonists' concern with the legal consequences of the justice or injustice of a war "led them to construct a doctrine of disobedience that appealed to the material welfare of a vassal similarly perplexed."[14] The theologians, on the other hand, were able to maintain their primary concern for justice as they offered their opinions on the "licit conduct and consequences of warfare."[15]

Secular Source: Chivalry

James Johnson considers the source of the chivalric definition of noncombatancy to be the knights' own interests. The code of chivalry seems to have served as a wall separating the "haves" from the "have-nots." It bound together those with the code (the knights) in a kind of mutual support, while it denied the same privileges to those outside it. The result was two kinds of treatment for the "have-nots": condescension or rejection.

Those who were "condescended to" are the weak and innocent: the "noncombatants" including women, children, the aged, clergy, etc. These had to be protected. As Johnson remarks, whatever the motivation, the chivalric relation of condescension "did help to produce a concept of noncombatant protection that went well beyond what the Church was willing to attempt in the twelfth and thirteenth centuries."[16]

On the other hand, during the Middle Ages the "rejected" included not only enemy nonknights but also the nonknight infantry fighting on a knight's own side. The "common soldier" was often taken from his farm by the knight and required to fight in that knight's army. The peasant or artisan was not treated during this period with the same protective, if condescending, attitude as the "condescended to."

During the same period, however, the Church tried to channel knighthood into its own conception of the social order and its benefits. This is evident in the various religious ceremonies associated with knighthood and in the Crusades, in which the church engaged the fighting capacity of the medieval knight to wage its battles for a religious cause.

The church and the chivalric tradition began to merge, then, until, by the last half of the fourteenth century, when as Honore Bonet states, the two lists of noncombatants were one: "bishops, abbots, monks, doctors of medicine, pilgrims, women, blind persons, all other men of the Church not named earlier, the deaf, the dumb, woodmen and farmers, [even] the farmer's ox and ass."[17]

The separate lists from the two traditions reveal two different foundations for noncombatant immunity: the canonical use of the category of "function in society" and the chivalric use of the category of "those unable to bear arms."

Johnson shows that these two different bases reveal a fundamental difference in the assumptions about the nature of noncombatancy. In canon law, noncombatants were spared according to the principle of justice, as has been noted. According to the chivalric view, the immunity of noncombatants follows from the relation of protector and protected; it was a "gift from the knight."[18] Indeed, in case of "military necessity," a knight could override the requirements of chivalry. This created a tension inherent in the new synthesis of noncombatants that emerges in the fourteenth century, a tension which, Johnson claims, "[became] central in the developing cultural consensus on just war, [a] contrast and... tension [that has] remained in that doctrine to the present day."[19]

One finds evidence of the same contrast and tension in the just war theorists who bridge the span of time from medieval culture to modern times.

Definitions

Noncombatants

AUGUSTINE

Augustine finds exceptions to the general commandment, "Thou shalt not kill." He says, "Included in this category are individuals whom God by means of some law or an explicit command, limited to a particular time and person, has ordered put to death. Anyone who acts as a delegate in this regard is not himself the slayer since he is like a sword that is a tool in the hands of its user."[20]

Paul Ramsey implies in his writings that in Augustine one finds the true basis for a doctrine of noncombatant, or "innocent," immunity.[21] That is, that each person is loved by God and deserves the care, respect and protection that God's love demands. However, Hartigan's examination of Augustine's notion of the place of justice in the State raises doubt regarding Ramsey's premise. Hartigan concludes that "the absolute imperative of Christian love did not include the demand that the morally innocent be spared the purely physical evil of death when the necessities of just war required their death."[22] According to Frederick Russell, Augustine believes that the real evils in war are not war itself, but "the love of violence and cruelty, greed and the *libido dominandi* or lust for rule that so often accompanied it,"[23] stressing the inwardness of Augustine's ethics which results in a position that justifies any hostile act provided it is motivated by charity.[23]

Although Augustine lived in the fourth century, it is evident that the interpretation of him that forms a part of the "seamless web" (if that is what it turns out to be) of the just war tradition, dates from Gratian's selection of texts in the *Decretum*. James Johnson points out that as Ramsey interprets Augustine, "the essential reason why noncombatancy should be recognized and respected by combatants is Christian charity... [requiring] that the Christian defend his neighbor against unprovoked, unjust attack."[24] The neighbor includes the "enemy neighbor" as well.

Augustine's focus is with the inner disposition rather than the outward act. Therefore, his imperative of Christian love "[does] not include the demand that the morally innocent be spared the merely physical evil of death when the necessities of just war require their death."[25] In fact, the just war makes possible an unlimited use of violence in order to avenge the violation of rights or a violation of the moral order,[26] according to the broad interpretation. Clearly, such an interpretation of Augustine does not represent all that was done during the Middle Ages to limit the ravages of war.

Classic Just War Theorists

AQUINAS

Like Augustine, Aquinas treats issues related to war in the context of broader questions, such as homicide and the proper conduct of defense; but he does deal with the issue of war itself in the *Summa Theologica*, II-II, Question 4. In this section, Aquinas is primarily interested in the *jus ad bellum* question; "Are some wars permissible?" He is less interested in the *jus in bello* issues of how wars are fought. He does not discuss noncombatant immunity as such. His four points of inquiry are (1) the permissibility of war; (2) whether clerics may engage in warfare; (3) whether belligerents may use subterfuge; and (4) whether war may be waged on feast days.[27]

During the wars of the thirteenth century, exceptions to usual military practice did occur. As has been noted, even the chivalric code was overridden by military necessity. The double standard inherent in the canonical limitations on warfare also permitted exceptions. The besieging of cities and subsequent atrocities were among these exceptions and Aquinas must have been aware of some of these. LeRoy Walters cites as examples of such sieges the Christians' assault against the Albigensians in Beziers in which eight thousand inhabitants, mostly noncombatants and Christians, were killed, and the assault on Damietta in Egypt, in which, of the eighty thousand inhabitants, three thousand survived; of these survivors, all but one hundred were not ill.[28]

In "The Crusader States, 1243-1291", Steven Runciman describes the horrors of the Christian sack of Antioch, and Walters cites Runciman to show that it is reasonable to believe that Aquinas would have been aware of this siege, and that "his stringent position on the protection of the innocent was, at least implicitly criticism of indiscriminate thirteenth century practice." Indeed, Walters claims this raises the question of whether Thomas would have approved of military action against cities under *any* circumstance. Killing innocents had not been discussed in detail by any theologians prior to Aquinas. It has already been shown that canonist/theologian were practically identical until the thirteenth century. Russell maintains that "[Aquinas'] extensive adaptation of Aristotle ... set [him] and his circle apart from earlier theologians, and emancipated them from dependence on the canonists." The Aristotelian influence is evident in Aquinas' reasoning that warfare is "rooted in the nature of human communities," that is that the safety of the community sometimes demands that the individual's life be put at risk in order to prevent large-scale killing and other spiritual and temporal evils in the larger community.

Hartigan maintains that Aquinas was more concerned in his writings about war in general than about the conduct of war. Thus, when examining his position on killing, and especially on killing the innocent, one errs in making an analogy between Aquinas' examples of individual killing and the killing in war. Hartigan concludes that Thomas gave no indication that unarmed civilians are innocent.

Walters disagrees with Hartigan and cites four reasons why he believes Aquinas did recognize the innocence of unarmed civilians. First, Thomas was opposed to collective guilt and insisted on the need to discriminate among persons. Second, he required the presence of a subjective and serious overt offense as prerequisite for just cause in war. Third, in Thomas' explanatory note to Deuteronomy 20:13-14, in which Israel's army killed only male soldiers and spared women and children, he added that the "enemy males" were the ones who had fought against God's people. Fourth, in Thomas' time, canon law had already exempted certain classes of people from harm in warfare. Thomas was silent on this matter, but was intent on formulating the general moral principle underlying the exemptions. Walters concludes that Aquinas' position was "at least implicitly criticism of indiscriminate thirteenth century military practice." Aquinas did not enumerate specific categories of protected persons, according to Walters since "he preferred to formulate his position in abstract terms, arguing in general that innocent persons [may] never be killed."[30] Aquinas condemned killing an innocent person because the killer (1) harms one who ought to be loved more, therefore infringing on charity; (2) inflicts injury on one who deserves it less, therefore infringing on justice; (3) deprives the community of a greater good; (4) despises God who takes rejection of another as rejection of God as well. Thomas added, "And the fact that an unjust man who is killed is brought to glory is purely incidental to the killing."[31] Russell believes this takes some of the sting out of Aquinas' condemnation and concludes that Aquinas really did "straddle" the issues of noncombatant immunity; he did not approve the killing of the innocent but neither did he unqualifiedly prohibit it. The tension which Johnson points out earlier is clearly apparent in Aquinas.[32]

Hartigan espouses the more rigid interpretation of Aquinas as well. Hartigan agrees with Emile Chanon whom he cites: "[Thomas d'Aquin] ne distingue pas entre les combattants et les non-combattants..."[33] Hartigan maintains that Aquinas seemed never even to hint at the possibility that there may be some among the enemy who are not sinners, that he did not mention children as an exception, nor the categories of innocents accepted in the "Peace of God." Rather than emphasizing the subjective moral guilt of the enemy, Thomas dwelt on the objective violation of a legal right as the basis of war's just cause.

According to Hartigan, Thomas left himself open to criticism and interpretation because of his failure to categorize innocents in war. Thomas assumed that "innocent" meant "in conformity to God's will." Russell asserts that Aquinas followed Augustine's theory of "war guilt," whereby the innocent may be legitimately punished even in an unjust war for sins they have committed that are unconnected with the war. In the debate regarding the moral status of captives in war, Russell finds Aquinas inconclusive, giving indications, perhaps, that Aquinas' own just war theory is inadequate to deal with all the problems involving noncombatancy that have emerged with the passage of time.

Later theorists supply what is lacking in Aquinas: they call for lessening of emphasis on the objective violation of a legal right as a basis for wars of just cause. In them one sees increasing evidence that the "bearing of arms" have become by their time the practical basis for exempting certain classes of people; that is, that the "innocents" of war have become the "noncombatants." In Hartigan's strict interpretation of the just war tradition prior to the time of the four later class theorists, however, "innocents" are not equivalent to "noncombatants," nor is there a *conceptual* place in the tradition for noncombatant immunity "understood in the modern sense as the exemption of certain classes of the enemy population from attack on the basis of their nonparticipation in the hostilities."[34]

Developing parallel to the theologians' and canonists' theories--and even in spite of them, as Hartigan claims--there is a general and growing sentiment that certain classes of people are exempted from war's violence. Johnson attributed the movement toward a unified doctrine of noncombatant immunity to the effort of a whole *culture*, and not just a part of that culture, to deal with the problem of war.[35] This may be partly attributed, as Hartigan claims, to humanitarian reaction to the "pitiless bloodshed and social insecurity" in Europe after the disintegration of the Roman Empire.[36] At any rate, the task of finding appropriate ways to limit the ravages of war would continue, thus revealing the contrast and tension between military necessity and protection of the innocent to which Johnson refers.

VITORIA

Hartigan singles out Vitoria as the "true bridge from the Middle Ages to the modern era,"[37] combining as he does ethical principles and customs to propose normative guides. Vitoria takes into consideration that *all* the enemy cannot be guilty. While holding that objectively war can be just only on one side, he believed that subjectively war can be just on both sides. He argued for the individuation of guilt and punishment, though, as Walters points out, in an early period Vitoria had supported punishing the whole state for a monarch's sin.[38] Hartigan cites Vitoria's use of the analogy of the nation-state as a moral entity, thereby permitting reprisals against all the people in an enemy state," even the innocent, provided the evil to be avoided or prevented is both certain and grave."[39]

Vitoria held that the killing of the innocent is forbidden by natural law. He seems to identify the "innocent" as those who do not aid or bear arms in the cause of the unjust belligerent, for he included among the innocent "'children', 'women, unless certainly guilty,' 'harmless agricultural folk,' 'foreigners, clerics, members of a religious order.'" He proposed a double standard for Christians and non-Christians, saying that it was "permissible to kill all who bore among unbelievers from whom it is useless ever to hope for a just peace on any terms. On the contrary, however, in a war against Christians, I do not think that this would be unlawful."[41] Walters concludes that Vitoria emphasized restriction more than permission and in "doubtful" cases urged that a compromise be worked out or that the *status quo* be kept intact.[42] Johnson points out that Vitoria acknowledges the use of seige weapons that might result in the accidental killing of noncombatants. The right to use such means, however, is limited in Vitoria by the principle of proportionality: "to see greater evils do not arise out of the war than the war would avert."[43]

SUAREZ, GROTIUS AND GENTILI

According to Johnson, Suarez states essentially the same view on "innocents" as Vitoria though he includes those who are able to bear arms but who have not obviously committed crimes or taken part in unjust war. Thus he says that natural law theory supports the inclusion among the innocent of children, women and all unable to bear arms. To these he adds ambassadors as provided by the *jus gentium*, and, among Christians--by the provisions of positive law--religious priests. The single feature shared by all these designated "innocents" by natural law, *jus gentium*, and positive law is that they are not bearers of arms, i.e., that they are noncombatants.

Grotius includes among the innocent old men and women, "unless they take the place of men," and those "'whose occupations are solely religious or concerned with letters,' as well as farmers and merchants," citing Vitoria as an authority.

Gentili includes in the category of the innocent, "children, 'boys who are not far from the age of puberty'; 'old people, farmers, traders, travelers, monks, clerics, contingent on their not aiding the enemy's war effort' and excluding 'pirates, brigands and rebels'" from protection by the laws of war.[46]

One may conclude that "innocent persons" are generally identified with "noncombatants" by the classic just war theorists but note, with Walters, two exceptions: (1) all adult males *capable* of bearing arms and not clearly innocent could be regarded as guilty;[47] (2) enemy combatants fighting under compulsion or because of invincible ignorance could be considered "subjectively" innocent. The class of "protected persons" has been enlarged by the classic just war theorists without compromising the status of "innocent" persons, Walters points out.[49]

The Principle: How binding is it?

AUGUSTINE AND AQUINAS

Swift points out that Augustine really never had a "theory of just war," but that his remarks were scattered throughout his work. Augustine seemed most concerned about *jus ad bellum*, not *jus in bello* limitations. At one point he says,

> The only thing a righteous man has to worry about is that the just war is waged by someone who has the right to do so because not all men have that right. Once an individual has undertaken this kind of war, it does not matter at all, as far as justice is concerned, whether he wins victory in open combat or through ruses.[50]

According to Hartigan, Augustine makes "no demands that [the] innocent be spared the evil effects of war whether these innocents be soldiers or civilians. Moral guilt was concerned not with *who* is killed but with *why* and *under what* circumstances they are killed.[51] This interpretation seems to imply that the principle of noncombatant immunity was not binding in a just war at all.

Aquinas denies the *intention* but not the *act* of killing the enemy with the intent of serving the common good.[52] In self-defense, Aquinas permitted the indirect killing of another; because of the very nature of self-defense, however, the "other" in these cases would not be "innocent." Aquinas states the principle as follows:

Accordingly the act of self-defense may have two effects, one is the saving of one's life, the other is the slaying of the aggressor. Therefore, this act, since one's intention is to save one's own life, is not unlawful, seeing that it is natural for everything to keep itself in *being*, as far as possible. And yet, though, proceeding from a good intention, an act may be rendered unlawful, if it be out of proportion to the end. Wherefore if a man in self-defense uses more than necessary violence, it will be unlawful; whereas if he repel force with moderation his defense will be lawful, because according to the jurists, it is lawful to repel force by force, provided one does not exceed the limits of a blameless defense.[53]

It is noteworthy that Aquinas speaks of *individual* self-defense during the conduct of war. Walters concludes that Aquinas would have regarded killing the innocent in warfare as two simultaneous acts. Killing the innocent is inherently immoral; waging war may be immoral or not, depending on many factors.[54] Walters cites six separate occasions where Thomas applies the parable of the "wheat and tares" to killing the innocent: in all these, "the guilty could be killed only when they were clearly separable from the innocent."[55]

The Doctrine of Double Effect

AQUINAS

Whether or not Aquinas applies the doctrine of double effect to killing the innocent in war, his enunciation of the principle for the first time has led to essential addition to the Christian just war theory."[56] Joseph Mangan, S.J. states that

> even though St. Thomas applied the principle explicitly only to one case, he at least enunciated the principle, according to our interpretation; and he seems to have been the first to do so. Furthermore, even if... St. Thomas did not teach the principle of double effect as we understand it today, he still gave the initial impetus to its explanation and application in the authors who follow him to the present.[57]

Cajetan, Mangan maintains, contributed to the historical advance of the principle in his sixteenth century commentary on the *Summa Theologica*. He was the first to apply the principle to killing innocents: "to intend to kill an innocent person as an end in itself or as a means to an end is contrary to all rights. But to kill an innocent person *per accidens*, by doing something that is lawful and necessary, as one does who is administering a public office, is not contrary to natural law, divine or written law."[58]

VITORIA

The principle is used increasingly in particular cases during the sixteenth into the seventeenth century. Moralists denied the necessity of using the principle in cases of self-defense, however, since they judged it already lawful to kill an unjust aggressor when necessary to save one's own life. It was during this period that the classic just war theorists applied the principle to the indirect killing of the innocent in war. Vitoria seems to apply the principle of double effect in the besieging of a city, where "[if] the death of the innocent is a consequence of the bombardment, let them die, since that consequence is incidental."[59] Hartigan claims Vitoria was the first to use the principle to justify killing the innocent in war. Walters cites Vitoria: "The proof is that war could not otherwise be waged against even the guilty and the justice of the belligerent would be balked."[60]

James Johnson, on the other hand, maintains that Vitoria did not base his position on the principle of double effect but on the *jus ad bellum* criterion of proportionality: "to see that greater evils do not arise out of the war than they would avert." If the justice of the war is in doubt, noncombatant immunity functions as an absolute principle and the innocent may not be harmed. Johnson suggests this is not a "sliding scale" argument, for the war is either known to be just or it is not. Even in a *just* war, noncombatants may be killed only collaterally, i.e., if they are in the immediate vicinity of a legitimate military operation. Johnson notes that justification for indirect killing of noncombatants does not lie in the *jus in bello* sense of proportionality, but in its *jus ad bellum* sense (total evil vs. total good). Therefore one may not move against noncombatants if this will merely help to subdue the enemy in a particular battle. He argues that Vitoria's use of *relative* immunity rather than "doubt effect" to justify indiscriminate weaponry and his use of *jus ad bellum* proportionality anticipates Ramsey's argument for the absoluteness of noncombatant immunity.[61]

SUAREZ, GROTIUS AND GENTILI

Suarez also states that the innocent may be killed incidentally[62] and appeals to the principle of double effect, for it would be impossible in any other way to "bring war to an end."[63] Elsewhere Suarez states that "'slaying of a great multitude' is allowed only if there is a 'most urgent cause.'"[64]

Grotius is more cautious than Suarez, says Walters. Where Suarez approves of "delivering a 'rebellious city' to fire and to the sword 'in case of necessity,'"[65] Grotius cautions, "such actions cannot take place without very serious harm to *many* innocent persons, and often are of little consequence for the result of the war; so that Christian goodness almost always and bare justice very often, shrinks from them."[66]

Hartigan attributes Grotius' urging for moderation to consideration of humanity, religion, and far-sighted policy.[67] Nevertheless, Grotius states, "[I]n war the things which are necessary for attaining the end are lawful."[68] Thus, "[s]ubjects, even when innocent, are liable to attack insofar as they impede the attainment of our right. For we wage wars for no other end than to obtain our right... by means of victory."[69] "We may bombard a ship *full* of pirates or a house *full* of brigands, even if there are within the same ship or house a *few* infants, women, or other innocent persons who are thereby endangered."

Walters believes Grotius considers "indirect intention" the moral basis for his position, that is, that he is appealing to double effect.[71] If one takes Mangan's meanings of *intendere* as referring to the ultimate end of the action and *also* to the *means* to the ultimate end, Grotius appears to hold that victory over an unjust belligerent is the ultimate end, while the incidental killing of the innocent "outside [the] intention" or *"per accidens."*[72]

Grotius is more cautious than Gentili, saying that if great numbers of innocents are involved, they should be pardoned after the war.[73] He also contradicts Gentili in stating that the belligerent should be "[d]iscriminate in the use of military means solely on the basis of moral considerations,"[74] and that one should keep faith with *all* enemies, even pirates:

> Since an enemy, although waging a just war, does not have the true and perfect right of killing innocent subjects, who are not responsible for the war, unless either as a necessary defensive measure or as a result and apart from his purpose..., it follows that, if it is certain that the enemy comes with such a spirit that he absolutely refuses to spare the lives of hostile subjects when he can, these subjects may defend themselves by the law of nature, of which they are not deprived by the law of nations.

In summary, Walters concludes that it is clear that "Vitoria, Suarez, and Grotius allowed the *unintentional* killing of innocent persons *during the period of actual combat* and *in cases of necessity."*[76] The theoretical basis for this position is generally the canonistic and Thomistic doctrine of indirect intention:

> the just warriors' aim was to injure only enemy combatants, but that unintentionally... and because of circumstances... he also harmed innocent persons or noncombatants. In their view this theory of indirect effect was valid even in cases where the damage to innocent persons could be foreseen and predicted.

Their position emerges as a result of their basic teleological just war orientation. The four later theorists thus "[agree] that the use of military force against innocent persons or civilians was justified *to the extent necessary* to ensure victory."[78]

In Walters' account, Vitoria and Grotius have broadened the possibility of innocence by introducing subjective complications, but these complications all lead to a logical difficulty and an irony since innocent persons on both sides justified in, or at least excused for, slaughtering innocent persons on the opposite side--but it is precisely the slaughter of innocent persons that Vitoria and Grotius are trying to avoid.

The term "innocent persons" is often confused with the term "civilians" or "noncombatants" today, although the three terms represent three different groups of people. Contemporary just war theorists do not all agree with the significance of the distinctions that are made. It will be important to note their own clarifications throughout their *jus in bello* discussions. Whatever distinction they make, however, they confront the possibility of nuclear war that may result in injuries and deaths among noncombatants many times greater than the injuries and deaths the classic just war theorists had to contemplate. Some argue that twentieth century wars *require* the killing of the innocent and that these wars must, therefore, be immoral.

Contemporary Just War Theorists and the Principle of Noncombatant Immunity

Introduction

Geoffrey Best notes that "the law of war... took a considerable beating during the Revolutionary and Napoleonic wars of 1792-1815 due mainly to two causes: first, that classes of people who engaged in these wars had not been educated to the Enlightenment ideals of improving the general happiness and welfare of peoples; and second, that changes in thinking about war, the state, and "the people" had taken place and contributed to enlarging the goals and, therefore, the capacity for destruction in wars. Civilian suffering during the period was enormous, especially in the Napoleonic Wars where the French armies relied so heavily on the civilian population for food and supplies. French armies were far more massive than any contemporary armies." Prisoners were treated mercilessly. Not until the mid and latter nineteenth century did the laws of war begin to develop to redress these inhumanities. One might expect that the twentieth century would have fared better; but, Best notes, "war in our century has become 'total' in ways not often, nor all at once, and in some ways not at all realized before."[79]

Not only is twentieth century warfare potentially total in the number of nations involved but also in the *degree* to which they can be involved in terms of goals and weapons. The determination of the morality of the use of weapons of mass destruction will be at the center of arguments regarding the applicability of just war tradition to nuclear war.

It is in total war that the line distinguishing "soldiers" and "civilians" becomes blurred, as Best describes. Civilians themselves often behave in ways that identify them with soldiers; for example, the occupied citizenry today become resistance fighters, use merchant ships to conceal weapons; and from the air, the line becomes even more blurred, especially when precision bombing is difficult. If one cannot find another means of identifying the innocent, some have recommended abandoning the principle as no longer a suitable criterion for determining who are the innocent who may never be killed directly.

The three contemporary theorists under consideration respond to this challenge. An examination of the positions of each is in order. This examination will deal first, with their definition of "innocents;" second, with the moral basis on which each founds the principle; third, with the degree of absoluteness each ascribes to the principle.

One may be aided further by Jeffrie Murphy's considerations on "murder." Murphy defines murder as the "intentional and uncoerced killing of the innocent." By definition, murder is morally wrong. Those who claim that modern wars require killing the innocent conclude that war is therefore morally wrong as well. To avoid reaching this conclusion, as the three theorists do, one must choose one of the following options: (1) that there are no innocent in war; (2) that modern war does not require killing the innocent; (3) that war involves the suspension of moral considerations and stands outside the domain of moral criticism; (4) that the deaths of the innocents, though foreseen, are not intended and therefore, not immoral according to the principle of double effect; (5) that the duty not to kill the innocent is a *prima facie* duty and therefore can be overridden.[81]

All three conteporary just war theorists agree that just wars are still possible. It would be well, then, to turn to them in order to see how they respond to Hartigan's challenge and to Murphy's choices.

PAUL RAMSEY

Definition

The principle to which Ramsey appeals in order to spare noncombatants in war is the "principle of discrimination." He defines it as "the moral immunity of noncombatants from direct attack."[82] James Johnson says it "is at the heart of the *jus in bello* limits of the prosecution of war" in Ramsey's development of his just war theory.[83] In order to understand more clearly a concept so central to Ramsey's just war doctrine, it will be helpful to see how he defines two of the key terms in his definition: "noncombatancy" itself, and "direct attack." Ramsey insists that these definitions must be clear and must be kept clear in order to understand the principle of discrimination.[84]

Noncombatancy

Ramsey gives a history of the concept of noncombatancy in chapter 3 of *War and the Christian Conscience*. There he accepts Father John Ford's identification of noncombatants as "innocents": i.e., those who are neither "fighters" nor who work in "close relation to" or "directly participate" in conduct of war.[85] Father Ford estimates that three-fourths of the populations in urban centers deserve noncombatant status, and that, where there is doubt about the classification of a given occupation or class or persons, these, too, have "a *certain* right not to be deprived of life, family, and property until the combatant or *guilty* status is proved with certainty."[86] "Innocence" and "guilt" apply, then, to the remote or close objective relation to the conduct of war and not to subjective innocence or guilt. No amount of personal guilt has ever given one the right to kill another at any rate, according to Ramsey.[87]

This classification is in keeping with the concept of noncombatancy as it had developed in the classic just war theories. Even during the sixteenth and seventeenth centuries, as Ford points out, "whole populations contributed in the war effort in a remote manner: they fed the soldiers, provided them with arms and encouragement." Though civilian participation may have changed and even increased in three hundred years, it can be argued that this increase is "comparatively insignificant." Thus, Ramsey concludes, the "innocent" person does not mean, as it did not in the past, "an altogether harmless person, even militarily speaking, but one who did not participate directly, or with immediate cooperation in the violent and destructive action of war itself."[88]

Ramsey is opposed, then, to those positions which say the combatant/ noncombatant distinction has been eroded in modern times so that only small children or the helpless may be considered noncombatants. "Standing outside the war effort," he notes, "has never been the criterion for noncombatant status. What does determine this status is the remoteness or closeness to the war effort."[89] Though he cannot give the precise point where noncombatancy stands on the remoteness/closeness scale, Ramsey insists the distinction can be made but, indeed, does not even have to be made with exactitude. One need only know *that* noncombatants are present in the area, not exactly *who* or *where* they are. Comparing the combatancy/noncombatancy distinction to twilight, Ramsey suggests, "The fact of twilight, as Dr. Johnson said, does not mean you cannot tell day from night."[90]

The combatancy/noncombatancy distinction is "relativistic and varying in application... a function of how the nations or the forces are organized for war and of military technology," according to Ramsey.[91] As a function of how nations are organized for war, Ramsey offers as an example, the kind of counter-insurgency warfare waged in South Vietnam, where combatants organized themselves for war among the people as "fish in water."[92] It is not clear exactly what Ramsey means by noncombatancy as a "function of military technology." Conceivably, the more complex the war machinery and the command structure, the weapons and launchers, the more workers there are who produce the many parts and play the many roles in political and military decision making, so that while those who made weapons in the past were more "closely" connected to the war effort, the same kinds of workers today may be considered only remotely related to it. Nevertheless, Ramsey appears to agree with Father Ford, who lists nearly 120 different occupations as having noncombatancy status during World War II and as constituting a large proportion of the civilian population. It may be assumed that the situation has not changed significantly in the past forty years. At any rate, what is important from a moral standpoint is not exactly *who* or *where* the noncombatants are, as Ramsey says, but *that* they are present in a given area. This brings one to Ramsey's important distinction between direct and indirect attacks.

Direct and Indirect Attacks

Ramsey defines "deliberate, direct attack [as]... a matter of the intentional acts of war, of their direction or thrusts in the world, of their targets and objectives, the planned design of the war to be executed."[93] Both words, "direct" and "indirect," in Ramsey's usage refer to the immediate material object of a physical act. The difference between the two lies in the *formal* object of the act--that is, its intention. Thus, in a military action, a decision may be made to attack a military installation. The attack on this installation is a direct attack on the formal object of the act; the destruction of the installation is the direct effect of the action. However, there may be noncombatants in the area of the installation. Death or injury to them is a foreseen effect of the action but "beside" the intention of the act. Therefore, Ramsey would call the destruction of the noncombatants in this action an *indirect* effect and the attack on them an "indirect" attack.

In order for the deaths of the innocent to be classified as an indirect effect of an attack, the deaths and injuries must not be the *means* to the direct effect. The deaths and injuries to noncombatants may occur later in time than the military effort, or they may occur simultaneously, but in order to qualify as indirect effects, they must be incidental to the intended effect.[134] Ramsey emphasizes that it is not numbers of noncombatants killed that accounts for the difference. If the same number of noncombatants were killed in a tactical nuclear strike at sea as in a strategic attack on a population center, only the former would qualify as an indirect attack on noncombatants. Even though much damage and death may qualify as indirect or "collateral" though foreseen, such facts could show that the action nevertheless violates the principle of proportionality and ought not to be done.[94]

As has been seen in the classic just war theorists, there is a recognition that warfare does result in noncombatant deaths and injuries. The assumption is made by them and by Ramsey that such will be the case or at least the possibility. Ramsey comes then to the question of justification. How can the violation of noncombatant immunity be justified?

Justification: "Twin-Born"

Ultimate Norm: <u>Agape</u>

Ramsey has followed Augustine in holding in the first place, that war is justified because of the necessity to protect noncombatants. This justification flows from *agape* or Christian love. Little cites Ramsey as again bypassing justice and going directly to agape.[95] Discrimination supplies a "feature-specific designation of certain proscribed forms of action",[96] while proportionality emphasizes the discretionary side of agape. Discrimination establishes "outside limits" beyond which military action may not go. In this sense discrimination emphasizes the formalistic side of agape. The "neighbor in need" obliges the Christian to come to his or her assistance, to resist by nonviolent means when possible, but by violent means when necessary.[97] From agape, then, springs both the duty to protect noncombatants and the permission to harm combatants. One cannot discuss the one without discussing the other.

War can be waged and in fact *must* be waged, for the sake of the innocent or the noncombatant: a *jus ad bellum* condition. At the same time, the war must be waged in such a way that noncombatants are protected. Thus Ramsey derives the principle of discrimination directly from agape. He recognizes, however, that in order to protect some noncombatants, others may be put in danger and thus he must account for violation of the principle. The formalistic side of agape requires certain kinds of action, "definite action-rules,"[98] to deal with these cases. The first such rule that Ramsey derives directly from agape is the rule of double effect.

The Rule of Double Effect

As has been seen, the classic just war theorists have used the natural law as justification for *jus ad bellum* and for killing noncombatants as an indirect result of military action. In this they have made use of the principle of double effect, first articulated, but never applied to the killing of noncombatants, by Aquinas (see p. 66 above), where Walters tries to show that Aquinas does recognize the innocence of unarmed civilians.) Ramsey, too, will use the principle of double effect, but he will derive it not from natural law, but from agape.

As Ramsey traces the history of the principle of discrimination, he finds its genesis in the movement of thought between Augustine and Aquinas on the subject of killing in self-defense. The relevant passage in Augustine, Ramsey takes from *De Libero Arbitrio*, in which Augustine acknowledges a difference between killing an unjust aggressor and killing the innocent. He sees the killing of the innocent as more opposed to natural justice than killing the unjust aggressor. On this basis alone, however, the Christian may not be permitted to kill the unjust assailant either, for the Christian must act not from justice alone but from charity.

If this were the only consideration, just war would not be possible. However, Augustine introduces the idea of the "public good" such that when this good is threatened and when the highest official authority (who is presumed to be more impartial than the ordinary citizen in judging the justice of the cause) so orders, "the Christian citizen finds himself called into responsible action because of allegiance of his will with the will (and love) that constitutes him with the rest of the multitude of people."[99] The Christian may, then, kill in defense of others, but not in his own personal defense.

Aquinas' answer to the problem of killing in self-defense is based on natural law: "it is natural to everything to keep itself in being, as far as possible. The act must be proportionate, not doing more harm than is necessary for self-protection, and it must also be "indirect": "it is not lawful for a man to intend killing a man in self-defense, except for such as have public authority, who while intending to kill a man in self-defense refer this to the 'public good.'"[100]

Aquinas demands that one withhold the *intention* to kill the other, but not the *act* of killing, while Augustine would withhold both (except in the case of the public good). Ramsey says that Aquinas reaches his position through "love-transformed justice," just as Augustine does, but not to the degree that Augustine does.

It has already been shown that the determination of noncombatancy was not the problem in the thirteenth century that it is today, and that Aquinas did not address the killing of noncombatants in war as such. However, Ramsey agrees with Joseph Mangan that his "'doubling' of the will's intention for love's sake produces... the first formulation of the rule of double effect." It is important, Ramsey claims, that those who maintain that Aquinas actually applies the principle to the act of self-defense are wrong. The one being killed in self-defense is the unjust aggressor, and according to Aquinas' interpretation of natural law, an unjust aggressor can be killed if the intention is to save one's own life.

Ramsey claims that Cajetan and other moral theologians elaborated the rule in later centuries and went beyond Aquinas in exactitude and "perhaps in substance." As the rule now stands with its four conditions, neither self-defense nor the killing of an unjust aggressor comes under it, according to Ramsey, for both of these are declared to be inherently just and therefore not wrong to use as a means to a good effect when proportionate and necessary. In the process of the change from Aquinas' first articulation of the principle to the modern understanding of it, Ramsey cites clarifications:

> 1) a fuller and clearer (or at least a different) distinction between intrinsically right and wrong means and the conclusion that intrinsically evil means might never be used for any good end;

2) a more careful formulation of the rule so that the determination of direct and indirect effects were not left altogether to the self-direction of the will;
3) the conclusion that the rule could be applied correctly only to the indirect killing of the innocent not to the unjust assailant who could be killed directly, however regrettable.

Ramsey's reaction to the changes is that "natural justice triumph[ed] over love in Christian ethical theory."[101]
Ramsey concludes that

> [t]he objective situation seems to be that Aquinas devised an early formulation of the principle of double effect. Yet at the same time, it is certainly true that he did not have in mind later augmentation of the rule which stipulates that in addition to the good as the only proper object of one's formal intention it must also be capable of being done directly, and with at least as much immediacy to the act as the evil effect.[102]

The tradition in moral theology has eventually ceased using the principle as applying to self-defense against an unjust aggressor and has limited its use to killing of innocent persons.

Range of Applicability:

Subsumption of Cases

Technological complexity has resulted in more legitimate military targets and, therefore, has put more noncombatants in a greater degree of danger than ever before in history. Yet Ramsey holds that the moral limit of directly targeting only legitimate military targets still holds. He is especially critical of those who have merged noncombatant destruction with other costs on a quantitative scale and have yielded "the problem of disproportionate devastation."[103] The problem, according to Ramsey, is not killing *more* people but the separate and absolute moral limit that prohibits the *direct* killing noncombatants regardless of numbers.

The Analogous Case: Ectopic Pregnancy

Ramsey reflects on the Roman Catholic struggle to escape from the limitation that prohibits the direct killing of the innocent in certain abortion decisions where Roman Catholic moral theology has been unable to apply the rule of double effect in such a way that merciful action, according to Ramsey, is morally possible.

The dilemma Ramsey poses is the one faced by the doctor in the case of the secondary abdominal pregnancy after the rupture of the tube in tubal pregnancy. In these cases, the fetus passes from the tube to the abdominal cavity and continues to grow. The fetus seriously endangers the mother's life before reaching viability and has no chance of surviving itself after viability. There is no organ or designated part of the mother to which the placenta is attached that can be removed directly, bringing about the "indirect" death of the fetus.[104] Some Roman Catholic moralists conclude it would be better to allow both mother and fetus to die (a physical evil) rather than directly to kill the one (a moral evil) in order to save the other.

Without repudiating natural law to which these Roman Catholic moralists appeal, Ramsey insists that natural law is not the only or main source of moral judgments in Christian ethics, but that one must be open to the guidance of Christian love.

> At the point of decision in a concrete case there takes place a convergence of judgments guided [by the application of the principles of natural justice and the application of charity], a convergence in which sometimes love does what justice requires and assumes its rules as norms, sometimes love does more than justice requires but never less, and sometimes love acts in a quite different way from what justice alone can enable us to discern to be right.[105]

Ramsey concludes that the surgeon can act morally to save the mother's life in the given instance because "charity enters into a fresh determination of what is right in the given concrete context, and it is not wholly in bondage to natural-law determination of permitted or prohibited means.[106] It is love that has first devised the rule of double effect yet this rule is "open for review and radical revision in the instant *agape* controls..." Thus, Ramsey approves of the application of the rule of double effect where it can be made to apply but not "where charity plainly requires that something be done."

Ramsey draws an analogy between military installations and the "entitatively distinct" organ of the pregnant woman. If the military installations are the direct objects of attack, the indirect deaths of noncombatants as collateral damage may be allowed. If, however, such installations are not entitatively distinct, and the whole enemy people are considered a threat to peace and order in the world, would a nation be justified in holding the noncombatants hostage or in area bombing? Ramsey answers, "No," that "[c]haritable action should be free and sovereign over its own limiting, self-direction prohibiting direct killing of the innocent [save] when the innocent are soon going to die anyway and where this is certain to save life." In war neither of these conditions holds. In fact, in modern war, the reverse is true: the enemy's noncombatants will die as a result of the attacks and those in whose name the action is performed will die if the immunity of the innocent from direct, wholesale attack is breached.[107]

Relation to Proportionality

The principle of discrimination and the principle of proportionality remain remain separate but related principles in Ramsey: "neither subordinates or absorbs or exhaustively interprets the other."[108] Yet elsewhere Ramsey calls discrimination "the primary of the two," with proportionality admitting the possibility of "significant reference to consequences while discrimination does not."[109] It has been shown that the principle of discrimination is "logically prior" to the principle of proportionality in Ramsey. Therefore, if the direct killing of noncombatants is put forth as a means of accomplishing a military end, the action may not be performed, according to Ramsey.[110] On the other hand, if a military action is aimed primarily against a legitimate military target and injuries to noncombatants are foreseen, the action may or may not be performed depending on the findings of discretionary judgment. The "good" resulting from the achievement of the military goal would have to outweigh the "evil" of the collateral damage on the proportionality calculus.

Ramsey claims that "all forms of consequentialist ethics in the modern period reduce the criteria for judging the morality of war to proportionality allowing the *final* adjudication of prudence to become the only test." He speaks of the "*moral* economy governing the use of force (noncombatant immunity) and of an *economy* governing the use of force (the principle of proportion)."[111]

Discretion or prudence acts to apply the principle of discrimination and to distinguish the real from the declaratory intention of an act. Ramsey cites as an example the decision to kill one thousand innocent civilians in order to kill one combatant. One might argue that killing the noncombatants is only indirect killing because the primary intention is to kill the one combatant. To say that only the latter is intended is, according to Ramsey, "insanity." One cannot ever apply the principle of proportion since the first condition of the principle of double effect is violated: the action is first of all, murder, and may not be done regardless of the calculation of "good" vs. "evil" effects. Elsewhere Ramsey argues that if an enemy establishes bases near population centers, it is "he who has deliberately enlarged the extent of foreknowable but collateral civil destruction."[162] Such an enemy noncombatant population should not be immune, at least on the grounds of the principle of discrimination, even at the nuclear level, according to Ramsey.

Other examples of the application of discrimination offered by Ramsey include the actual case from World War II in which a debate was held among Jewish leaders on whether or not to bomb Hitler's concentration camps directly, killing all the innocent inmates, but saving many more innocents during the time it would take to rebuild the camps. Ramsey concludes that in such discussions, "there were no reasons of morality except those that political prudence dictated for decision in the negative; "that is, such an action would not have been a violation against discrimination since the inmates of the camps were "neither objectively nor subjectively the objective attacked," but the action would have been a violation of proportionality.

A second example concerns the development of incapacitating and nauseating gases. Prima facie Ramsey concludes the gases may be more humane weapons of war than other explosive weapons: the gases would be less destructive and would cause less associated civilian damage. The international response, however, has been to maintain proscriptions against their use because of the anticipation of response and counter-response resulting in an escalation to more and more deadly gases and the possibility of epidemic diseases in the population. Again the decision-makers have reached this position on the basis of proportionality: "the best, rough judgment a prudent calculation can make of a possible consequences."[113]

Ramsey's third illustration is a consideration of the firebombing of Dresden. Ramsey quotes David Irving in *The Destruction of Dresden* in pinpointing the "decisive moral element" in the bombing of Dresden: "the extraordinary precision with which the residential sections of the city were destroyed, but not the important installations; not even the railway lines we marked out for 'carpet bombing'."[114] Ramsey concludes that the destruction of Dresden fulfills the lawyer's necessary and sufficient conditions for the criminal murder: intent and "objective characteristics in the deed actually done corresponding to a paramount intention to kill the innocent directly as a means to ulterior goals believed to justify such means."[115] The firebombing of Dresden is for Ramsey a violation of the principle of discrimination.

On the other hand, Ramsey cites an imaginary example in which the primary target is one combatant (a commander who plans to blow up a city of 100,000 that evening and against whom there is no alternate way of preventing the launching of the attack); yet it is foreseen that a thousand innocent persons will be killed as a result. Here Ramsey claims the principle of double effect may be applied, the attack permitted, and it is prudence that determines this.

Ramsey's final example gives an indication of the moral argument he uses in assessing the morality of deterrence, the topic of the next chapter.

WILLIAM V. O'BRIEN

Definition

It has already been noted that William O'Brien's position on the principle of proportionality begins to diverge from Paul Ramsey's position almost from the start. Divergence between the two men is even more evident as one examines their handling of the principle of discrimination. Once again the differences begin at the level of definition, notably at the definition of noncombatancy.

Noncombatancy

O'Brien's definition of the noncombatant follows from his view of modern war as "total": i.e., as war "waged by whole societies against other societies."[116] Total war is a "fact" of the contemporary world, according to O'Brien; and he claims that "[i]n a very real sense, all members of these societies are 'combatants'."[117]

Prior to the French Revolution, during the period from 1648 to 1792, wars were fought between professional armies and, practically speaking, it was not too difficult to avoid direct targeting of noncombatants. O'Brien claims that the combatant/noncombatant distinction has been eroding every since, however, due to the advent of mass armies and ideological objectives of war.[118] Modern wars have shown characteristics of the new type of warfare which O'Brien calls "total": "Economic warfare and starvation blockades, indiscriminate submarine warfare, strategic 'obliteration' bombing and now, nuclear warfare."[119]

Before World War I, "people who were not in uniform, not a part of the enemy's armed forces, and not bearing arms, could not be attacked... private property was protected from arbitrary seizure and destruction."[120] During and after World War I, however, it is evident from the conduct of war that the noncombatancy distinction has by now practically disappeared. O'Brien cites U.S. Air Force Pamphlet 110-31 as evident of this disappearance: here the interpretation of undefended localities "reduces the immunity of undefended localities to the vanishing point [in stating that] *'any place behind enemy lines defended place because it is not open to unopposed occupation'*."[121]

The confusion may stem from O'Brien's often desribing what *has actually* happened to the principle of noncombatant immunity. As a *legal* principle, he believes it actually died after World War I. As a *moral* principle, it is very much alive and O'Brien uses it to limit legitimate attacks to exclusively military targets or to targets that would have a high level of military damage in proportion to collateral concombatant deaths and/or injuries.

"Noncombatant" appears to be synonymous with "civilian" for O'Brien, yet he seems to exclude those civilians who are, in Ramsey's words, "remotely connected to the war effort"; i.e., even those who provide food and encouragement to soldiers.[122] He is thus subject to Ramsey's and Ford's criticisms previously discussed. O'Brien does not mention infants, children, or the sick or the aged, and it may be assumed that he includes these in the noncombatant category. O'Brien is insistent that the plea of "military necessity" is not sufficient to override the principle of noncombatant immunity. However, in the face of *legitimate* military necessity, the combatant/non-combatant distinction may be overriden because of the high level of military damage that may be anticipated.

The Principle of Discrimination

In *The Conduct of Just and Limited Wars*, O'Brien expands Ramsey's definition of the principle of discrimination to read: "The principle of discrimination prohibits direct intentional attacks on noncombatants and nonmilitary targets."[123] O'Brien reiterates this in "The Failure of Deterrence in the Conduct of War" in 1988.[124] Therefore, according to O'Brien's definition, protection from direct intentional attack is extended beyond persons to places and objects. This principle that limits war's destruction, therefore, is more and more called "the principle of discrimination" than the "principle noncombatant immunity." In "The Failure of Deterrence and the Conduct of War," O'Brien refers, however, to "the principle of discrimination or noncombatant immunity," but includes the prohibition of the direct intentional attacking of nonmilitary targets as well as noncombatants.[125] In Ramsey there is a close correlation between the human person and the target; in O'Brien there is a correlation between all "targets" (persons and nonpersons) and legitimate military necessity.

O'Brien adds the word "intentional" to his definition as if to elucidate the meaning of "direct" attack. Nevertheless, he maintains that interpretations of words like "intentional," "direct," "accidental," and even "noncombatant" and "innocent," which are used to justify the killing of noncombatants, are too obscure for ordinary statesmen, military commanders and citizens to understand.[126] Thus, "intentional" in O'Brien's definition does not seem to hold additional significance for the meaning of the principle. For O'Brien, when legitimate military necessity demands a military action, intentionality regarding the target is not a primary consideration in evaluating the oughtness of the action.

Though O'Brien rejects the literal, absolute moral prohibition approach of Ramsey to the principle of discrimination, he apparently views the principle as holding some *prima facie* obligation. He concludes that "[d]iscrimination is not an ironclad principle. It is a relative proscription that enjoins us to concentrate our attacks on military objectives and to minimize our destruction of noncombatants and civilian targets, i.e., in contemporary strategic usage, collateral damage." Thus, O'Brien no longer refers to discrimination as a principle but as a "prescription." In order to see how significant such a distinction might be, it will be necessary to analyze the way he validates such a prescription and the conditions which must exist before overriding it.[127]

Validation

O'Brien rejects attempts to justify killing noncombatants by both Ramsey's appeal to a direct/indirect distinction and the appeal of others, including classic just war theorists, to the principle of double effect. Using an inductive approach, O'Brien searches for the roots of discrimination in the history of belligerents' practice "rather than in the theological or philosophical formula of just-war doctrine."[128]   At times, he seems not to treat the principle of discrimination as a *moral* principle at all, but as a *legal* one determined not by natural law, but by *jus gentium*.[129] At other times, however, he seems to treat it as a moral principle, though one with limited relevance to modern war.

> I do not distinguish an absolute, moral just-war principle from a more flexible and variable international-law principle of discrimination. To be sure the moral, just-war understanding of discrimination must remain independent of that of international law at any given time. But discrimination is best understood and most effectively applied in light of the interpretation of the principle in the practice of belligerents.[130]

In keeping with O'Brien's approach, then, one may begin with his tracing the historical roots of the principle of discrimination. Once these are determined, one may examine O'Brien's own analysis of various historical contexts to see whether they reveal deeper underlying moral principles. These principles may account for the gradual erosion of belligerents' practice of discrimination.

General Principles

Chivalry, Utility, and Military Necessity

O'Brien finds the historical origins of the principle of discrimination in the codes of chivalry as practiced during the medieval and Renaissance periods. During this time, as described at the beginning of this chapter, attacking civilians was not ordinarily *useful* to the attainment of military goals and more seldom still, was it *necessary* to military victory. Wars were conducted by mounted knights and supporting infantry. "Attacks on unarmed civilians, particularly women and children, would have been considered unchivalric, contrary to the customary law of war, and military gratuitous."[131]   The noncombatant immunity of the principle of discrimination was, then, part of the chivalric code and practice and became recognized as a legal principle. O'Brien is quite clear, however, that the principle's relevance depended on the contemplated action's usefulness to the military effort.

Humanity

Underlying the chivalric code and the principle of utility or military necessity, however, is the deeper principle of humanity. This principle, identified in O'Brien's position on proportionality, forbids the infliction of suffering, injury or destruction not actually necessary for the accomplishment of legitimate military purposes. Once the basic presumption against killing and inflicting suffering is overcome, as in just wars, "the killing then permitted is limited to the enemy combatants, the aggressors."[132]

The principle of humanity continues as the basis for the international law proscription against both deliberate attacks on noncombatants and attacks involving a high degree of danger, death and destruction to noncombatants and nonmilitary targets when such attacks are disproportionate to military utility.[133] O'Brien makes a distinction between directly targeting *individuals* in some terrorist attacks, and targeting "cities" or "population centers." The first, against individuals, would be a violation against the principle of humanity; second, against cities or population centers, may or may not be a violation against humanity, but O'Brien seems to consider it a violation against legitimate military necessity and proportionality. He believes this view underlies the development of positive international law between 1648 and 1914 which is influenced by the Rousseau-Portalis doctrine concerning public forces of warring nations where what is primary is the relationship of states and not individuals.[134]

Humanity seems to be, then, the underlying principle for observing the principle of discrimination, at least as far as individuals are concerned. O'Brien states, "The distinction between combatants and noncombatants... does not in itself provide limitations recognized in fact by contemporary positive international law. This distinction may, however, be utilized as one of many factors to be considered in the determination of the limits of proportionality of permissible violence."[135] It is not yet clear whether forbidding unnecessary destruction of *property* is also grounded in the principle of humanity.

Grounding discrimination in the principle of humanity would hardly be a surprise. What is surprising to some is the relative ease with which discrimination can be overridden in O'Brien, and the question arises as to whether the reasons for overriding are also grounded in humanity.

Interdependence of Peoples

One of the values or principles which O'Brien stresses in his early writings is the "interdependence of peoples." It is interesting to note that this phrase does not appear in his latest book, *The Conduct of Just and Limited Wars*, and one may ask why O'Brien has deemphasized it. When O'Brien first wrote about the interdependence of peoples in the late 1950s and early 1960s, there was still optimism that the United Nations might become a world organization able to effect a more just and peaceful world order. Pope John XXIII's *Pacem in Terris* reinforced this hope. Within a few years, however, it became apparent to many that such optimism was not warranted, at least not for the foreseeable future O'Brien has apparently shared this more pessimistic view, for though he seems not to have abandoned the concept of the interdependence of peoples, he pays little attention to it after 1960. Nevertheless, because the principle, usually expressed as a statement or proposition, received O'Brien's early support and emphasis and because he still recognizes its validity, it is worthwhile to examine it at some length.

In his attempt to find guidelines "to construct an effective modern law of war," O'Brien contends that new interpretations of military necessity are necessary. He speaks of the need to pay attention to what he calls "the higher necessities," and seems to include in the latter "the necessities of the entire international community" and "the ultimate supremacy of natural law and divine law... The respect for human life and dignity [are] required by the higher necessities."

In addition to reasons of morality, O'Brien states that selfish interests lead states to consider "*long-range* State necessity and... the immutable higher necessities of the international community and of God," in reinterpreting military necessity. Thus, the states will see that brutal destruction and loss of life and private property are destructive of international relations in the long run, after the hostilities are over. "The most practical policy happens, in this instance to coincide with the most ethical policy. Thus, "the ultimate goal of war is a just and lasting peace"; military necessity must contribute to this goal. O'Brien notes that "unrestricted destruction" of the material wealth of the earth and degradation of human beings on a massive scale affect the entire international community. Thus, the principle of the interdependence of peoples reinforces the principle of humanity, and subsequently, the principle of discrimination. Nevertheless, the principle of discrimination may be violated, not for the sake of preserving the existence of a particular State in and of itself but only if the disappearance of a particular State would result in the loss of freedom of conscience or freedom of the citizen's lives. Both the principle of discrimination and the principle of the interdependence of peoples are always morally relevant as they enter the proportionality calculus but they are not always morally decisive there: i.e., the morality of the action will be determined by the balance of good outweighing evil effects of a military action. Among the goods that must be weighed are the conditions which support respect for the individual human life and promote the interdependence of peoples.[136]

The interdependence of peoples is a principle or a value that supports a higher value; namely, respect for the individual human life. O'Brien sees this interdependence as a necessary condition for human beings to live on this plane and to meet their needs. O'Brien ranks the two principles highest in the hierarchy of values revealed by contemporary *jus in bello* practice and positive international law. The principle of proportionality must serve to enhance the two ultimate values. The principle of discrimination must sometimes be overridden, but that does not imply that respect for the human person is less binding. Rather, the principle must be overridden when legitimate military necessity demands it for the sake of preserving the conditions necessary for securing that respect. Chief among these conditions is the maintenance of a world structure that allows for the interdependence of peoples.

In summary, the principle of discrimination is related to O'Brien's highest value, the respect for the individual person. The interdependence of people follows from this highest principle. The interdependence of peoples is closely related to McDougal and Feliciano's "the principle of humanity" and to Georg Schwarzenber's "principle of civilization."

Range of Applicability

Conditions for Overriding: Proportionality

O'Brien has allowed the overriding of the principle of noncombatant immunity in cases where a high level of military damage could be expected, as has been seen.

This indicates that O'Brien does view the principle of discrimination as a *moral* as well as a *legal* principle but that he ranks it lower than most other just war theorists have done. In support of this position, O'Brien notes that historically, when weapons are banned, they are banned more on the basis of disproportionality than on the basis of discriminatory effects.[137] In addition, recent Catholic teaching on war stresses large-scale destruction and not the principle of noncombatant immunity from direct intentional attack in its various condemnations.[138] Therefore, proportionality is the decisive principle. Looking at positive international law, O'Brien notes that it "does not proscribe any general limitation on means for war aside from the principle of proportionality as the heart of the principle of legitimate military necessity." One must remember that O'Brien looks on law as possibly in error; nevertheless he views contemporary international law "as a reflection of the values, authoritative decisions and expectations of the holders of power in the world public order..."[139]

In attempting to find guidelines for international law that must deal with nuclear war, O'Brien looks not to the "inviolability of noncombatants" or "outlawing inhumane weapons" but to the concept of legitimate military necessity and therefore to the principle of proportionality.[140] He says that what is at issue in modern war, conventional and nuclear, is not intention or preference but the predictable amount of collateral damage to noncombatants and nonmilitary targets and this is a matter of proportionality.[141] O'Connor draws the following conclusion: "William O'Brien notes that this principle is not declared apart from the context of widespread destruction. Thus, [the absolute principle of noncombatant immunity] may express the principle of proportionality rather than the principle of discrimination.[142]

O'Brien seems to confirm this interpretation in a recent statement: "The standard of judging the sufficiency of the effort to minimize civilian damage is one of proportionality."[143] It has become evident that the principle of discrimination in O'Brien retains a separate identity in his just war theory though it has a secondary function. The discrimination principle enters into the proportionality calculus in some instances and plays a role of its own in others, which will become more clear in an examination of its range of applicability that follows.

It will be helpful to examine various strategies belligerents adopt in order to search out those instances in O'Brien's theory where the principle of discrimination is morally decisive and those where it is only morally relevant. One can divide the strategies into four types for this purpose: (1) counterforce targeting (CF); (2) countervalue targeting (CV); (3) mixed counterforce/countervalue targeting with the countervalue effects following as concomitant or "undesired" consequences (CF/cv); (4) mixed countervalue/counterforce targeting where counterforce destruction destruction is the concomitant effect (CV/cf). In addition, each of these types must be considered as it relates to two values: military utility and legitimate military necessity.

Morally Decisive Role: Conditions of Military Utility

CF and CF/cv Targeting

According to a CF targeting strategy, either military utility or military necessity may be the military objective of the action. If the goal is consistent with legitimate military necessity, the injury and deaths of noncombatants and damage to nonmilitary property are weighed in the proportionality calculus to determine the morality of the act. If the goal of the action is only that it would be *useful* militarily, however, the principle of discrimination plays a morally decisive role for O'Brien. In this case, if noncombatant death or injury or, it seems, even destruction of nonmilitary property, is the foreseeable result of such military action, the action may not be undertaken. Such a decision would have to be made, for example, in a situation where it would be useful to destroy a military supply depot located near a farming community. Though destruction of the depot would be useful for military purposes, it may not satisfy O'Brien's conditions of necessity: that is, it may not be an immediately indispensable measure to secure a legitimate military end. The principle of discrimination is lexically prior to that of mere military utility. In cases of CF targeting, then, when only military utility would be served, the principle of discrimination is morally decisive.

The same reasoning can be applied to the CF/cv strategy. When *only* military utility is at stake, the principle of discrimination forbids military action. Cases of CF targeting where legitimate military necessity is being served and where danger to noncombatants is present, fall under the treatment of necessity below.

Morally Relevant but Nondecisive Roles:

Legitimate Military Necessity

CV

A purely CV targeting strategy is proscribed by O'Brien not on the basis of the principle of discrimination, but on the basis of the principle of proportionality. Thus a strategy which aims to destroy cities and population centers is disproportionate to any war aim. As previously stated, O'Brien contends that the trend in contemporary wars is toward not observing the combatant/noncombatant distinction in which case strategists would acknowledge only CF strategy (recognizing, however, that CF strategy includes among its targets industrial complexes having military value). However, as O'Brien analyzes contemporary positive international law, he sees that the development of the law is running contrary to that trend. He takes as fact that international law doctrine is unsettled regarding the practice of noncombatant immunity but that "the majority of modern authorities do *not* recognize the original principle of inviolability of noncombatants and nonmilitary targets." They have, however, reached a compromise with those who maintain the distinction is valid such that contemporary international law forbids attacks directed *solely* against civil populations.[144] O'Brien recognizes, however, that instances of targeting *solely* civilian populations can hardly be imagined since there is almost always *some* military benefit to be derived from this strategy. Even in the British strategic bombing of German cities (O'Brien contends that even though the declaratory policy was ostensibly a CF/cv mixed strategy, in reality it was a CV strategy), *some* military objectives were destroyed. In theory, however, CV attacks would be proscribed since they would not satisfy the requirements of legitimate military necessity, i.e., they would violate international law. Once again, it is not the principle of discrimination but the principle of proportionality that is morally decisive in this case though it may have played a morally relevant role in determining the immorality of CV warfare. The question of whether a CV *deterrence* policy would be morally permissible for O'Brien will be dealt with in the next chapter.

CF/cv

Instances of a mixed CF/cv strategy used in cases of legitimate military necessity include situations where the primary target is military but where noncombatant death and destruction are likely to occur. In these cases O'Brien would count the noncombatant deaths and destruction, the secondary effect of the proposed action, in the proportionality calculus as physical evils. These would be weighed against the "good" effects which result from attainment of the primary military objective, and in this way the morality of the action could be determined in cases of legitimate military necessity where, one is reminded, O'Brien identifies three essential elements: (1) the military action is immediately indispensable proportionate to a legitimate military end; (2) the action is subject to the limiting of the laws of war and natural law; (3) it is determined by a responsible commander and subject to judicial review.[145]

In a mixed CF/cv strategy, then, it is only when the conditions for legitimate military necessity are met that the principle of discrimination can be overridden.

O'Brien gives as an example of this type of tactical strategy the rules of engagement in force during the U.S. "Christmas bombing" of Hanoi in 1972, providing for bombing accuracy at the sacrifice of protective maneuvering. According to this rule "*[b]ombers on the first raids were required to stabilize flight for approximately four minutes prior to bomb release. It was a long four minutes. Unfortunately for some, it lasted less than that.*"[146]

O'Brien claims that advances made in the bombing accuracy since World War II have made possible this type of strategy and have enhanced the capability for discrimination. "[C]onventional strategic air war is technically capable of respecting the principle of discrimination and should be held to that basic *jus in bello* requirement."[147]

Of his own approach, O'Brien says that he "would be more likely to accept major collateral damage in essentially CF attacks or in CV attacks against enemy command, control and communication centers and industrial complexes (current U.S. policy) than would the approaches that employ double-effect reasoning."[213]

CV/cf

This mixed strategy differs from the one previously discussed in that the destruction of military targets is the concomitant aim of the military action. An example of CV/cf strategy is illustrated by the Casablanca Directive issued by Roosevelt and Churchill in 1943 with respect to strategic bombing:

> Your primary objective will be the progressive destruction and dislocation of the German military, industrial and economic system, and the undermining of the morale of the German people to the point where their capacity for armed resistance is fatally weakened.

Though the words of the directive indicate a CF/cv strategy, O'Brien maintains that in practice, the British CV strategy dominated, though the U.S. Air Force made costly efforts "to prove the efficacy of daylight precision bombing on military targets.[150] O'Brien concludes that if the attacks on German and Japanese cities had been confined to precision bombings of military targets, the bombing policies would have satisfied the requirements of proportionality and even of discrimination in those cases where indirect targeting of noncombatants nevertheless led to disproportionate damage. He seems to be making a distinction here between *raison d'état* and *jus in bello*, with *raison d'état* sometimes acting as a sufficient reason to override *jus in bello* requirements. It is, then, proportionality and not discrimination that takes precedence in these mixed CV/cf cases.

In judging the morality of the atomic bombing of Hiroshima and Nagasaki, O'Brien also notes the unique aspect of the issue of proportionality involved: the calculus included *raison de guerre* calculations related to attaining particular military goal and *raison d'état* calculations related to the successful conclusion of the war. In terms of military necessity, it was estimated that Japan could have been defeated by conventional means but probably at a higher cost of lives and damage. O'Brien agress that the decision to use the atomic bomb satisfied the demand of proportionality in that it accomplished the completion of the war with less loss of life than would otherwise have occurred. He does not seem to have addressed the question as to whether the alternate policy involving conventional weapons and more deaths would itself have been disproportionate.

O'Brien does not believe the atomic attacks can be reconciled with the principle of discrimination, however, since although there were some military targets within the area, the vast majority of persons and targets were noncombatants and nonmilitary. "The proportions were such that the destruction of the cities emerges as the primary purpose of the attacks while the incidental destruction of military targets appears to fall into the category of collateral damage, thus reversing the usual and preferred ratio."[151]

It appears, then, that in CV/cf attacks the principle of discrimination is morally decisive, taking lexical priority over the principle of proportionality in O'Brien. However, O'Brien is ambiguous in his conclusion about the atomic bombings. As the long-term and permanent consequences of nuclear contamination are still unclear, and as positive international law has still not prohibited the use of nuclear weapons, O'Brien concludes

> that if the use of nuclear weapons can be justified in the context of World War II, the attacks on Hiroshima and Nagasaki are about as defensible as can be imagined, since they did foreseeably and in fact end the war quickly and preclude greater losses to the belligerents and the Japanese society.[152]

Regarding the principle of discrimination, O'Brien says that "there is little to do except admit [its violation] openly and accept the fact that, ever since, major powers operating in the nuclear age have been confronted with the fact that the principal means of deterrence and defense in existence is incompatible with the principle of discrimination."[153] This sounds as if O'Brien is saying that because use of nuclear weapons did violate the principle of discrimination and yet accomplished the *raison d'état* goal, the violation was justified. Justification of the violation is grounded in the principle of proportionality.

This conclusion lends support to the contention that O'Brien has virtually collapsed the principle of discrimination and proportionality into the one principle of proportionality--at least as discrimination relates to nuclear weapons. Although the United States and its allies in World War II violated the principle of proportionality and even more extremely, the principle of discrimination, O'Brien judges the overall efforts against Germany and Japan to have been just. He finds Truman's decision to end the whole war quickly by means of one or two bombs "very persuasive," although he acknowledges that this decision may well have been *sui generis*. The U.S. was the only nation that possessed nuclear weapons at that time and there was no danger of nuclear escalation. This has left the United States at the outset of the nuclear age with concepts and practices that seem to common morality contrary to just war requirements. However, before dealing with this subject in chapter 4, we must see whether Michael Walzer has resolved the problems resulting from the conflict of the principles of discrimination and proportionality.

MICHAEL WALZER

Definitions

Walzer says that the rules of war cluster around two sets of prohibitions connected with the principles that soldiers have an equal right to kill: first, when and how they are to kill; the second set limits whom they may kill.[154] If the first principle of war is that soldiers are subject to attack at any time, the second principle of war is that noncombatants are not to be attacked at any time.[155] But who are the "soldiers" and who are the "noncombatants"?

An article entitled "World War II; Why Was This War Different?" (*Philosophy and Public Affairs*, 1971) helps to sort out the distinctions Walzer makes between combatant and noncombatant. One of the reasons for the uniqueness of this war, as Walzer sees it, is the Allied bombing policy that seemed to deny the combatant/noncombatant distinction. One may well look to this article and to chapters 9, 10 and 11 of *Just and Unjust Wars* (1977) to find the distinction Walzer does make and to see how he defines the principle of noncombatant immunity.

Noncombatants and Combatants

Like Ramsey and Ford, Walzer admits there is difficulty in determining exactly where combatancy begins and noncombatancy ends. That there are noncombatants, however, he has no doubt. Like Ramsey, Walzer seems to indicate that combatancy is relative to the times, a function of the way nations organize for war and of weapons technology, and "subject to social revision."[156]

Using the inductive method, Walzer says that one must look to the conventions of war to see who are currently recognized as noncombatants. "It is the acceptance of these conventions and the recognition of the clear cases that is generally useful and that is all the rule requires."[157]

Walzer is somewhat more specific than this approach might suggest, however. For example, in his article on World War II already cited, Walzer defines combatants as soldiers "who are armed and trained and committed to fight us (whether or not they are actually engaged in combat)."[158] In *Just and Unjust Wars*, he recognizes the categories of noncombatants listed by the just war theorists of the Middle Ages: "Women and children, priests, old men, the members of neutral tribes, cities, of states, wounded or captured soldiers," and he says what all these have in common "is that they are not currently engaged in the business of war."[159] The two definitions contain an apparent contradiction: that is, in the first, Walzer includes among *combatants* soldiers who are not actually engaged in combat, while in the second, he explicitly includes these same unengaged soldiers in the category of *noncombatants*. On closer examination, however, the "wounded or captured soldiers" in the second list are *incapable* of engaging in combat and this is what makes them like the others in the list.

Walzer devotes a large part of his chapter on noncombatant immunity in *Just and Unjust Wars* to the topic of combatants who in a sense move in and out of combatancy during warfare. He uses several examples of soldiers' recollections of wartime behavior to illustrate this. When these soldiers encountered the enemy "acting like a human being" more than like a soldier (smoking a cigarette, taking a leisurely walk, or eating a meal, for example), they often held their fire. This behavior reveals for Walzer a natural hesitation to kill a "fellow-creature," yet stops short of saying that these "human being-soldiers" are not still, strictly speaking, combatants. Rather, he attributes the decisions not to fire in the cases as "[r]ooted in a moral recognition of these individuals as human beings and therefore of the decisions not to fire as acts of kindness, acts of supererogation involving "doing less than is permitted."[160]

Probably Walzer does not consider possible discrepancies in categorizing combatants and noncombatants significant because he is not really concerned with determining the precise point at which combatancy begins and noncombatancy ends. "Doubtless, the precise marking of the limit, the definition of noncombatant, proves in every war a troublesome and ultimately an arbitrary matter."[161] Walzer comes closest to the positions of Ramsey, Ford, and Anscombe when he says. "The relevant distinction is not between those who work for the war effort and those who do not, but between those who make what soldiers need to fight and those who make what they need to live, like all the rest of us."[162] He, too, recognizes the complexity of contemporary society and the possibility of a category of "partial combatants," for example, those who work in munitions plants. Even these, however, he says are subject to attack only in their factories and "not at home,"[163] that is, "when they are actually engaged in activities threatening and harmful to their enemies."[164]

Thus Walzer explicitly denies the claim that there are no noncombatants in modern war, even given the complexity of the war effort and the demands it makes on the industrial force of a nation. In this he remains within the classic just war tradition.

Walzer departs from the position of Vitoria and Grotius, however, on the topic of subjective guilt. He cautions that in wartime, words like "responsibility" and "moral agent" are used in a special sense. This statement reflects the complete separation Walzer makes between *jus ad bellum* and *jus in bello*. As far as *jus ad bellum* is concerned, the ordinary citizens, civilians or soldiers, may not be held personally responsible; they are "innocent" in the ordinary sense of word and may not be punished, according to Walzer, though they may be resisted and attacked. This is because they are not "engaged in harming." Their only choices in time of war are to hide, flee, surrender, or work and fight. Therefore, Walzer claims, one must pay attention to the activities in which people are actually engaged in order to treat them as persons in the only way one can.

Walzer is somewhat uncomfortable with his position on subjective guilt, however. He points out that nations cannot punish people *because* they are guilty but only *guilty* people are punished--apparently, Walzer is saying that *innocent* people are "harmed" as opposed to "punished." In addition, the theory that distinguishes combatants from noncombatants does not distinguish the enemy's noncombatants from one's own noncombatants. Yet Walzer somehow "feels" that it would have been worse in World War II, for example, to have bombed French cities than to have bombed German cities, even though presumably more Germans were "responsible" for the unjust conditions leading to war than the French.[165]

Walzer's examination of positive international law to reveal underlying moral principles suggests that the rule requires respect not only for the human lives of noncombatants but for nonmilitary property as well. In regard to the aerial bombardments in World War I, for example, Walzer cites the findings of an international comission of jurists meeting in The Hague in the 1920s: "Aerial bombardment destined to terrorize the civilian population, or to destroy or damage private property which has a military character, or to wound noncombatants, is prohibited."[166]

The strategic bombing of German cities in World War II leads Walzer to his deepest reflections on what he calls the "rule" of noncombatant immunity. Having determined that he does recognize a combatant/noncombatant distinction and roughly *who* these combatants and noncombatants are, one can now turn to a closer analysis of the rule itself.

The Rule of Noncombatant Immunity

In 1971, Walzer defines the principle as "the rule against the deliberate killing of civilians (noncombatants) in wartime."[167] In 1977, he refers to it as "the second principle of the war convention [which provides] that noncombatants cannot be attacked at any time. They can never be the objects or the targets of military activity."[168] Whether he speaks of it as a rule or as a principle, Walzer considers it a *moral* rule or principle. He uses the two terms interchangeably and means by both, a "precept to be followed." His later definition differs from both Ramsey's and O'Brien's in that he does not mention "direct" or "deliberate" attack. It will become evident, however, that Walzer does want to continue to include this notion in his definition and it continues to be relevant in his analysis of the morality of military strategies. Elsewhere in *Just and Unjust Wars*, for example, Walzer speaks of the *legal* rule as banning "the deliberate killing of civilians."[169] The fact that the restrictive words are not always included in the definition may relate to Walzer's description of moral rules: "moral rules... are usually stated and probably should be stated (in international law, for example) in absolute terms."[170] He says this because some people will always think they are justified in breaking the rule when such violations should not be justified. He does go on to say that moral rules are not absolute, however, but that they "establish a strong presumption against certain sorts of actions," and then he adds, "like the *deliberate* killing of noncombatants"[171] (emphasis added).

As with the other theorists, it is often helpful to look at the reasons for violating a principle in order to find out what validates it in the first place. Attention will now be given, then, to Walzer's validation of the principle of noncombatant immunity.

Validation

Even though O'Brien considers the principle of noncombatant immunity as a relative principle and Ramsey considers it an absolute principle, both theories recognize its moral validity and ground it in their ultimate norms. Before reaching its own conclusions, Walzer notes that the rule against *deliberately killing civilians, or noncombatants, in warfare has a very long history and that its moral value is widely recognized.[172] In keeping with his inductive approach, he examines the long-standing social patterns and the religious, cultural, political and legal judgments for clues to the reason why the rule has enjoyed such respect over the centuries.

General Principles

Utility

In classic just war theory, Vitoria allows collateral harm to noncombatants in certain extreme cases. He seems to justify his position by means of the proportionality calculus, weighing the total evil caused by war against the evil war would avert.[173] James Johnson says that the closest comparison in contemporary just war theory is with Walzer, since "in both cases the argument is to override the accepted immunity of noncombatants in order to protect the very values that ultimately guarantee the safety of such persons: two different phases but an argument within the same family."[174]

Walzer notes that the application of the rule to problems of aerial bombardment was, in 1940, "fairly recent, not yet incorporated in international treaties and conventions, but there could be no doubt as to the practical requirements of the rule, broadly understood." He points out that it can be defended in many ways of which he chooses only two: first, as a "limit upon the destructive force of warfare which is generally useful to mankind--useful over time, that is, since its violation might at any given moment serve the interests of one party or another; second, because of the intrinsic value it attaches to human personality."[175]

The first value which can be said to have given rise to the principle of noncombatant immunity is utility. Elsewhere Walzer shows that this is not the ultimate ground for the principle, however: "the deliberate slaughter of innocent men and women cannot be justified simply because it saves the lives of other men and women." Like O'Brien, Walzer rejects the argument that the Nazi concentration camps be destroyed knowing that innocents would be killed while possible future victims would be saved. His conclusion regarding the allied aerieal bombing in World War II follows the same form of argument. Even if Bomber Command ended the war sooner and at lower cost of human lives, Walzer says, "this claim [is] not sufficient to justify the bombing."[176]

The Human Person

The second value that Walzer singles out in defense of the principle of noncombatant immunity is the "intrinsic value it attaches to the human personality." In his discussion of this way of defending the principle, Walzer appeals to respect for the person: "It requires that we pay attention to what men and women are actually doing, that we regard and treat them as responsible agents." In the same place, he describes the bombing of cities as situations where the inhabitants are, in effect, "hostages," "degraded from moral agents to human persons."[177]

Civilization

It is not only individual human life that is at stake in violating the principle of noncombatant immunity, for there is much else that we might plausibly want to preserve--the quality of our lives, for example, our civilization and morality, our collective abhorrence of murder, even when it seems to serve, as it always does, some narrow purpose.[178]

It is with the value of "civilization," understood as the conditions under which individuals exercise their rights to life and liberty in a shared life with others in political community that Walzer seems to reach his ultimate concern: "[I]f civilization itself is really at stake... I find myself moving uneasily toward the decision Churchill made, though not, perhaps, for his (or all of his) reasons."[179]

The values that Walzer believes the principle of noncombatant immunity is revealing are, then, in order of priority from lowest to highest: utility, civilization (which is valued for the sake of the individual human person), and the human person *per se*.

The Role of Rights

As the analysis of Walzer's treatment of proportionality has shown, Walzer claims that he always starts from "a doctrine of human rights."[180] So with the principle of noncombatant immunity, the values which are its source-- utility, civilization, and the human person--can be traced to individual rights: the right to life itself and the right to live in a society where one is free to live out one's moral, religious and political convictions in a cultural setting, i.e., in civilization. As with proportionality, these rights underlie and restrict the application of the principle.

The right to life and the right to liberty seem more obviously distinct from each other in their relation to the principle of noncombatant immunity than in their relation to proportionality, however. The right to liberty may be more adequately understood in terms of the right to live out one's beliefs and preferences in the context of society, in a civilization supportive of this liberty. In his article on World War II, Walzer speaks of the duty of the state to preserve the conditions needed for both of these rights:

> the rulers of the state have a very strong obligation to preserve the lives of their people, and so calculations of this sort should never be foreign to them. But the social union is something more than a pact for the preservation of life; it is also a way of living together and (inevitably) of living with other peoples and other unions, and there is something here that needs to be preserved as well.[181]

The "right to liberty" conceived as possibly the "right to live in a civilized society" is of a higher order than the "right to life" taken by itself. The right to individual life is obviously a precondition for the right to liberty. It must precede the right to liberty in the temporal order, yet it ranks below the right to liberty in the moral order.

One of the considerations that gives evidence of this moral ranking in Walzer is the fact that the right to life may and must be forfeited when the value of civilization, the only milieu in which individuals' right to freedom can be exercised, is seriously threatened. Thus states must protect the lives and liberties of their individual citizens but they must also protect "their shared life and liberty, the independent community they have made, for which individuals are sometimes sacrificed."[182] This sounds as if Walzer places the value of many lives above the value of one life, but at closer examination, this is not true. The reason for valuing civilization is, at the core, that civilization is necessary to protect and enhance the rights of the individual human person. Therefore, it appears that the value of the human person is actually Walzer's ultimate value. Further clarification of this emerges as one examines situations where the two values, civilization and the individual human person, conflict. The area of conflict of values introduces a consideration of the range of applicability of the principle of discrimination.

Range of Applicability

Walzer has stated that moral rules are not absolute but that they hold strong presumptions against certain sorts of actions like the deliberate killing of noncombatants.[183] What, then, is to count as a moral reason for going against this presumption? As with Ramsey and O'Brien, Walzer declares that noncombatants must not be the *direct* objects of attack. Ordinarily purely countervalue attacks are violations of the rule of noncombatant immunity. However, when noncombatants are near a battle site, Walzer recognizes the moral permissibility of military attack if "due care" is taken not to harm the noncombatants.[184] This he justifies by use of the principle of double effect.

The Principle of Double Effect (Revised)

"Double effect," Walzer states, "is a way of reconciling the absolute prohibition against attacking noncombatants with the legitimate conduct of military activity."[185] He wants to argue, however, that this reconciliation has traditionally come too easily. In keeping with his own moral foundation of human rights, Walzer holds that questions of coercion and consent must precede any question of direct and indirect effect.

Walzer cites John Ford's articulation of the four conditions of the double effect principle in "The Morality of Obliteration Bombing" as representing its classical formulation:

(1) the act must be good or indifferent;
(2) the act's direct effects must be morally acceptable;
(3) the intention of the actor must be good: i.e., aim at the acceptable effect;
(4) the good effect must be sufficiently good to compensate for allowing the evil effect.[186]

Walzer claims that the third condition carries the burden of the argument: the act must be directed toward the good and not the evil effect. Thus Walzer cautions: "We have to worry, I think, about all those unintended but foreseeable deaths, for their number can be large and subject only to the proportionality rule--a weak constraint--double effect provides a blanket justification."[187] He therefore proposes a revision to "condition 3" of the double effect rule in order to make the rule more defensible: "The intention of the actor is good, that is, he aims narrowly at the acceptable effect; the evil effect is not one of his ends, nor is it a means to his ends, and, aware of the evil involved, he seeks to minimize it, accepting costs to himself."[188]

With this restatement, Walzer claims to permit invoking the rule of double effect only when the two outcomes are the product of a *double intention*: first, that the "good" be achieved; second, that the foreseeable evil be reduced as far as possible. The second condition is the "due care" clause which marks a significant contribution to a more adequate formulation of the *jus in bello* rule of noncombatant immunity. Not only must death and/or injury to noncombatants or their property be an indirect effect of an attack, but in addition, the attacker must take positive steps to minimize these effects. Walzer's use of the rule of double effect has definite implications for military strategies.

Implications for Military Strategies

CV Strategies

In his analysis of the aerial bombing of the Second World War, Walzer claims that many in the Tory government of Britain viewed the Nazi government as not evil in itself but as having imperialistic ambitions to the detriment of Britain's own interests. Even if this were true, Walzer concludes, the policy of aerial bombardment of German cities could not be "a justified response to a conventional imperialism."[189] Whatever the declaratory policy was during the Second World War, Walzer is in agreement with O'Brien that the actual strategy was a CV strategy against residential areas. This, he believes, is prohibited by the rule of noncombatant immunity.

If the Nazi regime was not simply a conventional imperialist regime but was evil *in se*, and presented an imminent danger of an "unusual and horrifying kind,"[190] i.e., a threat to the values of Western civilization itself and the annihilation of a people, then the point of supreme emergency would have been reached. One has to consider the implications of this unique situation as a separate category.

CF Strategies

Walzer's conditions for double effect determine that CF strategies have the greatest possibility for being the most moral, since they offer the most possibility for "due care" to be taken to avoid harming noncombatants.

One may recall that O'Brien's position on the dominant role of proportionality regarding CF strategies subjects him to criticism that too much damage is permissible. In Walzer, however, the principle of noncombatant immunity is allowed to play a role, though limited, even in situations involving combatants alone. This may help Walzer avoid the same kind of criticism that O'Brien must bear.

It has already been pointed out, for example, that reflection on some of the actual combat experiences of World War II veterans led Walzer to conclude that although soldiers forfeit their individual rights to life and liberty, they do so only "when they are actually engaged in activities threatening and harmful to their enemies." When they are relating to one another *qua* human beings and not *qua* soldiers, as in Walzer's accounts of the "funny-looking soldier" running along holding up his pants, or the "naked soldier" taking a bath and believing he was unobserved, one may well hesitate in claiming that these "partial combatants" may be targeted or killed. Walzer concludes that refusals to attack these individuals involve "doing less than is permitted." Thus he does not go so far as to say the rule of noncombatant immunity is being disregarded here; these are, after all, combatants albeit inactive ones at the moment. He does find evidence in positive law that "partial combatants" are protected, however, as in the code of military conduct drawn up by Francis Lieber for the Union Arrmy during the American Civil War. This code provides that "Outposts, sentinels, pickets are not to be fired upon, except to drive them in."

One can imagine a war in which this concept could be extended so that the war would become "a series of set battles,... announced in advance, and broken off in some clear fashion." However, Walzer claims that though some wars actually have begun in this way, the larger and better equipped army has soon gained the upper hand, and the weaker side pleads "military necessity" in violating the limits on the vulnerability of noncombatants.[191]

This plea of necessity is what has been previously labeled "necessity$_1$." As far as Walzer is concerned, necessity$_1$ is not sufficient to warrant violation of the rule of noncombatant immunity. Walzer stops short of saying combatants retain the same rights to life and liberty as their civilian counterparts in certain non-combat situations, yet he does introduce limits that may be motivated by "kindness and magnanimity." He seems to end up somewhat uncomfortable about how easily the rights of "partial combatants" to life and liberty may be violated under the strict interpretation of noncombatant status, as, for example, O'Brien has concluded.

CV/cf Strategies

Walzer is in basic agreement with O'Brien regarding the nature of declaratory policy of Allied Bomber Command during World War II and actual practice: i.e., that the declaratory practice was an example of a CF/cv strategy while the real policy resembled more of a CV/cf or even a CV strategy. As either a CV/cf or a purely CV strategy Walzer condemns it as violating the principle of noncombatant immunity. His position is strengthened by the addition he makes to the principle of double effect: i.e., that due care must be taken to minimize harm to noncombatants.

The siege or blockade may be an example of this type of strategy. Because the inhabitants of a city under siege have not chosen to live under siege, Walzer claims that the siege is itself an "act of coercion," and therefore a violation of the noncombatants' rights. "The systematic starvation of civilians under siege is one of those glaring military acts which 'though permissible by custom is a glaring violation of the principle by which custom professes to be governed.'[192]

Walzer's addition to the principle of double effect obliges soldiers to help civilians leave the scene of battle. The implications of this for something like siege warfare, then, would be to provide an exit route for civilians. Only then would it be morally possible to engage in battle.

CF/cv Strategies

A belligerent may honor Walzer's obligation to provide "due care" that noncombatants be protected and yet know that regardless of his efforts, some noncombatants will probably be harmed or even killed. In an attempt to destroy a military target, the belligerent may nevertheless be morally justified in engaging in such an action. The addition of the emphasis of "due care" ensures minimal harm to noncombatants to a degree perhaps not guaranteed by either Ramsey's or O'Brien's accounts. "The principle... rules out... every sort of strategic devastation, except in cases where adequate provision can be made, and is made, for noncombatants."[193]

Guerilla warfare is a type of contemporary CF/cv warfare that offers the greatest challenge to this principle. (The challenge posed by the threat of nuclear warfare is the topic of the next chapter.)

Walzer points out that even if vast numbers of civilians could be relocated so that the war could be fought combatant vs. combatant (and this relocation and its consequences might well violate the principle of proportionality), there may yet be a problem related to civilians who refuse to move. In attacking the invading soldiers one may be "covered" by the principle of double effect, but as long as the noncombatants provide only political support, they are not legitimate targets. Regardless of their political allegiance, due care must still be taken to minimize harm to them. This, Walzer claims, the Americans did not do in Vietnam. Rather they distinguished not between combatants and noncombatants but between friendly or hostile, loyal or disloyal noncombatants. Walzer appeals again to rights for the ultimate justification of their protection: "They have done nothing to forfeit their right to life, and that right must be respected as best it can be in the course of attacks against the irregular fighters the villagers both resemble and harbor."[194]

Conditions of Supreme Emergency

As chapter 2 has shown, Walzer holds that necessity can rightly be claimed only at the point of "supreme emergency," that is, the danger must be such as to threaten disaster for a political community. Walzer bases this position on his claim that "the survival and freedom of political communities... are the highest values in international societies."[195] It is only here that "the heavens are (really) about to fall." And this is where Childress claims Walzer finally surrenders to utilitarianism: "In supreme emergencies, Walzer contends we are compelled to say both 'right' and 'wrong' about the same act and perhaps refuse to honor those who have dirty hands even for sufficient reasons."[196]

Childress claims that Walzer also offers a less than adequate response to Ramsey and others who hold that once certain rules are formulated, it is never right to break them.

Walzer seems to believe he deals adequately with this difficulty in his account of supreme emergency as an event that occurs only when a disaster to the political community is at stake. As one may recall, Walzer claims this is an improvement over the "sliding scale" utilitarian argument and is ultimately justified by the right to live in a political community in order to preserve the rights to life and liberty.

Walzer admits that he does use a utilitarian calculation here and therefore, proportionality determines whether or not the principle of noncombatant immunity may be violated. He ends up with a paradox in which one is left with no honorable course: one is justified in violating the principle, yet one is "guilty" for performing a justified act.

As the conclusion of chapter 2 indicates, Walzer may have a way around this paradox by using the concept of "proportionate reason" as it is articulated by Richard McCormick. McCormick claims that the notion of proportionate reason is analogous to but not reducible to the utilitarian calculus that Walzer wants to avoid and seemingly cannot.[197]

Walzer's dilemma seems to satisfy the possible and general sense of proportionate reason as appropriate to a situation where "the only alternative to causing or permitting evil is greater evil."[198] In Walzer's case, the two evils presented are first, the death and injury of innocent persons, i.e., the violation of the individuals' rights to life and liberty; second, the destruction of a political society, the only setting in which the exercise of the rights to life and liberty are possible. As has been seen, Walzer claims the second option sacrifices the very possibility of the first and is, therefore, a greater evil.

McCormick's position supports Walzer in his consideration of the distinction between indirect and direct intention as playing a subsidiary role in determining moral rightness or wrongness. So McCormick argues, "that our moral posture must be measured by a broader intentionality that related it to a plurality of values... it is the presence or absence of a proportionate reason which determines whether my action--be it direct or indirect psychologically or causally--involves me in turning against a basic good in a way which is morally reprehensible."[199]

One may question whether or not sacrificing the lives of noncombatants undermines the value of civilization. Walzer would have to argue that permitting the destruction of a political community could lead to greater deterioration in respect for individual human life than permitting the death of noncombatants while trying to protect the shared life of the community. It appears that such a case can be made in situations like Nazi Germany. The concentration camps alone give evidence that allowing a Nazi-type takeover can lead to the degradation of the value of individuals' lives and the deprivation of freedom. Even the unintended deaths of noncombatants would seem in these cases to enhance the value placed on individual human life rather than undermine it.

Cases of supreme emergency give a proportionate reason for choosing to defend the political community while seeming to turn against the value of respect for individual human life. In McCormick's way of thinking, however, one is obliged to respect the *ordo bonorum*, the order of goods or values.[200] Walzer's case of supreme emergency appears to do this by satisfying McCormick's three requirements for proportionate reason:

(1) the value at stake is at least equal to the value sacrificed (in this case the value of the political community makes possible the value for respect for human life and liberty);
(2) there is no less harmful way of protecting the value here and now (the danger is imminent and threatens utter destruction of the political community);
(3) the manner of its protection here and now will not undermine it in the long run (if the political community is not defended, the evil regime will not merely threaten the freedom to live in this political community but will actually eliminate it, thereby undermining the value of the human person).[201]

The final requirement of proportionate reason holds implications for nuclear warfare and deterrence that go beyond military strategy using conventional weapons. This is the topic of the next chapter.

Chapter 4

The Military and Political Uses
of Nuclear Weapons

Introduction: "Use" and "Non-Use" Defined

The word "use," as applied to nuclear weapons, ordinarily connotes the military employment of these weapons in actual war fighting situations. Likewise, "nonuse" ordinarily refers to a policy of nuclear deterrence. These ordinary connotations of "use" and "nonuse" can be misleading, however, since nuclear weapons are "used," in a broader sense of the word, in both military and political contexts. "Use" in war fighting refers to the predominantly *military* use of the weapons. There are two *political* uses of nuclear weapons: "use" in deterrence policies and "use" as bargaining chips in arms control negotiations. The three theorists share the more ordinary definition of "use" as "use in war fighting," however. Therefore, "nonuse" will apply throughout these chapters to nuclear deterrence and/or to nuclear weapons as bargaining chips.

Before analyzing the three theorists' positions on the uses of nuclear weapons, it will be helpful to dwell briefly on various aspects of the two uses; that is, the military use of nuclear weapons in war fighting; and the political uses of nuclear weapons as deterrents and as bargaining chips.

Nuclear Weapons in War Fighting

An examination of various positions on the use of nuclear weapons in war fighting reveals three questions addressed by political and military strategists and moral theorists: (1) *When* ought nuclear weapons to be used? (2) *Where* ought nuclear weapons to be used? (3) *How* ought nuclear weapons to be used? These are questions related to the nature of the targets, and the nature of the weapons themselves respectively.

In analyzing a given theorist's position on use, then, it will be helpful to see how he or she stands on policies of "first use" and on retaliatory or "second use." A position on first use may even vary according to whether that use is made by one's own state, an ally's or a lesser power's state, or an enemy superpower's state. A position on first use may also include a stand on a preemptive strike[1], or the first use of nuclear weapons during a previously conventionally waged war.

A theorist may also distinguish *where* the use of nuclear weapons ought and ought not to be deployed: (1) against population centers (countercity or countervalue targets; these will be referred to as CV); (2) against nuclear forces or (3) against "countercombatant" targets, which are more extensive than attacks against nuclear striking forces alone but less extensive than countercity strategies (both of which will be referred to as CF). These may include basic nuclear striking forces, their immediate support facilities (missile silos, bases, etc.) as well as weapons and military equipment-manufacturing plants.[2]

In addition to determining when and where nuclear weapons should be used, theorists may also make distinctions regarding the type of nuclear weapon that ought to be deployed: (1) strategic, (2) theatre, or (3) tactical. The precise meanings of these terms is not always clear. For example, some writers speak of "strategic" when relating certain decisions regarding the deployment of weapons to the overall war aims of a particular nation. In the same way, "tactical" often refers to the limited aim of a particular military maneuver. When applied to nuclear weapons, however, "strategic" generally includes missiles with nuclear warheads of high yields and capable of reaching targets at distances of more than 600 km. "Strategic" may also refer to "long-range," the distance over which a nuclear weapon of high or low yield might be capable of travelling. Strategic missiles include ICBMs, SLBMs and ASBMs (air and surface ballistic missiles) capable of a range in excess of 600 km and installed in or on an aircraft.[3]

"Tactical" nuclear weapons include shells fired from howitzers or other forms of artillery with yields of 1/2 kt to 10 to 100 tons of TNT and with a range of from 3 to 160 km. "Theatre" nuclear weapons are "grey area" weapons which include the U.S. Cruise and the U.S.S.R. Backfire weapons with warheads of 100 kt each.

The destructive power of all these weapons is such that some strategists, including Herman Kahn, claim that "the only reason to own the weapons is to deter, balance or correct for their ownership and potential use by others.[4] Bernard Brodie claims as much in 1945 when he stated, "[T]hus far the chief purpose of our military establishment has been to win wars. From now on its chief purpose must be to avert them."[5]

This position leads one to consider the "non-use" of nuclear weapons: as a deterrent.

Deterrence

Leon Wieseltier calls the doctrine of deterrence "the exact opposite of the doctrine of use,"[6] though, as has been observed, nuclear weapons are "used" in deterrence policy as well as in war fighting policy. Before discussing the distinctions theorists make in deterrence theories and the relationship between use and deterrence, it will be helpful to analyze the nature of deterrence itself and to find a definition which is best suited to the comparative study of the three contemporary theorists under consideration.

Patrick Morgan maintains that "deterrence is not a clear and precise notion."[7] He offers a generic definition of "deterrence" as "manipulating someone's behavior by threatening him with harm."[8] He cautions, however, that one must narrow such a definition when speaking of an international policy of deterrence. Everyone is familiar with the meaning of generic deterrence as it is used in the primary domestic scene--the family. Children, for example, respond to the anticipation of punishment or the withholding of something pleasant by adjusting their behavior to their parents' wishes. So in the larger domestic society, it is commonly assumed that criminal activity is discouraged at least to some degree by the threat of punishment. Even in international society, nations are discouraged from acting in certain ways because of the harmful consequences that may result in the form of economic or even military sanctions.[9]

The term, "nuclear deterrence," as it is used to describe international foreign policy, however, is much more specific. Each word of the generic definition has a specific meaning and ought to be spelled out if one is to arrive at a more clear understanding of deterrence in the *nuclear* context. In the analysis of each theorist, then, one will be interested in seeing how specifically the theorist answers the following questions:

What is to count as "manipulating" and when is it allowed?
Who are the "someones" involved?
What kind of "behavior" does deterrence address?
What are the characteristics of the "threat?"
What sort of "harm" is threatened?

In shorter form, what must be asked of each theorist is:

(1) *Who* are involved in making the threat and in being threatened? (the nature of the actors)
(2) *What kind* of threat is it? (the nature of the threat)
(3) *When*, if ever, is such a threat morally justified? (the nature of the justification)

When referring to an international policy of nuclear deterrence, the actors are assumed to be national *governments* that are related to each other as *adversaries*. Thus the U.S. nuclear arsenal may be said to act as a deterrent to the USSR while it makes little sense to say it is a deterrent to a Canadian attack. A nuclear arsenal may or may not act as a deterrent to individuals, such as terrorists, but at any rate, the nuclear deterrence *policy* of a given nation is not directed at individuals but at adversarial governments.

One is likely to find less disagreement among the three theorists on the question of the nature of the actors than on the last two questions--the nature of the threat and the nature of the justification.

Ordinarily, as Morgan says, by "threat" one refers to a *military* retaliation to forestall a *military* attack. Though "deterrence" can be used during wartime to prevent certain kinds of attacks, it is ordinarily used in the context of *preventing* war rather than *containing* it. In addition, deterrence is a particular kind of threat (retaliatory) offered for a particular purpose (to prevent an attack). Morgan also suggests that there are two kinds of deterrence: (1) pure (or immediate) deterrence and (2) general deterrence: *"Immediate deterrence* concerns the relationship between opposing states where at least one side is seriously considering an attack while the other is mounting a threat of retaliation in order to prevent it. *General deterrence* relates to opponents who maintain armed forces to regulate their relationship even though neither is anywhere near mounting an attack."[10] Identification of the *kinds* of deterrence should help answer the second question about the "behavior" of the adversaries and the "manipulation" involved as well as the sort of "harm" that is being threatened.

When nuclear weapons were first developed and used against Japan in World War II, many hoped they would deter all war in the future, so great was the harm their use caused. However, it soon became evident that nuclear weapons did *not* deter all *conventional* wars, though they may have deterred wars between the superpowers (twenty-five million people have died in war since Hiroshima.)[11] Wieseltier asserts that nuclear weapons only deter nuclear weapons. It may be impossible to prove whether or not this statement is correct since a direct cause and effect relationship between deterrence and war may not be verifiable.[12]

The claim that deterrence prevents nuclear war introduces the problem of counterfactuals, a philosophical controversy engaged in by William Kneale and Karl Popper, among others. Kneale's analysis may prove helpful here. The deterrence argument may be stated in "Knealean fashion" as the following counterfactual conditional statement: "If a deterrence policy were not in place, a nuclear war would take place." This would be equivalent to the conjunction of three sentences, *mutatis mutandis*: (1) There has never been a nuclear war while a deterrence policy was in place. (2) There has never been an unobserved nuclear war while a deterrence policy was in place. (3) There will never be a nuclear war while a deterrence policy is in place.

Statement (1), Kneale says, is well confirmed by evidence and what is being claimed is that this evidence is enough to confirm (2) and (3), but, "only in the sense in which the fact that it is raining provides some confirmation for the conjunctive statement that it is raining and the moon is made of green cheese." Thus, Kneale shows that a precisely formulated material implication cannot be derived from the contrary-to-fact conditional, "If there were no deterrence policy."[13]

Carl Hempel also claims through logical analysis that a given hypothesis can be *disconfirmed* with certainty, but that it can be *confirmed* only to a certain degree of certainty. However, as Hempel points out, this is true of *all* empirical reality, assuming a Humean causality. Thus, the lack of certainty may be seen as a limitation on a given theory but not as a defect of that theory.[14]

Patrick Morgan expresses the deterrence argument this way: "[t]o conclusively demonstrate that deterrence worked (or is working) means proving why something did not happen (is not happening) [and] that is never really possible."[15]

Bruce Russett says that "in instances of successful deterrence, the causes are complex and not easily ascertainable."[16] However, he concludes that the wars that have been deterred are wars between the major powers, presumably because engagement in these wars increases the risk of escalation to "all-out" war: "[W]e have ample reason to feel now that nuclear weapons do act critically to deter wars between the major powers, and not nuclear wars alone but any wars."[17]

It is beyond the scope of this study to analyze each war in the last forty years to see where deterrence is and is not proving successful. It seems reasonable to conclude, however, that policies of nuclear deterrence are ordinarily understood as deterring at least nuclear wars and possibly escalation of any smaller-scale wars that threaten to lead to nuclear war.

The last question concerning justification will further explore the nature of "threat" as it relates to use.

The relation between use and deterrence is not immediately obvious. Some theorists will want to say that a nation cannot have a meaningful deterrence theory unless it has the will to move to use should deterrence fail.[18] Others maintain that "having the weapons is enough," that one does not have to be committed to their use in order to deter the enemy because the enemy is never certain whether or not the weapons will be used.[19] Still others say that one may have a "bluff" deterrent where the declaratory policy states that nuclear weapons will be used, but the operational policy calls for non-use.[20]

There is yet a third opinion regarding the relationship between use and deterrence. That is the position of theorists like David Hollenbach: "No simple logical argument can be made from the illegitimacy of use to the moral evaluation of the intentions involved in deterrence."[21]

Hollenbach distinguishes between the actions implementing the intention of using$_2$ nuclear weapons and the actions of actually deploying the weapons:

"The actions implementing these intentions are not the actual use of nuclear weapons but military and political steps which attempt to prevent nuclear conflict.[22]

What distinguishes the intention behind a deterrence policy from the intention to use the nuclear weapon is "a reasoned judgment that the policy in question will actually prevent use."[23]

According to Hollenbach's position, the morality of a given deterrence policy is at least partly determined by the nature of a weapons system and whether it is more or less *likely to lead to use,* and not simply by the nature of its target. Hollenbach believes that whether a target is CV, CF, or countercombatant is secondary to the likelihood of use. According to someone like Germain Grisez, however, this target determination is key to deciding on the morality of a given policy. Thus, if current United States policy includes moving to countercity nuclear strikes "if necessary," Grisez judges such a policy to be immoral. In fact, it may be claimed that even if the U.S. does not need to include countercity nuclear strikes, it still requires the threat to take the lives of millions of innocents. Though these are claimed to be "collateral" deaths, they are not merely a side effect, according to Grisez: "When destruction which is a side-effect of one's outward behavior is essential to the attainment of one's purpose, such destruction is included in what one morally does."[24]

The U.S. targeting options in SIOP-5 include such targets in at least the fourth category, "Economic and industrial targets," insofar as these are located in or near population centers. Options 1, 2, and 3 seem to fall under Russett's "countercombatant" category. If the latter options do not depend on large numbers of "collateral" deaths of the innocent, presumably Grisez could accept this as a moral deterrence policy.

Bargaining Chips

Another political use of nuclear weapons is the part they play as bargaining chips in arms control negotiations. None of the three contemporary just war theorists in this study pays much attention to this role. It is likely that many theorists apply the same reasoning to nuclear weapons seen as bargaining chips as they do to these weapons considered as deterrents. The two do have some aspects in common: their military "non-use," by which the "actors" involved use the weapons for political reasons; and their primary purpose, which is to prevent the war-fighting use of these weapons.

Nuclear bargaining chips also have a deterrent quality although the state that possesses and develops them does so for a different intention: it is interested in using them to eliminate additional nuclear weapons and not to threaten an adversary. A deterrent both threatens, usually in a declaratory fashion, and offers risk; a nuclear bargaining chip does not threaten in a declaratory fashion but its very possession does present risk and could be interpreted as a threat by some states.

Having examined some of the key elements inherent in the concepts of use and non-use of nuclear weapons, one may now analyze the positions of the three theorists on these issues. Their application of the principle of proportionality and the principle of discrimination to nuclear use and nuclear deterrence will be of special interest.

The Contemporary Just-War Theorists and the Military and Political Uses of Nuclear Weapons

PAUL RAMSEY

War Fighting

The announcement by Secretary of Defense Robert McNamara in June 1962 that U.S. nuclear targeting strategy is a "mixed option" plan and not simply a strategy of mutual assured destruction prompts Paul Ramsey to praise the apparent change of declaratory policy, though, as has been seen, it was the Eisenhower Administration that first moved away from a plan of massive retaliation to one of flexible response in 1959. In a 1962 pamphlet, Ramsey chides those who seem to gloss over the "qualitative moral distinction" between countercity and counterforce warfare as not recognizing the significance of this change in strategic planning. Ramsey's support of counterforce targeting indicates that he subscribes to the use of some nuclear weapons either in war fighting or as a deterrent or both. Attention will be given first to the possibility of the use of nuclear weapons: use in actual war-fighting situations.

The Nature of the Weapons

"I say simply that any weapon whose every use must be for the purpose of directly killing noncombatants as a means of attaining some supposed good and incidentally hitting some military target is a weapon whose every use would be wholly immoral."[25]

This statement of Ramsey's in *War and the Christian Conscience* leaves room for the moral use of nuclear weapons that have at least some use, the purpose of which is *not* directly killing noncombatants. Ramsey's use of "directly" here means more than directly *intending* to kill noncombatants; he is including even the intention to destroy military targets but with such disproportionate collateral death and injury to noncombatants that the act would be immoral. For example, Ramsey considers thermonuclear weapons, i.e., megaton weapons like the hydrogen bomb, and even some fractional kiloton weapons, to be so devastating that their destruction of military objectives would always and only be "incidental to the destruction of a whole area thereby passing beyond all reasonable or justifiable limits."[25] This condition, however, is subject to empirical change, and Ramsey finds it conceivable that historical events and/or changes in the concentration of political and military power could make it possible to justify morally the use and/or possession of these same weapons: "the *Grenzmoralität* of its [the megaton weapon's] merely military possession and use depends on whether in fact, now or in the future, there are any conceivable circumstances in which it would have importance against military targets against which less powerful weapons would not serve as well."[27]

Meanwhile, even at the present time, there exist military targets of fifty or more miles in diameter against which conventional weapons or smaller nuclear weapons would be ineffective.[28] Such military targets, Ramsey finds, are located at sufficient distances from population centers to offer the occasions for the moral use of nuclear weapons, though not of thermonuclear weapons. In justifying their use, Ramsey "begins with the traditional immunity from direct killing surrounding noncombatants in the just-war theory [and not] with only the limitation of proportionate grave reason or lesser evil."[29] Thermonuclear weapons used "all-out" are definitely proscribed as no longer being weapons of *war* since war must be fought with a national purpose in mind. Ramsey concludes that it would be impossible for a nation engaged in full-scale thermonuclear war to continue as a nation with a purpose. In other words, thermonuclear or "all-out" war is not the continuation of politics by other means.

A great many nuclear weapons, however, have what Ramsey calls a "dual use": they can be used properly against military objectives or improperly against populations. This dual possibility, Ramsey insists, rests in the weapons themselves and not in the way a nation-state possesses them or declares how it plans to use them.[30] Ramsey's "dual use" will have broad implications for his position on deterrence which will be addressed later.

Strategic Weapons

Ramsey speaks of strategic weapons as those that have a "long range," not necessarily as having a certain amount of megatonnage. Strategic weapons, then, have a "dual use," according to Ramsey: they may be directed against the enemy's own strategic military forces, a pure "counterforce" use, or they may be directed against population centers, a "countervalue" use. In other words, when Ramsey speaks of strategic weapons, he is referring to the distances they can travel and not to their targets.

Tactical and Theater Nuclear Weapons

Ramsey does not usually differentiate between strategic and tactical or theater nuclear weapons. The distinction for him is not morally significant in most cases in which the terms merely refer to the distances from launcher to target. If there is a legitimate military use, that is sufficient to allow at least *consideration* of the morality of that use.

Ramsey has maintained that no argument can be given for any morally defensible or politically beneficial use of multimegaton weapons. He holds that rational nuclear armament should tend to be confined to the firepower of the conventional weapons that would be needed to perform the same function. Thus, for example, where it is impossible to destroy a legitimate military target because of the number and physical size of conventional bombs necessary to accomplish the objective, only nuclear weapons approximating the same firepower ought to be used. Ramsey bases this on the danger of escalation and on the likelihood of moving beyond just war limits.[31]

Ramsey argues from the "cause of justice" that a nation should be able to repel "a force that justly should be repelled"; the force a defending nation can use, however, is still subject to *jus in bello* limitations. He is concerned not only with multimegaton weapons but also with the upper range of kiloton weapons. If there is a militarily efficient use for kiloton weapons, these may be classified as rational armament in a just war. However, Ramsey maintains it would still have to be shown that conventional weapons or weapons of less destructive power, and "less damaging to civilian life indirectly, would not have equal or greater military effectiveness against the target."[32]

Ramsey's concern regarding escalation, which he expresses in *War and the Christian Conscience* (1961), appears to increase in his essays appearing in *The Just War* (1968). In "The Limits of Nuclear War," first published in 1963, Ramsey recommends a policy that tactical weapons be used only against military forces and not strategically against the enemy's homeland. The implications of this will be spelled out more clearly when "first use" and "retaliation" are considered. Further evidence of Ramsey's increased concern about escalation is evident in his agreement with Thornton Read regarding the necessity to preserve the distinction between conventional weapons and nuclear weapons. Ramsey states that "[Read has] satisfactorily demonstrated the essentially escalatory character of tactical nuclear weapons themselves because of the relation of their weight and their firepower in comparison with conventional explosives, a relation which places a great gulf between conventional weapons and tactical nuclears as possible instruments of controlled warfare."[33]

What Ramsey must consider, then, is whether there are any circumstances that do not seem to lead to escalation and that, therefore, might warrant approval.

First Use

"The proscription of a first use of force may very well be a conclusion of statecraft; it ought never to be its universal premise."[34] "First use" is an option Ramsey clearly wants to keep open but whether he wants to keep it open as a possible *nuclear* policy is the question that must be addressed.

Ramsey recognizes that not every important policy decision is an ethical decision but that ethico-political analysis can offer "regulative moral guidance" to political decision-makers. With this in mind, he recommends the following policy regarding "first use" of nuclear weapons: "This nation should announce that as a matter of policy we will never be the first to use nuclear weapons-- *except* tactical ones that may and will be used against forces only and not strategically against an enemy's heartland, to stop an invasion across a clearly defined boundary, our own or one we are pledged by treaty to defend."[35]

By "invasion," Ramsey includes the action of conventional forces as well as or instead of nuclear forces. In order to secure its own borders, he would permit a nation to launch a nuclear strike *over its own territory* against such invading forces. Ramsey believes this policy has a moral advantage over one which allows the first use of nuclear weapons, albeit defensive, against the aggressor's homeland. In Ramsey's recommended policy the area of nuclear use is not predetermined; it is designated by the attackers themselves and not by the defending nation. In addition, Ramsey agrees with Leo Szilard that allowing first use only over one's own territory (or that of one's allies') is not so likely to result in nuclear retaliation as would a policy allowing first use over the attacker's territory. Presumably, he is not allowing for strategic use in support of one's allies and the reasons for this are not clear. His recommendation seems to require actual placement of nuclear weapons on allies' territory. It is reasonable to suppose that the use of strategic weapons might be open to misinterpretation by the attacking nation and thus lead to escalation.

Ramsey concludes that his policy suggestion is more credible and more likely to deter invasion. Whether the policy should be permanent or should be in effect just long enough (Ramsey gives Szilard's projection of five years) to mount the necessary defensive conventional forces in Europe, Ramsey leaves as an open question. Having sufficient conventional forces would, according to Ramsey, invite the Soviet Union to renounce first use of tactical nuclear weapons as superfluous and escalatory since the Soviets could mount a counterattack with sufficent conventional forces.

In summary, then, Ramsey's position regarding the first use of nuclear weapons has three provisos: (1) that their use be defensive against an invasion already underway; (2) that the targeting be counterforce only; (3) that the target area be confined to one's own territory.

If, as Ramsey concludes, first use of certain nuclear weapons defensively is not inherently wrong, second use in reprisal also seems justifiable. Ramsey addresses this second use as "retaliation."

Retaliation

The right of reprisal is solidly established in *jus gentium*, but Ramsey agrees with O'Brien that it is severely challenged by the means of warfare available in the twentieth century. The right of reprisal is meant to serve two purposes, according to William O'Brien: "'it provides a sanction for the law and it tends to restore the balance upset when one belligerent uses illegal means.'"[36]

The issue at stake in "nuclear retaliation" is "reprisal in kind," i.e., a nuclear "tit-for-tat" exchange. In the past, most actions warranting reprisals in kind were not *malum in se*; but the right of reprisal, according to O'Brien, is not an "All-embracing rule for the conduct of men or nations."[37] What must be determined, then, is whether there are uses of nuclear weapons that are inherently wrong. Ramsey proscribes all uses of thermonuclear weapons because they cause too much collateral damage. It would, therefore, be immoral to use these weapons even in retaliation for their first use by an opposing force. Ramsey's reason for reaching this conclusion is based primarily on the resultant death and injury to noncombatants and the fact that this result cannot be claimed an "indirect" result of the use of weapons of mass destruction. This conclusion is determined in large part by the nature of the target. It will be helpful, then, to address this issue more carefully.

The Nature of the Target

The Countervalue Distinction

Ramsey distinguishes two broad categories of targeting strategies, the first of which is ordinarily referred to as countervalue (CV); the second, counterforce (CF). Ramsey identifies strategies within the first category as "[those which] aim at civilians, except for the sort of '"countervalue"' warfare which proposes to allow time for cities to be evacuated." Countervalue targets, then, include the following types of warfare: "pure-city, cities-plus, and devastation war; controlled or unlimited countercity retaliation; counterforce-plus-countervalue, or counterforce-plus-bonus; and limited strategic city reprisal."[38]

The common element in all these strategies is that they directly target civilians. Ramsey finds them morally unjustifiable, first, because they violate the principle of discrimination, and second, because they violate the principle of proportionality. They differ from a second set of targets, counterforce targets, which will be considered in detail below. Counterforce targeting strategies include "counter-force warfare; no-city war; controlled or unlimited counter-force retaliation; straight counter-force or counterforce-plus-avoidance."[39] The common element in the second set is the fact that they do not directly target noncombatants.

For Ramsey, these two sets of targeting strategies are non-continuous in the sense that there is no "grey area" between them. The radical break between them is accounted for by the principle of discrimination: the direct vs. indirect targeting of noncombatants and the fact that Ramsey cannot morally justify direct targeting of noncombatants.

In his 1963 pamphlet, "The Limits of Nuclear War," Ramsey states his thesis clearly: "Counterforce nuclear war is the upper limit of rational, politically purposive military action." He considers three possible reasons why one might oppose his position. The first two reasons offer *opposition* to the use of any nuclear weapon; the third argues for *expanded use*. The three reasons are (1) that general disarmament is about to be accomplished and therefore no plans should be made for the use of any weapons; (2) that balanced deterrence can be stabilized and kept perfect enough to ensure the nonuse of nuclear weapons except for deterrence reasons; (3) (and a more uncommon view) that during actual war a decision might be made to go to "a slow lobbing intercity exchange," i.e., a policy of "limited attacks on cities," 'controlled counter-value,' or 'counterforce-plus-bonus civilian damage'." The first option Ramsey discounts as unlikely to occur soon. The second, he maintains, still necessitates consideration of fight-the-war strategies should deterrence fail.[40] The third demands a closer analysis.

CV Lower Limit: "Limited Exchange of Cities"

The lower limit to the first set of CV targeting strategies Ramsey takes to be the "limited exchange of cities." In doing so, he seems to ignore the distinction he has made elsewhere that another limited strategic plan might be an attack on cities allowed first to be evacuated. Presumably, "counter-combatant" areas would be targeted and noncombatants themselves would not be *directly* attacked, although noncombatants' possessions and other non-military areas would be destroyed. Ramsey does not wish to treat this possibility as a genuine CV strategy.

Ramsey makes the judgment that only if the alternative in a given situation is to go to all-out countercity retaliation, can limited city exchange be done or even genuinely considered.[41] In this he agrees with Klaus Knorr, who writes that limited strategic retaliation is "'a calamity' so great that 'a rational person will consider it only if all available alternatives are appreciably worse.'"[42] What Ramsey seems to mean here is that one may *think* of such a strategy's being put into effect but that it might be immoral to do so; he concludes that "value-for-value war plans" are "intrinsically intolerable." Only a "supposed rationality" resulting from the transformation of "political man" into "economic man" would lead to such a conclusion.[43]

Ramsey has considered the possibility of limited strategic retaliation for the purposes of argument only. His conclusion is that it is not a moral policy to pursue[44]: "even limited city exchanges must be judged politically un-do-able, as no longer having political purpose."[45] Limited strategic war, meaning limited attacks on strategic *forces*, however, is an option that must be considered under CF targeting.

Counterforce Targeting

Countercombatant Targets with "Collateral Damage"

In CV strategies, it is helpful to consider the *lower* limit that might be justifiable as the upper limits more easily violate proportionality once they are put into effect. In CF strategies, it is helpful to consider the *upper* limit since, as has been stated, Ramsey does justify some uses of CF nuclear warfare.

The upper limit of CF war that Ramsey must deal with is "all-out" or "unlimited CF warfare." This strategy includes what Russett calls "countercombatant targets (*tactical* objectives, munitions dumps, supply lines, bridges, etc.)." Russett's and Ramsey's use of "tactical" refers to the type of missile or weapon being used and not the distance the missile travels to destroy its target. The destruction of tactical objectives may result not only in the destruction of the enemy's military forces but in "collateral" death and injury to civilians as well.

On the basis of discrimination alone, such attacks may be judged as moral, but the morality of a military action is also determined by the principle of proportionality. It appears that many CF strategies will be determined to be immoral on the basis of violating the principle of proportionality. Robert Tucker argues that whether or not death and injury to the innocent is "collateral," that is, whether it is indirectly or directly intended, is not relevant to the morality of the action. What determines the morality, according to Tucker, is "*the scope of this death and injury.*" Ramsey calls this a false account: "an end's being secured without another effect is not the same as the effect's being a *means* to that end."[46] In CF warfare, death and injury are not the *means* to the end of destroying the forces of an unjust attacker. *Unlimited* CF warfare, however, may well and most likely would, according to Ramsey, violate the principle of proportionality. It would be thinkable but "politically un-do-able," because it would destroy more individuals than would be proportionate to the value of preserving the State. This position rests on the value Ramsey assigns to the State vs. the value he assigns to the individual, but this is dealt with more fully in chapter 5.

The CF strategy that Ramsey recommends, then, must be one in which care is taken to avoid death and injury to noncombatants as much as possible.

This is the "CF-plus-avoidance" strategy: "Only CF-plus-avoidance may be called a just way to conduct war, since traditional and acceptable moral teachings concerning legitimate military targets require the avoidance of civilian damage as much as possible even while accepting this as an unavoidable indirect effect."[47]

This strategy, according to Ramsey, is most likely to keep war limited and marked off as clearly as possible from "general war." Ramsey allows first use of CF warfare to secure one's borders and defend the country. He also allows CF retaliatory strikes or "strategic strikes against forces" against the enemy's own territory "to bargain effectively about the limits and rules by which war is to be fought." The main purpose of a strategic CF war is "to enforce *lower* limits, punish violations of them, and in any case decrease the enemy's military capability and affect the balance of power in the world after the war is over."[48]

An additional purpose of any limited war, Ramsey states, is its deterrent value, i.e., the indication of a possible willingness to go to higher levels. Morally, Ramsey would not advocate actual use of nuclear weapons, but as previously indicated, the ambivalence inherent in the very nature of the weapons threatens such a possibility. Like it or not, the "CF-plus-avoidance" strategy includes a CV deterrent effect. In order to appreciate the moral significance of this effect, one must analyze Ramsey's account of nuclear deterrence in greater detail.

Nuclear Deterrence

In *The Just War* (1968), Ramsey alerts his readers to a change in his position on the morality of deterrence, or rather, an elaboration and further probing of the morality of deterrence since the time he first addresses the issue in *War and the Christian Conscience* (1961). In *War and the Christian Conscience*, Ramsey concludes that no force may be used for purposes of deterrence which is immoral to use in war fighting. In *The Just War*, Ramsey claims to have paid more attention to findings of fact and findings of the moral law "to show how a *possible* deterrence posture and governing moral principles mesh together.[49] It seems worthwhile, then, to focus on Ramsey's writings after 1961, many of which have been collected in Parts II and III of *The Just War*, in order to find his more considered conclusions regarding deterrence. His 1973 essay, "A Political Ethics Context on Strategic Thinking," is especially helpful in summarizing his position and in elaborating certain aspects of the deterrent threat.

The Nature of the Threat

Relation to Use

In *War and the Christian Conscience* (1961), Ramsey stated that "the manufacture and possession of a weapon whose every use is [for the purpose of directly killing noncombatants as a means of attaining some supposed good and incidentally hitting some military target] and the political employment of it for the sake of deterrence, is likewise immoral."[50]

Ramsey states the same position in "A Political Ethics Context" (1973): "Whatever is wrong to do is wrong also to threaten, if the latter means 'to do.'" He admits that the doing of the action (indiscriminate war fighting) may be a *different* wrong from the threatening to do it for the sake of the good to come (deterrence); nevertheless, "[t]he question... of the ethical justification of deterrence depends crucially on a question of fact, or of plannable policy." It is the answers to the "question of fact" that change in Ramsey's developing theory of deterrence.[51]

It is evident from the statements cited that the deterrence Ramsey ordinarily refers to in his writings corresponds to Patrick Morgan's concept of "general" deterrence, a long-range policy, as opposed to "immediate" deterrence, a policy operative in crisis situations. In addition, Ramsey usually speaks of deterrence as preventing *nuclear* attacks or *nuclear* wars. Ramsey's interest, then, is in determining a deterrence policy which would remain in effect over a long period of time to prevent primarily *nuclear* wars.

Ramsey also seems to be a deterrence theorist of Morgan's first type, i.e., he assumes that one cannot have an effective deterrence policy unless one has the will to use nuclear weapons should deterrence fail. However, for a time, Ramsey is ambiguous on this point as is evident in his changing position on the "bluff" deterrent.

The "Bluff" Deterrent

In "The Limits of Nuclear War" (1963), Ramsey seems to be operating on the assumption that threat does not imply use. He argues that although it would be immoral to use nuclear weapons against population centers, it might be moral to threaten to use them as long as such a threat results in deterring the adversary from launching a nuclear attack. Such an act is not an example of lying, according to Ramsey; rather it is like the example in "The Case of the Curious Exception," where withholding the truth from someone to whom the truth is not due does not qualify as lying.[52] Ramsey's critics, however, deny that deterrence can be credible without the intention actually to *do* the act--in this case, an act that is immoral according to Ramsey's argument. The critics attack the bluff deterrent as being imprudent, but not necessarily immoral.

Ramsey counters his critics in 1963, saying that they "fail to show that there can be no deterrent effect where there is no actual intention to use nuclear weapons directly against cities."[53] He holds that the argument from bluff is underrated and that it is moral because it does not imply a conditional commitment to CV warfare.

However, on further reflection, Ramsey changes his mind about the morality of the bluff deterrent. By 1965, Ramsey states that he withdraws the "bluff" from his analysis of a moral deterrent for two reasons:

> First, one's real intentions not to go to such use will be found out, and the bluff will fail to deter; and, second, even if our top political and military leaders were pure in heart, they must count on thousands of men in missile silos, planes and submarines to be conditionally willing, under some circumstances, to become murderers. One should never occasion mortal sin in others, tempt them to it or enlist them for it. It is never right to do evil, or to intend to do evil, so that good may come."[54]

Ramsey's first reason shows that he has become convinced after reflection on the facts that the bluff is ineffective because it lacks credibility and is, therfore, imprudent. His second reason is a claim that the bluff deterrent is also immoral, that is, if the stakes are high enough, those "thousands of men [and women]," ignorant of actual operating policy, would be willing to use the weapons against CV targets.

Most of Ramsey's critics find the more convincing reason for dropping the "bluff" deterrent to be the prudential argument. In accepting this argument, Ramsey appears to agree with Philip Green that a key element in an effective deterrence policy is *credibility*: "A rational man does not (a) make threats that are not credible, or (b) allow himself to be deterred by threats that are not credible or (at least) are incredible."[55] However, Morgan suggests the perfectly "rational" human being does not exist; the most one can hope for are "reasonable" or "sensible" actors. It is important to analyze Ramsey's view of these human actors in order to understand why he reaches certain conclusions about deterrence.

The Nature of the Actors

Ramsey, like Morgan, identifies the actors in deterrence theory as the nation-states. Unlike Morgan, however, Ramsey does not limit the actors to present adversaries. In fact, he speaks of nation-states as collectivities, each of which is an "autonomous actor," a "stranger," even "a potential enemy." Each state, then, must respond to the perennial unpredictability of other states by, "*among other things*, preparedness, threat, and perhaps an actual use of force."[56]

Such language seems far removed from the agape language Ramsey uses to justify the principles of proportionality and discrimination. His phrase, "among other things," however, may include such responses as "care and concern," and the willingness to help defend against an unjust attacker. Thus, the picture Ramsey draws of the nation-states may be considered as consistent with his earlier insistence on the need to act out of love for neighbor. Love of neighbor is stressed less in his treatment of deterrence than, for example, in his treatment of discrimination. To be consistent, Ramsey must continue to insist on love of neighbor as the moving force behind deterrence. To see whether he maintains this consistency, one must see how Ramsey views the nation-state as collectivity *vis a vis* the individuals within not only one's own nation-state but also within the adversary's nation-state.

The actors Ramsey speaks of are "peoples." Each collectivity expresses its purposes as a people. The "rules of practice" which allow these people to effectuate their purposes must be "systemic," according to Ramsey. They must originate with a people and not be an ethics imposed from outside. Even the "just war criteria for limiting warfare, although possibly a product of Western ethics, concerns the very nature of the international system and is really an articulation of principles required by this system of peoples, the 'interstate system.'"[57]

The stress Ramsey places on the potentially hostile, and at least unpredictable, intentions of nation-states points to a possible weakness in his overall position on nuclear war and deterrence. The systemic rules of practice should function in such a way that they enhance the possibility for the continued existence of the various collectivities or peoples. While limiting warfare is one of the means to this end, it is not yet clear from Ramsey's position how far an individual nation-state can go in its own defense before endangering the physical conditions necessary for the continued existence of third parties. If just war limitations have not had to address this possibility in the past, they must address it now since nuclear war presents a risk of destruction unprecedented in the history of warfare. The nature of the target has implications because of the nature of the risk nuclear weapons pose.

The Nature of the Target

CV Targets

In "The Limits of Nuclear War" (1963), Ramsey argues that it is morally wrong directly to target population centers mainly because targeting them would be a violation of the principle of discrimination. However, the strategic nuclear weapons that would be needed to destroy cities have what Ramsey calls "dual use:" they can be used effectively either against an enemy's strategic military forces or against cities. Despite the fact that a nation's declaratory policy may be to target only an adversary's forces, the *possibility* that they may be used against cities inheres in the weapons themselves. The mere possession of nuclear weapons, then, may act as a deterrent to any nation contemplating attacking an opponent's cities. This kind of deterrence strategy is called a "suspended" deterrence strategy: it considers the worst possible case, the nuclear attack on cities, and hangs or "suspends" all the other possibilities of nuclear attack from it in such a way that only the threat of the worst case is considered to deter CF or countercombatant attacks effectively. However, Ramsey has already made it clear that he rejects the idea that mere possession is an effective deterrent; that is, Ramsey says possession or threat must carry with it the willingness to move to use should deterrence fail. If the adversary knows there is no willingness to deploy the weapons should deterrence fail, Ramsey believes possession would not deter an attack.

Ramsey's change of position on this issue has direct implications for the targeting policy he recommends. A "bluff" CV targeting policy rests on the assumption that a nuclear adversary will be prevented from attacking another's cities only if its own cities are threatened in retaliation. Ramsey has re-examined this assumption and as a result revises his deterrence policy recommendation.

"The Graduated Deterrent": CF and Countercombatant Targets

Ramsey's analysis of nuclear and conventional war indicates that modern warfare becomes disproportionate, and thus immoral, long before it becomes indiscriminate. This conclusion leads him to reconsider the effectiveness of various targeting policies as deterrents.

What Ramsey concludes is that the threat of damage at a lower level than the upper limit of CV damage suffered in CV attacks is sufficient to deter even CV attacks to one's own cities or other CV targets. If, for example, certain strategic forces are destroyed, a nation-state may not be able to maintain an effective defense. Since it could no longer secure its borders without certain support services to its military forces, it would be unable to continue to pursue its national goals or maintain its political independence.

What Ramsey recommends, then, is a policy of "graduated deterrence" as opposed to the "suspended deterrence" policy. The latter policy assumes CV threats are necessary to maintain an effective deterrent. The graduated steps Ramsey recommends begin with the minimum deterrent he believes necessary to deter an aggressive nuclear attack. It provides for deterrence from

(1) the perceived likelihood of unacceptable combatant or military target or nuclear force destruction,
(2) the perceived likelihood of unacceptable collateral damage from quite discriminate acts of war in a nuclear age,
(3) from the ambiguous possible uses of nuclear weapons, or from an irremovable perception as to their possible uses, and
(4) from deliberate ambiguity as to the weapons' intended use.[58]

Ramsey reaches the conclusion that graduated deterrence would be "a theory of responsible deterrence" as early as 1963. In his essay, "Can a Pacifist Tell a Just War?",[59] he compares his method of reasoning with Herman Kahn's. Kahn became convinced on the basis of strategic analysis that CF threats were sufficient to deter an enemy from launching a nuclear attack against one's own cities.[60] Ramsey reaches the same conclusion as a result of further reflection on the morality of deterrence.

Ramsey's first step of his graduated deterrence strategy appears to be a just CF retaliation, provided that the collateral effects do not cause death and injury to noncombatants. Whether this is possible will depend on empirical facts regarding fall-out, etc. Conceivably, however, CF retaliation could be a moral use of nuclear weapons consistent with Ramsey's overall moral theory. The second step involves collateral damage that Ramsey justifies by "indirection," i.e., that noncombatant death and injury are the result of indirect targeting. Ramsey appeals here to double effect reasoning. As such, it is subject to Michael Walzer's criticism. Walzer has asserted that if CF warfare had no collateral effects, it could not play a part in Ramsey's strategy. Ramsey "relies so heavily on the deaths he supposedly doesn't intend [that the standing of indirection] is undermined here." Though indirection has some moral significance, it seems insufficient to stand as the "cornerstone of a justified deterrent."[61]

Even if Ramsey can maintain that the second level, deterrence from the threat of collateral noncombatant death and injury, does not violate discrimination (and this argument, Walzer shows, is weak at best), he still must show that it does not violate the principle of proportionality. In his 1963 statement, Ramsey says that "[a] threat of something disproportionate is not necessarily a disproportionate threat."[62] It appears that deterrence from the threat of collateral noncombatant damage fits such a threat for Ramsey.

To the criticism that if graduated deterrence threatens something disproportionate, it is itself disproportionate and therefore an immoral threat, Ramsey offers three replies. First, as mentioned above, the threat of something disproportionate is not necessarily disproportionate itself. Second, the issuance of disproportionate threats is the nature of deterrence in *any* kind of war. Should deterrence fail and the disproportionate damage be actualized, this is both the tragedy of war and the immorality of a warfare that has lost its objective. "It is not a question of the morality of deterrence oriented upon its objective." Third, "there is an obligation never to mean to do and accept damage disproportionate to political goals."[63] By this Ramsey apparently means that one cannot *intend* to move to CV targeting since this would only make retaliatory CV strikes more likely and with them, the destruction of the very values for which a defense is mounted in the first place.

Ramsey's use of the term "proportionality" seems to stretch the meaning of the term beyond its ordinary moral connotation. According to Ramsey's reasoning, it would appear that anyone who wants something enough may take whatever means (*non mala in se*) necessary to get it. According to Ramsey's position, it is not the "ideal observer," or the disinterested party who weighs the goods and evils in the proportionality calculus and determines the morality of the act. "Good effects" are not necessarily *objectively* good effects; they are *subjectively* good effects. what is good for the actor (in this case, the one who deters by CF threats with heavy collateral damage) is an evil for the one acted upon (the adversary). Step 2 of Ramsey's graduated deterrence policy is an example of this extended meaning of proportionality.

Steps 3 and 4 of the graduated deterrence policy seem subject to Ramsey's own criticism of the "bluff" deterrent in that they may not appear credible to the enemy and would not actually deter the enemy. This, however, would be a prudential and not necessarily a moral criticism. Morally, they, too, seem to offer too easy a way out for Ramsey and are subject to Walzer's criticism that "men and women are responsible for the threats they live by, even if they don't speak them out loud."[64]

Ramsey maintains that his "graduated deterrence" policy promises an escape from the moral dilemmas posed by other deterrence policies, and that it promises to be effective in preventing all but the *ultimate* destruction, presumably mutual assured destruction (MAD). He leaves the threat of ultimate destruction to the *possession* of nuclear weapons since this destruction would be "the subjectively unintended consequence of the mere possession of these weapons."[65]

Despite what Ramsey has tried to do, he seems ultimately to have failed to find a moral deterrent, for Walzer appears correct in saying that "men and women are responsible for the threats they live by, spoken or unspoken." If the mere possession of nuclear weapons threatens MAD and nation-states "live by" this inherent threat, it would seem that they are responsible for the risk the possession of these weapons imposes. Whether this risk is less than the risk taken by disarmament and whether either risk is a moral choice are questions that must be addressed; but they are not questions that Ramsey's "indirect targeting" and extended concept of proportionality seem capable of answering.

Walter Stein contends that William O'Brien offers "exactly contrary arguments" to Ramsey's.[66] It will be important to see if O'Brien succeeds where Ramsey fails.

WILLIAM V. O'BRIEN

War Fighting

As has already been noted, William O'Brien approaches the study of war like a "twentieth century Grotius": that is, he analyzes the actual practices of present-day belligerents and measures their behavior against natural law principles. The result of his inductive approach is a blending he sometimes refers to as a "state of nature-natural law" approach.

This approach is especially evident in O'Brien's analysis of the morality of nuclear war and deterrence, for as he enters the nuclear age, he enters uncharted waters. Not only does he find no positive international law on nuclear warfare to guide him, but he also encounters a further obstacle impeding his search for principles that will act as moral guides to nations in the nuclear age. This obstacle is a preoccupation on the part of most contemporary theorists with *means* of warfare to the exclusion of *ends*. What O'Brien intends to do, then, is to return the focus to the ends of war and to analyze *means* in relation to those ends: i.e., to ask not merely whether fighting a war with nuclear weapons is permissible, but to ask first whether fighting such a war can be a legitimate military necessity.

In addition to changing the focus in the analysis of nuclear warfare, O'Brien emphasizes international political differences among nations and among blocs of nations to a greater degree than Paul Ramsey has done. In particular, O'Brien's analysis of the "Communist World" and the "Free World" lead him to the conclusion that contemporary warfare has "transnational" *raison d'état* implications and that just-war principles must be adapted to fit this reality.

O'Brien views the Communist bloc of nations as a coalition which does not abide by the same ethical code as the Free World bloc. The so-called "Great Powers" who have the power and prestige to lead these two transnational societies are the Soviet Union and the United States, respectively. Other nations may qualify as "Near-Great Powers," but it is primarily their superior nuclear capabilities that give the Soviet Union and the United States true "Great Power" status.[67]

This view of the political structure has implications for the use of nuclear force in contemporary warfare as well as for deterrence. This becomes more apparent in the analysis which follows. Unless otherwise stated, O'Brien refers to the duties of the "Great Powers" when he speaks of the duties and conditions limiting the uses of nuclear force.

The examination of O'Brien begins with his own analysis of the nature of the weapons that give the United States and Soviet Union their Great Power status.

Strategic and Tactical Weapons

"Strategic" in O'Brien's usage ordinarily refers to both the long range and the high-yield capacity of nuclear weapons. Strategic attacks, then, may be launched against CV or CF targets. "Tactical" weapons have short range and lower firepower capabilities and are, therefore, more approriately used as battlefield weapons against CF targets. O'Brien also relates the terms, "strategic" and "tactical," to the ends associated with them. This leads to some "overlap." In *The Conduct of Just and Limited Wars* (CJLW), O'Brien explicitly distinguishes the two types:

Tactical means will normally be judged in terms of their proportionality to tactical military ends (for example, the tactics of attacking or defending a fortified population center will normally be judged in terms of their proportionality to the military end of taking or holding the center). Strategic means will normally be judged in terms of their proportionality to the political/military goals of the war (for example, the strategy of attacking Japanese cities, first conventionally and then with atomic bombs, in order to force the surrender of Japan will be judged in terms of its proportionality to the just cause of the war)."[68]

O'Brien stresses that in assessing the proportionality of nuclear policies there will be "*more than two dimensions*" to consider. With conventional weapons, one must measure the costs and benefits to the belligerents. In nuclear warfare, especially with strategic megaton weapons and sometimes even with kiloton weapons under certain fallout conditions, one must take five sets of effects into account: the effects on

(a) the enemy--military and civilian
(b) one's own side--military and civilian
(c) the allies--military and civilian
(d) neutrals
(e) the earth and mankind in general.[69]

Theater Weapons

"Theater" nuclear weapons refer to what O'Brien calls "an important but elusive middle category" with a "somewhat vague" definition necessitated primarily by the need to distinguish among categories in arms negotiation agreements. "It embraces weapons systems that have a greater range than tactical, battlefield weapons but less than what is necessary to reach from one nuclear superpower's homeland to the other's."[70]

In certain geographical areas, theater weapons can be used to attack a superpower's homeland: from Cuba against the United States, for example, or from a West European country against the Soviet Union. Theater nuclear weapons play a critical role in O'Brien's targeting analysis because they present a threat of radiation and of escalation much more dangerous than that posed by tactical nuclear weapons. They therefore affect the proportionality calculus to a greater degree than tactical weapons. The greatest difference O'Brien sees between tactical and both strategic and theater nuclear weapons is "the minimalization of the problem of radioactive fallout." The fallout from tactical weapons can conceivably be limited to the battle area, and the need to calculate the evil effects of more widespread fallout is practically nonexistent, according to O'Brien.

Given O'Brien's distinctions among the kinds of nuclear weapons, when, then, does he consider their use to be moral and appropriate?

Legitimate Military Necessity

Obviously one can begin to find justification for the use of nuclear weapons by appealing to the principle of "military necessity" or even "military utility." O'Brien, however, has shown that there are limits to both military necessity and military utility, especially for anyone who takes a natural law approach to nuclear war. O'Brien's joint inductive-deductive method allows him to combine the findings of positive international law with the requirements of natural law and results in his formulation of the principle of legitimate military necessity. Legitimate military necessity "provides a normative basis for the law of war and a standard for measuring the limits of permissible violence." In applying this principle to nuclear war, O'Brien identifies four points of inquiry that must be addressed:

(1) the measurement of the true necessity and proportionality of nuclear means;
(2) the positive law limitations in effect;
(3) relevant considerations of natural law; and
(4) the application of the principles of command responsibility and judicial review to nuclear warfare.[72]

The results of these inquiries should indicate under what circumstances nuclear weapons should be used.

O'Brien begins by assuming that the resort to armed force between nations is "abnormal" and must be justified by compliance with certain standards. From the standpoint of international law and ethics, the fact must be established that "all reasonable peaceful means of resolving the conflict have been exhausted."[73]

O'Brien acknowledges that it is difficult to find agreement on the moment of "necessity" and one must look to the consensus of "reasonable" people to find the working standard. One looks for the "Reasonable State" with the "reasonable" *raison d'état*. Though no such state actually exists, O'Brien believes it is possible to find limits to *raison d'état* through an analysis of past experience.

In the nuclear age, one must also deal with the "necessities" of various "blocs" of nations: the bi-polar Communist and Free World blocs as well as the regional blocs like NATO and the Warsaw Pact countries. Few individual states at the present time can assure their own security and, at any rate, more than individual self-interest is at stake. More will be said of collective security in the analysis of deterrence which follows. In general, however, O'Brien notes "(a) the self-interests of *all* members of a security group are affected by change in the power position of *any* member; (b) the collective self-interest of all is particularly and most seriously affected by changes in the power position of the leading State or States in the coalition."[74]

Within these blocs are certain states whose power and prestige entitle them to be Great Powers and these Great Powers must to a large extent equate the interest of the entire group to their own. Great Powers have needs and responsibilities that have implications for the use of nuclear weapons. They "need" Power and Prestige; they need other kinds of power than military power, but they do need the latter and, in this age, that power includes *nuclear* power. Their prestige is in danger of being lost in two obvious ways: "(1) Commitment of power resulting in defeat; (2) Promise to commit power and failure to do so or failure to do so fully and reasonably."[75]

The nuclear implications for a Great Power are evident in situations where conventional weapons are inadequate to defend a smaller nation within a bloc, for example. The Great Power's individual self-interest may be in conflict with the self-interest of the larger bloc. The use of nuclear forces, limited or strategic, to help a member of the bloc *risks* nuclear retaliation against the Great Power. If the Great Power does not assume the risk, its prestige begins to fall.

International law allows the use of force only against aggression. Positive international law, as expressed in the U.S. Army Field Manual on *The Law of Land Warfare* (1956), concludes that nuclear weapons in themselves do not violate international law, since there are no positive international laws that forbid them. The definition of "aggression," however, is elusive and O'Brien says that "today... it is more likely that 'aggression' is what the General Assembly says it is."[76] Despite what the legal definition is, a state must make a political and ethical determination of what the definition means. The state will then weigh risks and values in order to determine whether it should have recourse to force. "Among those who do not hold in principle that nuclear war may never be justified, there will be wide differences of opinion as to the calculus of determining the degree of threat to basic values and the risk involved in different forms of defense of those values."[77]

Certainly, recourse to nuclear force will impose the requirement to be much more conservative and pessimistic in estimating risks than has been necessary in any previous war.[78] International law proscribes "first use," that is, first aggressive use of *any* weapons. The only time a nation may strike first is to prevent an imminent attack (a preemptive action). Positive international law says nothing about what is permissible regarding nuclear weapons and preemptive actions.

Nevertheless, there is a guide to determining legitimate military necessity in the nuclear age and this, according to O'Brien, is the natural law. The natural law does not provide the answers to every question, but it does give the "right terms" and the proper frame of reference within which to base decisions.

A "twentieth-century Grotius" would attack the problem of nuclear war, according to O'Brien, by seeking to establish the facts about the reaction of men to the ethical dilemma of the nuclear age. "[He] might seek the normative basis for a future positive international law of nuclear war in the universal conscience or ethical consensus of mankind with respect to such events as the original dropping of the A-bombs on Japan, nuclear testing and well-known preparations of the Great Powers for nuclear war."[79]

The "preparations of the Great Powers" will be dealt with in more detail in the analysis of deterrence which follows. Concern over "nuclear testing" in the atmosphere was the topic of the test-ban treaty between the United States and the Soviet Union. O'Brien does treat the use of "A-bombs on Japan" in somewhat greater depth than these other issues, however, and it may be helpful to reflect on his findings. In so doing one finds that O'Brien reaches certain conclusions about "first use" of nuclear weapons as well as retaliatory use.

First Use

Hiroshima/Nagasaki: A Unique "First Use?"

The waters of the nuclear age are uncharted as far as positive international law is concerned, but not as far as use is concerned: Hiroshima offers the example of the absolute first use of a nuclear weapons in war fighting. O'Brien's inductive approach makes his reflections on this example of actual use especially relevant to the development of his position on nuclear use in general.

As discussed in chapter 2 on proportionality, O'Brien finds adequate grounds for claiming that the United States and its allies had satisfied the *jus ad bellum* requirements for going to war with Germany and with Japan, though O'Brien tries to show that Japan's war aims were not so dangerous as Germany's, especially since Japan's did not include genocide. However, Japan's unwillingness to negotiate a termination of the war, led to the United States decision to use the atomic bomb on Hiroshima and Nagasaki. At this stage, O'Brien claims, the political goal, the *raison d'état*, and the military task, *raison de guerre*, coincided: "complete the defeat of Japan and end the war" (CJLW, 1981).

In applying the principle of proportionality, O'Brien is in basic agreement with the U.S. decision that the use of the atomic bombs was proportionate in that they accomplished the strategic task with less loss of life than would have been entailed had they continued the war by conventional means. However, he finds it impossible to reconcile the use of the bombs with the principle of discrimination.[80]

In *War and/or Survival* (1969), O'Brien had written, "The only two uses of nuclear weapons in war against Hiroshima and Nagasaki were wrong because they introduced this new and terrible weapon." He finds no fault with the argument from proportionality, however; nevertheless, he concludes that this "first use of the atomic bombs was wrong."[81]

In CJLW (1981), O'Brien concludes that since the "total war-effort" against Japan was just and if the use of nuclear weapons in the context of World War II can be justified at all and he seems uncertain that it can, "the attacks on Hiroshima and Nagasaki are about as defensible as can be imagined, since they did foreseeably and in fact end the war quickly and preclude greater losses to the belligerents and the Japanese society."[82]

It appears that O'Brien has moved to a more permissive position on the use of nuclear weapons in recent times, although he recognizes that this case was "unusual" and "may never happen again." It was *sui generis* in that only one nation possessed nuclear weapons at the time and no escalation was likely. His later position allows him to admit the violation of discrimination openly along with accepting the fact that the use of nuclear weapons in defense and deterrence is incompatible with the principle of discrimination.

Once the nuclear threshhold is crossed in Japan, O'Brien seems to be saying, "We can never go home again"; that is, no one can will the possibility of nuclear use out of existence and we must revise *jus in bello* conditions accordingly if warfare is to be limited in the nuclear age.

In *Nuclear War, Deterrence and Morality* (1967), O'Brien states, "If one totals up the possible objections to tactical nuclear weapons, and then adds a more pessimistic estimate of the dangers of escalation, the presumptions are against such a war satisfying the condition of proportionality of probably evil and good effects."[83]

In *War and/or Survival* (1969), he writes: "As one who once thought that limited nuclear war was practically necessary and morally permissible, I have come to believe that the critics of limited nuclear war were right when they contended that nuclear war represents a *threshhold* that ought not to be crossed."[84]

O'Brien seems to be taking a position against first use; however, he also says in *Nuclear War/Deterrence and Morality* (1967), "It would be a hard saying to maintain that this event [first use of nuclear means] would never under any circumstances be justified, but certainly it is one that may increasingly attract the support of morally responsible persons in all nations."[85] Thus, he shows that in 1967, at least, he considered the topic of first use still an open question.

Evidence of this openness appears in the 1981 publication of CJLW as well. Here O'Brien discusses the issue of preemptive nuclear attack. He points out that present international law forbids the first use of any armed force, but that his own interpretation of that rule would allow for the defender to take defensive action once the aggressor's intent is manifest and the aggressor is taking measures to carry out that intent. In a 1983 statement, O'Brien speaks of "a strong moral presumption against the use of nuclear weapons,"[86] and this seems to include a presumption even against the *defensive* use of nuclear weapons.

A preemptive attack is more an act of retaliation for an imminent attack than the kind of attack one ordinarily thinks of as "first use," i.e., first use of nuclear weapons would occur during a war already in progress.

Nuclear Retaliation

O'Brien cites as "the most crucial showdown on nuclear war and deterrence" the Cuban situation in the early 1960s, when President Kennedy threatened "retaliation in kind" against the Soviet Union if Soviet missiles in Cuba were launched against the United States. O'Brien asserts, "This I defend as morally permissible because it was not a threat of first use but of retaliation in kind."[87]

O'Brien appears, then, to justify the use of nuclear weapons if these weapons have been used first by the aggressor. However, the use of nuclear weapons in retaliation is still subject to *jus in bello* limitations. One must continue to probe O'Brien's analysis of the possible use of nuclear weapons to see what limitations his state of nature-natural law approach places on their use.

Higher Goods

Professor O'Brien gives as the starting point of applying natural law to nuclear problems, "the establishment of the hierarchy of international goods and the recognition of the normative obligation of the state not to violate that hierarchy, no matter what its necessities."[88] An "indispensable" starting point is with the natural law principle: "Good ends do not justify bad means." But how does one recognize "bad means"? Using his state of the nature-natural law approach, he looks for an "internal immanent limitation" on military necessity and finds his answer in Suarez' concept of the international society, which he cites:

> The reason for the Law of Nations, under this aspect, is, that the human race, though divided into no matter how many different peoples and nations, has for all that a certain unity, a unity not merely physical, but also in a sense political and moral. This is shown by the natural precept of mutual love and mercy, which extends to all men, including foreigners of every way of thinking. Wherefore, though any one state, republic or kingdom be in itself a perfect community and constant in its members, nevertheless each of the states is also a member, in a certain manner, of the world, so far as the human race is concerned. For none of these communities are ever sufficient unto themselves to such a degree that they do not require some mutual help, society or communication, either to their greater advantage or from moral necessity and need, as is evident from custom.[89]

Because the state cannot supply all that is needed for the good life of its citizens, it must acknowledge its mutual dependence upon other states. The individual member of a state must also acknowledge that he or she is a member of the human race--a race which owes its existence to a common Creator and which is destined to seek its common supernatural end in life side by side on this earth. The notions of the international common good and the higher necessities are derived from this truth and must prevail over particular national common goods.

Regarding nuclear means of warfare, O'Brien concludes, "Specifically, the subordinate place of the State in the natural law hierarchy of values clearly precludes the use of nuclear means which would result in disproportionate injury to the earth and its resources, to mankind, to the international society."[90] In other words, national "necessities" do not justify recourse to nuclear war. O'Brien reiterates the idea of international obligation in *War and/or Survival* when he says, "Strong nations have a right, and possibly an obligation to extend *such protection as they can*," presumably to their allies or to weaker nations who seek help. Whether this can be a *nuclear* "protection" cannot be assumed given O'Brien's adoption of Suarez' position.

O'Brien places responsibility for determining whether the use of nuclear weapons is a legitimate military necessity in the hands of those who are responsible for policy making at the strategic level. Obviously, the risks involve demand that those officials be well aware of the implications of moving to nuclear means. Judicial review for errors made regarding conventional weapons may result in courts martial, but errors made at the nuclear level may make any previous court martial decision "look like a juvenile court case," if, indeed, there are military or civilian superiors living to conduct the case. In all probability, O'Brien suggests, a nuclear war in which the West is likely to engage would be fought under the direction of an organization like NATO (though not on a NATO nation's soil). Allied authorities are not likely to permit moving to nuclear weapons of mass destruction: "All in all, it seems pretty clear that the one untouchable cloak of 'military necessity' will not protect the commander who uses grossly disproportionate, superfluous, nuclear means."[91]

According to the application of the principle of legitimate necessity, O'Brien draws four conclusions:

(1) He rules out *prima facie* the use of large "dirty" megaton bombs as out of all proportion to any reasonable military objective. This leaves open the possibility of the use of lower levels of nuclear weapons.

(2) No relevant positive law proscribes the use of these weapons and so they can be used legally.

(3) Regardless of legality, means of injuring the enemy are not unlimited but are subject to proportionality and the requirements of morality. Presumably the principle of humanity and the interdependence of peoples play significant roles in this determination. Military utility itself must yield to these higher principles.

(4) Responsibility and accountability fall primarily upon those who establish, approve, or authorize general nuclear policies and the employment of a nuclear weapons system.[92]

Now that O'Brien has determined that nuclear weapons may be justifiably used but under certain conditions only, he can address the question of *where* they may be used: i.e., what is the nature of the targets against which they may be justifiably used?

The Nature of the Target

CV

One of the operative "rules" of nuclear war and deterrence is, according to O'Brien, "the rule prohibiting countercity warfare except as a last-resort deterrent against countercity warfare by an enemy."[93] Experts in arms control express this as "no cities first," and with this, O'Brien is in agreement: "Large population centers should not be attacked first, no matter how many important military targets and communications centers are located in them."[94] This conclusion appears to be at odds with O'Brien's previous justification for the atomic bomb attacks on Japanese cities. O'Brien, however, could be interpreting these attacks as CF attacks with collateral damage or as CV retaliation against conventional attacks by the aggressor. Otherwise, there seems to be no way to reconcile these two conclusions.

In *War and/or Survival* (1969), O'Brien does leave open the moral possibility of CV nuclear retaliation in the situation where such action would be a protection of the cities of one's own nation, the cities of an ally or of a nonnuclear nation which is a member of a pact with guaranteed protection from nuclear blackmail or aggressive first strike attack.

> Just as first use of nuclear weapons is unjustified, first crossing of any of the thresholds that can be discerned in a nuclear war is unjustified. By thresholds I mean, first of all, that covered by my third rule, no first attack on cities. Nuclear retaliation *which may lamentably become necessary* [emphasis added] should be as much of a counterforce character as possible."[95]

Later, in CJLW, O'Brien clarifies what he means by such countervalue attacks. He calls them "selective strategic countervalue attacks," and allows the moral possibility of these attacks during an actual war if they deter a continuation of antecedent selective countervalue attacks by the aggressor.[96] O'Brien justifies this strategy on the basis of *defending* remaining cities and populations unlike countervalue attacks launched in *retaliation* for all-out countervalue attacks. What would need to be determined is whether the reasons of proportionality would be sufficient to override the requirements of discrimination, for O'Brien maintains that the literal application of the principle of discrimination is incompatible with nuclear war as explained more fully in chapter 3.

Destruction of "cities as such," however, seems to be such a violation of proportionality that O'Brien concludes that "even [d]iscrimination modified by some form of the principle of double effect cannot salvage it."[97] This 1983 statement, along with a statement in CJLW, reflects a change in O'Brien's thinking.

> As to the intention and possible refuge of the principle of double effect in a countervalue attack on a population center, it certainly cannot be maintained that the actor "aims narrowly at the acceptable effect," or that "the evil effect is not one of his ends," or that the evil effect is not "a means to his ends." Nor may it be contended that "aware of the evil involved," the actor "seeks to minimize it, accepting costs to himself."[98]

By 1986, O'Brien abandoned his justification for CV, counterpopulation, attacks "raising the perennial question of loss of deterrence potential as the price for threatening only what is permissible under just war standards."[99]

In CJLW, O'Brien singles out the possibility of a nuclear war, not fought between two nations but between blocs or coalitions of nations. In coalition wars, "the 'self' that is defended is multiple."[100] This multiple self has implications for the application of the principle of proportionality, for one might offer the argument that one or more member-states might be destroyed while the coalition fights on.

Formerly, O'Brien would have allowed countervalue retaliation when a single nation was a belligerent if it meant protecting the population centers of other nations who were not presently at war with the aggressor nation. He based the legitimacy of this he based on the closeness of ties with the neutral states (making this relation almost a "bloc" as above) and the likelihood of the aggressor's attacking or blackmailing the neutral states. By 1986, however, O'Brien urged a policy that would exclude others from the U.S. strategic umbrella of extended U.S. deterrence in order to limit the scope of a desparate strategic predicament.[101]

It appears, then, that O'Brien's most recent position is consistent with the "openness," albeit an extremely cautious openness, expressed in the 1960s allowing for the moral possibility of countervalue attacks.

CF/Countercombatant

O'Brien maintains that nuclear weapons can be used in both a proportionate and discriminate manner "in limited, flexible response, counterforce strikes at military targets sufficiently removed from population centers so that collateral damage would not be disproportionate." In th same article in *The Washington Quarterly* (1982), O'Brien writes of the danger of escalation in CF warfare but objects to demands for certainty of control:

> As a longtime student of just-war doctrine, I must say that this is the first time that I have encountered the requirement that a belligerent must guarantee the outcome of the use of the military instrument. ...The *jus ad bellum* requirement of proportionality requires that the *probable* good outweigh the foreseeable evil. *Jus in bello* proportionality requires the effects of military action be *reasonably* proportionate to the military objective. Noncombatant immunity requires reasonable efforts to avoid collateral damage.[102]

By 1986, O'Brien appears to have modified his position on the moral permissibility of using₁ nuclear weapons against political-military control and assets and the Soviet supporting infrastructure: "My own understanding of the principle of discrimination is that it prohibits disproportionate collateral damage in addition to prohibiting attacks on population centers, noncombatants, and nonmilitary targets as such."[103] "There are many military targets in the Soviet Union that could be legitimately attacked under the principle of discrimination were it not for the fact that their location... means that the collateral damage of nuclear attacks on them would surely be unacceptable."[104]

CF weapons may be strategic, theater or tactical. They are not limited to an enemy's nulcear forces[105] but include other military targets as well; for example, in *Nuclear War, Deterrence and Morality* (1967), O'Brien mentions a possible use of limited nuclear weapons that would not violate proportionality or discrimination: "a one-kiloton device exploded against the staging area for an armored attack in an area from which all known refugees had been evacuated."[106]

In CJLW (1981), however, O'Brien cautions against the use of nuclear weapons in CF attacks:

> Nuclear weapons should not be used simply because they would have military utility but because there is no reasonable, alternative, conventional means. Thus, while the proportionality of a nuclear defense against conventional attack is conceivable, the presumption is against such a defense. This presumption must be overcome by a clear showing that conventional defense against conventional aggression is insufficient, and that the advantages of nuclear defense will be proportionate to the damage and dangers it entails.[107]

The only defense in a nuclear war, O'Brien states,

> is preemptive destruction of the enemy's capability to devastate the just defender. That, however, does not call for an all-out CV attack; a CF attack is sufficient. As a general proposition, an all-out strategic counterforce attack may be proportionate to the legitimate requirements of defense from strategic nuclear attack, dependent upon its collateral effects in the enemy state and worldwide.[108]

O'Brien has said previously that theater nuclear weapons offer greater danger of radiation and escalation than tactical nuclear weapons. If deterrence fails and theater nuclear war ensues, O'Brien believes the principle of proportionality may allow for a CF theater nuclear war "keyed to defense against nuclear attack." It has already been pointed out that O'Brien allows for *strategic* selective CV attack during a war already in progress in order to deter antecedent CV attacks by the enemy. He would also allow for selective CV *retaliation* at the *theater* level "based on the fact that not all of the participants in the theater defense had been the victims of CV attacks, and that the need and right to deter such attacks continued."[109]

O'Brien concludes,

[I]t is certainly possible to envisage use of nuclear weapons proportionate to legitimate military necessity but the proportionality of any intended use of nuclear means must be judged in the full context of contemplated use and of the probable outcomes and effects of each case.[110]

CF attacks in which collateral damage to civilians will occur must be subject to the standard of proportionality and an effort must be made to minimize civilian damage. This is similiar to Walzer's "due care" clause in his revised principle of double effect. It has already been pointed out, however, that O'Brien does not appeal to double effect to justify collateral damage but appeals to the non-absolute character of the principle of discrimination. Discrimination may be overridden by the requirements of proportionality.[111]

O'Brien claims that even strategic CF nuclear war may conceivably comply with the just war principle of proportionality and the principle of discrimination as long as the values that constitute the just cause for the war survive. The major problems in fighting such a war would be the maintenance of a command, control and communications and information (C^3I) environment, the uncertainty about the accuracy and penetrability of such long-range weapons, the uncertainty over the extent of collateral damage, and the fear that a strategic CF attack could be interpreted as a first strike threat which could result in destabilization and escalation.

Theater intermediate CF attacks and tactical battlefield CF attacks are other nuclear options. In Western Europe, where such a strategy may be employed, O'Brien contends that the calculus of *jus ad bellum* proportionality of probable good and evil, in light of the probablity of success, indicates that such a strategy should be discouraged.[112]

O'Brien's concerns about escalation from limited nuclear war to unlimited nuclear war have seemed to increase over the years. In a recent article, for example, he states,

[N]uclear war in any form is such a drastic step, given the potential for disproportionate and indiscriminate effects in many circumstances and, above all, the dangers of escalation, that it is virtually impossible to separate the political or strategic ends held out as the just cause of the war from the proximate military ends.[113]

O'Brien seems to be saying that the proximate military ends must be related to the strategic or political ends of war. Attacking a military objective must be done with a view toward contributing to the achievement of a just end; but when that objective is attacked with nuclear weapons, the disproportionate destruction that results cannot contribute to the just cause.

If nuclear means are neither prohibited by positive international law nor by the *jus gentium/jus naturale*, their use remains restricted to the prescriptions of *jus in bello* like any other weapons of conventional warfare. Yet their destructive capacity gives them a use not really addressed by the *jus in bello* conditions that have been discussed thus far. This is their role as a deterrent.

Deterrence

In 1969, O'Brien states that "nuclear war represents a *threshold* that ought not to be crossed," and that nuclear weapons' deterrent function is their "only rational and morally defensible *raison d'être*." O'Brien himself admits that he is speaking here only of *unlimited* nuclear war which he condemns as violating the principle of proportionality. He clarifies his "threshold" position later in the book: once a nation is attacked, he allows for retaliation with nuclear weapons but with as much CF character as possible.[114]

Recently, O'Brien has been critical of those whose position on deterrence is characterized by an "abstractness" that fails to appreciate the need to consider what happens if deterrence fails. He believes that the U.S. Catholic Bishops, especially, have reflected this sort of thinking in their 1983 Pastoral letter. The weakness of their position, O'Brien asserts, is due to (1) their "deterrence-only" strategy in that they consider no war-fighting mode should deterrence fail; (2) their unrealistic arms control expectations. O'Brien points to the arms control record to show that there is no evidence that indicates nulcear weapons will be eliminated in the foreseeable future nor that a new world order based on "peace, justice and cooperation" is likely to be established in the near future, and he concludes, "In any event, the foundation of all modern arms control theory and practice has been the assumption of stable deterrence between nuclear powers."[115]

Walter Stein has said that Paul Ramsey and William O'Brien have offered contrary arguments about the use of nuclear weapons in "limited nuclear war." However, he maintains, "They agree only in disclosing that nuclear deterrence has been proved morally unusable... and in facing the fact that it is the morality of nuclear *deterrence* that most urgently calls for present decisions.[116]

What Stein perhaps should have said and maybe even means to say is that *some* deterrence policies are morally unusable. At any rate, deterrence (and the use of nuclear weapons as "bargaining chips") is fortunately the only "real use" being made of nuclear weapons today. It is, therefore, of great importance that one strive to determine the morality of the deterrence policies now in effect and those that might be determined in the future.

O'Brien defines deterrence as follows: "Nuclear deterrence is based on the credible threat of unacceptable damage to a potential aggressor. The threat consists of a sufficient nuclear-war potential and communication to an enemy of the intent and will to carry out the threat if certain eventualities occur."[117]

The "unacceptable damage" to which O'Brien refers corresponds to an earlier description of the "paradox" of deterrence: "whereas the basic principle governing military coercion is that of proportionality of ends and means, the essence of deterrence is the threat of *disproportionate* reaction to aggression."[118] [Emphasis added.] More will need to be said of this "disproportionality" in the analysis of O'Brien's choice of appropriate targets. By speaking of "disproportionate *reaction* to aggression rather than of "disproportionate *damage*," he clearly identifies the referent of proportionality. "Disproportionate reaction" may be consistent with an attack causing *proportionate damage*, where in the latter case the referents of proportionality are the *jus ad bellum* and *jus in bello* conditions. O'Brien's distinction allows him to avoid Ramsey's problem of having a disproportionate threat be proportionate at the same time.

The "eventualities" to which O'Brien refers above in his definition of deterrence include "conventional aggression, nuclear aggression, and first use of nuclear weapons in a conventional war [against] self and an ally or other state [by means of] CF or CV... strategic..., theater..., or tactical [attacks]."[119]

O'Brien's definition thus includes most of the elements in Morgan's definition of "general deterrence," but it also covers the "immediate deterrence" eventuality. As will become more evident, O'Brien departs from Morgan's concept of deterrence as only *preventing* war; he clearly allows for deterrence as a means of *containing* war once it is underway.

Before one addresses each of the "eventualities" O'Brien has identified and the type of threat appropriate to each, it may be helpful to focus first on the relation of deterrence to actual use of nuclear weapons.

O'Brien is of the opinion that a nation cannot have a meaningful deterrence theory unless it has the will to move to use should deterrence fail. "Deterrence without credible intention to carry out the deterrent threat will not be effective. If it is known that a nation considers its deterrent force morally unusable, this undermines deterrence."[120]

Apparently O'Brien is so confident of the effectiveness of deterrence that he can say in 1969: "I, for one, can write about the morality of nuclear war and deterrence, because I doubt that there will ever be a nuclear war, certainly not a major one."[121]

He is especially critical of the "bluff" deterrent once held by Ramsey and now held, he contends, by the U.S. Bishops as described in their 1983

Pastoral. O'Brien claims that the bluff deterrent is the "foundation of the Bishops' position" as expressed in that document.[122]

A bluff deterrent, O'Brien believes, reflects an "extreme nominalism," a kind of abstraction which does not take into account the reality that no one will be deterred for long knowing there is no commitment to act on the threat.

O'Brien, then, is a theorist who maintains that use and threat are closely related, that one must be willing to *do* what is threatened if the threat is to be credible. If an action is immoral to *do*, it is immoral to *threaten* to do it. Since this is his position, he must allow that some war-fighting use of nuclear weapons is moral, and it has been shown that this is indeed the case. O'Brien has identified circumstances in which the following uses of nuclear weapons might be justified: selective strategic CF and counter combatant attacks, theater CF and CV attacks. The only uses for which O'Brien can find no moral possibility are the all CV or counterpopulation attacks, including such "all-out" CV "city-for-city" exchange or general CV retaliatory "vengeance" attacks launched for no other military or political purpose than revenge.

Once it is acknowledged that there are some uses of nuclear weapons that one may morally threaten to employ, there remains another aspect of the nature of threats that is worth considering. That is whether there might be anything immoral inherent in the nature of even an otherwise "moral" threat; that is, whether the threat actually includes, in a kind of "undeclaratory" way, more use of force than that which is morally permitted.

Ramsey includes this possibility in his concept of "dual use," which, as has been seen, presents certain difficulties concerning the morality of his "graduated deterrent" proposal. Thus far, it appears that neither Ramsey nor O'Brien has given an adequate analysis of this "risk" that nuclear weapons inherently present. Neither addresses in much detail the risk of "accidental" nuclear war, i.e., the risk of an unjustified war, which the mere *possession* of nuclear weapons "threatens." O'Brien does treat "possession" as a "discrete part of the problem of deterrence."[123] He claims that the use of nuclear weapons as "bargaining chips," for example, is subject to the same conditions with regard to the willingness to use them as are deterrents. Therefore, a nuclear bargaining chip that cannot be used morally in war-fighting cannot be bartered either. A merely *potential* weapon may still be a *real* bargaining chip in arms negotiations. O'Brien does not address this possibility but would probably reach the same conclusion as he does with bargaining chips in general. That is, even the concept of a nonexistent weapon that cannot have a moral use in war-fighting has a certain deterrent value in the very possibility that it *could* be developed. However, a possible bargaining chip that can never be morally used cannot be bartered, either.

O'Brien's meaning of the word "threaten" requires conscious deliberation and this requires human actors. In addition, it is conceivable that both Ramsey and O'Brien consider the "risk" of nuclear war from mere possession of the weapons to be less than the risk of nuclear war resulting from a decision for nuclear disarmament, at least *unilateral* disarmament. Attention now shifts to the decision-makers, the "actors" on the deterrence stage.

Like Morgan, O'Brien specifies that the actors involved in threatening and being threatened by the use of nuclear weapons are the nation-states. However, O'Brien gives added emphasis to the fact that these nation-states belong--in the present day and in the foreseeable future--to various regional and ideological blocs.

The reality of international society, according to O'Brien, holds an "external immanent limitation" on military necessity. Like Suarez, O'Brien, at least in his early writings (1957 and 1960), dwells on the political and moral unity existing within such blocs: i.e., the mutual dependence on other states, and the individuals living as members of a state but also as members of the human race sharing a common destiny. This expanded concept points to notions of an "international common good" and of "higher necessities" than the limited military necessities of a single state. "[T]he subordinate place of the State in the natural law hierarchy of values clearly precludes the use of nuclear means which would result in disproportionate injury to the earth and its resources, to mankind, to the international society."[124] The "subordinate place of the State" follows from the claim O'Brien makes elsewhere. "The End of the State is the protection of the natural rights of man... it exists for the people in the State, not the opposite."[125]

The state and the people who compose it have reciprocal duties but always "for the sake of" the rights of individual human beings. So the State and international society have reciprocal duties but also "for the sake of" those same individuals. The restriction put onto the State by placing individual human beings at the top of the priority of values places the same restriction on blocs of states for the same reason: "It means no merely *national* military necessity, or even the necessities of many nations joined together to protect their rights, can justify disproportionate injuries to the higher good of the international society."[126]

The notion of the international common good and the higher necessities receive much less attention from O'Brien with the passage of time and for reasons which it would be useful to explore. Among these may be the failure of the United Nations to provide effective structures to prevent unjust aggression and the fact that, for O'Brien, the ideals of Pope John XXIII's *Pacem in Terris* seem beyond reach in the foreseeable future. However, it is obvious that O'Brien does derive the "higher goods" from natural law, and that he cannot disregard them.

The "national actors" and the regional/ideological blocs of nations, then, are restrained by the higher goods, and though O'Brien admits that it is difficult in reality to persuade the states of the necessities of such restraint, it is in fact a moral restraint that cannot be pushed aside.

Not only is there a human reluctance to admit limitations on the military necessities of one's own State, there is the further complication that participants in deep ideological conflicts are prone to persuade themsleves that what they are fighting for is so important to the whole world that no limitation of the means of ensuring "moral survival" is admissable. But means which cause disproportionate harm to the international common good are bad means and are not justified, even by so lofty an end as the protection of free peoples from totalitarian tyranny.[127]

The implications of these statements for the international system are "double-edged" in a sense. For example, they place a duty on the "Great Powers," and especially on the *leaders* of the Great Powers, to defend not only their own national boundaries but also weaker nation-states against injustice, presumably by nuclear means when recourse to these is a legitimate military necessity. On the other hand, they place a duty on the Great Powers to consider the good of the entire international community before engaging in either self-defense or defense of an ally or non-allied nation.

According to O'Brien's methodology, one cannot "derive" practical solutions to the defense-dilemma offered by this double-edged implication. Where positive law is silent, one must use natural law as a guide to find the "right terms" and the "framework" in which such dilemmas must be argued.

O'Brien's particular dilemma, which appears to assume greater importance over time, seems to be, "Is nuclear warfare as a means of resisting Communism permitted?" ...[that is], "Is nuclear warfare against Communist armed attack a legitimate military necessity?" and, *mutatis mutandis*, "Is the *threat* of nuclear warfare against Communist armed attack moral?"[128]

O'Brien's later writings emphasize the bipolar political reality of today's world, albeit a rapidly changing one: the ideological split between the Western and Soviet bloc. Consequently, much of what O'Brien has written previously about the concern one must have for the "higher necessities" and the "international common good" has not been emphasized in more recent writings. O'Brien seems to be responding to what he perceives to be an increasing Soviet threat. His position is that the Soviets do threaten "totalitarian tyranny." What he is wrestling with is the other half of his earlier statement, that some things cannot be done morally "even by so lofty an end as the protection of free peoples from totalitarian tyranny." Given the nature of Communism and the state of the international order, O'Brien concludes in 1983, "Deterrence will continue to be a necessity for states such as the U.S., and it will be nuclear as long as there are nuclear powers--and the trend is toward more nuclear powers."[129] However, this statement also shows that O'Brien sees the world as moving in a less bi-polar direction and toward greater plurality. With this in mind, one may consider O'Brien's views on the nature of targets in the context of the present political and nuclear reality, a reality that reflects less of a totalitarian tyranny and more of a tolerance for freedom.

CV Targets

In *War and/or Survival* (1969), O'Brien states, "Absent the deterrent dilemma, there are no adequate grounds for violation of the prohibition against countercity warfare."[130]

This statement leaves open the possibility that though the use of nuclear weapons against cities is immoral, the *threat* to use nuclear weapons against CV targets like cities *would* be morally acceptable. This conclusion is inconsistent with O'Brien's later insistence that one must be willing to carry out the deterrent threat. It could be that O'Brien's earlier statement is limited to those who think there could be an effective bluff deterrent.

O'Brien's most recent statements on deterrence are consistent with his position on the use of nuclear weapons in targeting: that is, threatening cities "as such" is immoral. O'Brien admits that the CV/CF distinction has in fact become "blurred" by the present U.S. deterrence doctrine which threatens those assets most "valued" by the Soviet Union: not the population centers, but "the military assets, the means of political control and their supporting infrastructure. It is these which are threatened in a U.S. strategic posture that threatens enemy force as a value."[131] O'Brien's position on use allows him to include these expanded countercombatant targets as morally permissible. He explicitly rejects the MAD doctrine of deterrence as failing the test of *jus ad bellum* and *jus in bello* proportionality and of offering no "probability of success." His alternative is to propose a CF deterrence/defense posture that remains consonant with just war principles.[132]

A type of deterrent that has not been discussed by either Ramsey or Morgan but has been proposed by O'Brien is the deterrent which *contains* but does not prevent war. In CJLW (1981) O'Brien allowed this type of countercity attack called "selective strategic CV attacks," the threats of which can be made during the course of the war "to deter a continuation of antecedent selective CV attacks by the aggressor."[133] It is difficult to see, however, how the use of nuclear weapons during a time and in a place already engaged in battle can be effectively controlled. O'Brien did not seem to give enough attention to this consideration, and his proposal seems to entail more risk than a moral calculus of proportionality can allow. In fact, in "The Future of the Nuclear Debate" (1986), O'Brien says he has "abandoned justification of any CV, copunterpopulation attacks," acknowledging that the price he must pay is a loss of deterrent potential: "As usual, the choices are between undesirable alternatives."[134]

CF and Countercombatant Targets

O'Brien remains concerned with the limitations each state must place on its own right of self-defense for the sake of international society. His proposal for an effective CF deterrent depends on many "ifs": if the level of nuclear war could be limited to CF attacks and, therefore, if the deterrence policies could be limited to these as well, and if nuclear operations were conducted so as not to threaten neutrals and the world with dangerous amounts of radiation--such rules of conflict could be more effective than all of the formal paper declarations, condemnations, and promises made by statesmen since Hiroshima.[135]

The "deterrence/defense posture" which O'Brien recommends is based on the following:

(1) targeting which permits proportionate, discriminate attacks,
(2) accurate weapons capable of destroying the targets contemplated,
(3) command, control and communications (C^3I) that can operate effectively in a nuclear environment,
(4) decision-makers with the ability and will to control nuclear weapons,
(5) protection of one's own population.[136]

This proposal represents a deterrence policy consistent with O'Brien's argument for moral use, but it can almost be viewed as "wishful thinking." The uses that O'Brien permits seriously challenge most of the conditions that must be maintained if the war is to be kept limited. "Pure" CF strikes, which he has said previously can be "without limit," (presumably as long as there is no collateral damage) are not possible given the colocations of legitimate military targets and population centers. Once a nation moves to theater weapons and targets, it would be even more difficult to preserve an effective C^3I environment: either in neighboring countries or, as importantly, within the country being attacked--thus adversely affecting the ability of decision-makers to control the war. If one includes in (5) above, protection of an ally's or lesser power's population, which O'Brien is committed to do by his higher principles, theater nuclear warfare is especially threatening.

What must be kept in mind is the perspective from which O'Brien approaches deterrence. He imagines himself, as it were, as a political or military decision-maker at a point in time *after* a nuclear or sufficiently threatening massive conventional attack has taken place, and he is faced with what to *do* then. The other theorists under consideration seem to be looking at deterrence from the perspective of the actual present time: that is, no nuclear attack *has* taken place and the chief concern is to *prevent* it from happening. This difference in perspectives, perhaps, accounts for some of the risks O'Brien seems willing to include in a moral deterrence policy, while these same risks appear too great for someone viewing deterrence from the different perspective to allow. His position opposing first use confirms this interpretation.

What O'Brien is proposing is to develop CF deterrence capabilities that could conform to just war conditions in order to replace the current modified version of countervalue MAD."[137] Despite the "serious problems with control," O'Brien concludes in a 1983 article,

[G]iven the just cause of protecting the United States and its allies from nuclear aggression, intimidation, and subjugation by an enemy dedicated to the destruction of our society, our values, and of the Church itself, it seems to me that we have no alternative but to attempt to find a deterrence strategy that will be both practically effective and morally permissible.[138]

O'Brien admits that if one employs limited nuclear defense systems that reduce substantially the damage of a nuclear exchange, then perhaps the odds ("50-50") on keeping such a war within just war limits would improve.[139] Such odds suggest the risks of damage are disproportionate when taken into account by the *jus ad bellum* proportionality calculus. If one then compares this 1986 statement with O'Brien's 1960 statement below, O'Brien himself offers one of the strongest criticisms of his own position: "But means which cause disproportionate harm to the international common good are bad means and are not justified, even by so lofty an end as the protection of free peoples from totalitarian tyranny."[140]

MICHAEL WALZER

War Fighting

Aside from what is contained in his chapter on nuclear deterrence, Michael Walzer does not devote a particular portion of *Just and Unjust Wars* to the use of nuclear weapons. However, Walzer reveals his position when he writes about other aspects of war, especially of World War II, and when he reflects on the experience of Hiroshima and Nagasaki, the only instances of actual use of nuclear weapons in war-fighting. His judgments about past use should shed light on where he stands *vis a vis* future use. One may begin, then, by addressing the three questions of when, where and how nuclear weapons may be morally used.

Throughout *Just and Unjust Wars* (JUW), Walzer strives to counter "war is hell" thinking by stressing the limits that must be placed on war fighting strategies. The introduction of nuclear weapons in actual war fighting at Hiroshima challenged these limits.

According to Walzer's analysis, the politicians and scientists who originally decided to develop the atomic bomb seemed to be proceeding as though the United States were facing a genuine "supreme emergency." Walzer implies that if such were the case, the development, but not necessarily the use, would have been warranted. However, since intelligence revealed in November, 1944 that German scientists had made little progress in their own development of the bomb and would not do so in the foreseeable future, no condition of supreme emergency existed. The technicians and politicians who took over the program first launched by the scientists, therefore, risked violating the limits of proportionality and noncombatant immunity.

Walzer claims that Truman's reason for using the bomb was primarily to "shorten the agony of war." This was not a supreme emergency, then, but a case of using the utilitarian sliding scale. This would presumably be Walzer's criticism of O'Brien's position on Hiroshima.[141]

Walzer concludes, then, that it is sometimes necessary to move beyond the limits established for war fighting. In cases of supreme emergency, therefore, he leaves open the possibility for the moral justification of the development of nuclear weapons though he says nothing definitive about their use in these circumstances. Whether these weapons may be used against cities such as Hiroshima and Nagasaki or only against CF or countercombatant targets will determine what kind of nuclear weapons Walzer would allow.

The Nature of the Target

CV Targets

First-Use

Walzer calls the war born at Hiroshima "[a] new kind of war... [a war where though] fewer people were killed than in the fire-bombing of Tokyo, they were killed with monstrous ease."[142] The attack on the people of Hiroshima and Nagasaki violated their rights to life and liberty, according to Walzer, because large numbers of them were either not combatant or were only remotely contributing to the war effort.

> Perhaps their taxes paid for some of the ships and planes used in the attack on Pearl Harbor; perhaps they sent their sons into the navy and air force with prayers for their success; perhaps they celebrated the actual event, after being told that their country had won a great victory in the face of an imminent American threat. Surely there is nothing here that makes these people liable to direct attack.[143]

For Walzer, then, massive attacks on population centers violate the principle of noncombatant immunity and are not morally justified. One might ask, however, whether such CV attacks may be morally justified in times of supreme emergency.

Nazi Germany did present a supreme emergency, according to Walzer. Would he, then, have permitted nuclear weapons to be used₁ against cities in Nazi Germany? Walzer does not address the issue explicitly. However, he does consider the threat Nazi Germany posed to the West to be a supreme emergency in which the *jus ad bellum* requirements were met. Even in this case, however, one may conclude that Walzer judges that in the case of Germany, the use of nuclear weapons would have violated the principle of proportionality and the principle of discrimination to a greater degree than necessary to pursue the conduct of the war. Conventional weapons were adequate to defeat the unjust aggressor, and the use of nuclear weapons would have resulted in vastly more death and destruction than was necessary for victory. But what if conventional weapons had not been adequate? Would the U.S. have been justified in what would have amounted to a "first-use" nuclear attack?

Walzer seems to answer this question in the negative. He holds that the war aims of the American government calling for Japan's unconditional surrender were unjustified. Even if unconditional surrender were morally desirable, however, as in the case of Nazi Germany, "it might still be morally undesirable because of the human costs it entailed."

> In any case, if killing millions (or many thousands) of men and women was militarily necessary for their conquest and overthrow, then it was morally necessary--in order not to kill those people--to settle for something less. . . . If people have a right not to be forced to fight, they also have a right not to be forced to continue fighting beyond the point when the war might justly be concluded. Beyond that point, there can be no supreme emergencies, no arguments about military necessity, no cost-accounting in human lives.[144]

It is quite clear, then, that even in supreme emergencies, Walzer considers first use of nuclear weapons against cities morally unjustified.

Massive Retaliation

If Walzer does not permit first use of nuclear weapons, however, where does he stand on retaliatory strikes against cities: i.e., "massive retaliation?" Walzer is quite clear on his position: "If the bomb were ever used, deterrence would have failed. It is a feature of massive retaliation that while there is or may be some rational purpose in threatening it, there could be none in carrying it out."[145]

Such a war, Walzer says, could not be *won*. Therefore, it would violate the *jus ad bellum* principle of "reasonable hope of success." In this case, the anticipated violation of the *jus in bello* principles of proportionality and discrimination is sufficient to warrant the judgment that one could not engage in a just war under conditions of massive retaliation.

CF/Countercombatant[146]

If Walzer does not allow the use of nuclear weapons against cities, one may still ask whether he would justify their use against opposing nuclear forces of against other military targets.

Walzer notes that during the 1950s and 1960s there was an attempt to make nuclear war fit the war convention by the development of tactical nuclear weapons. Walzer's descriptions of these weapons shows that he considers them as directed at CF targets, i.e., "resisting conventional or small-scale nuclear attacks," and also the broader "countercombatant" category, i.e., "directed at the enemy's military installations and also at major economic targets (but not at entire cities)."[147]

Walzer concludes that these targets offer "a difference without a difference," however. Although "[t]actical and counter-force warfare meets the formal requirements of *jus in bello*... [t]hat is not to say, however, that it makes moral sense." The use of nuclear weapons in this type of targeting strategy would be immoral, according to Walzer, for two reasons. First, he concludes that the collateral damage likely to ensue would violate the limits of both *jus ad bellum* proportionality and *jus in bello* proportionality: the number killed would not be warranted by the goals of war and the number killed in individual actions would be disproportionate to the value of the military targets directly attacked. Second, Walzer believes that "these limits would almost certainly not be observed." "[T]he danger of escalation is so great as to preclude the first use of nuclear weapons except by someone willing to face their final use."[148] Determination to use nuclear weapons is, for Walzer, tantamount to committing "national suicide," and he applies this reasoning to large-scale conventional war as well.

It appears, then, that he would also judge CF or countercombatant retaliation to be immoral because of the danger of escalation. Since he disallows the moral use of nuclear weapons on either a CV or a CF/counter-combatant target, it is not even necessary to address the "how" question. Walzer states in this regard that strategists have "suggested (rightly) that the crucial distinction in the theory and practice of war was not between prohibited and acceptable weapons but between prohibited and acceptable targets."

Walzer does seem to open the door for some kind of "use" for nuclear weapons, however, even for CV weapons, for he states, "Against an enemy actually willing to use the bomb, self-defense is impossible, and it makes sense to say that the only compensating step is the (immoral) threat to response in kind."[149]

An analysis must now be made of Walzer's position on deterrence, the political use of nuclear weapons.

Deterrence[150]

Walzer discusses nuclear deterrence in the context of "Dilemmas of War." In Part IV of JUW, he identifies four such dilemmas: (1) winning and fighting well; (2) aggression and neutrality; (3) supreme emergency; (4) nuclear deterrence. The first two dilemmas he arranges in pairs; the last two he names singly. Yet every dilemma must have two horns, and the horns implicit in Walzer's concept of supreme emergency seem to be "acting to ensure the survival and freedom of the political community," and "acting to protect the rights of the innocent." The horns of the nuclear deterrence dilemma may be expressed similarly: "the state's defense of its citizens' rights to life and liberty" and "the mounting of a credible and moral defense."

It has already been noted that Walzer holds that any use of nuclear weapons, CV, CF, or countercombatant, in actual war fighting is immoral. In order to prevent such immoral attacks from occurring, nations threaten an "immoral response," according to Walzer. He calls this "the basic form of nuclear deterrence," and "it is in the nature of [the closeness between killing and threatening to kill] that the moral problem lies." The doing in this case seems to be so terrible that the threat in comparison seems to many to be morally defensible. Yet, for Walzer, it is evident that, though he does not argue for it, he assumes the deterrent threat implies the commitment to act on it should deterrence fail: "Nuclear weapons are politically and militarily unusable only because and insofar as we can plausibly threaten to use them in some ultimate way. And it is immoral to make threats of that kind."[151] This statement also rules out Walzer's acceptance of a "bluff" deterrent.

Walzer knows that he is caught on the horns of the nuclear dilemma. He has already eliminated use as a moral means of war fighting, yet he does not want to shut out all possibilities for mounting a moral nuclear deterrent of some sort. He begins his exploration for a moral deterrent by "redescribing" the problem of nuclear deterrence.

One direction Walzer could choose to pursue in order to find a moral justification for a nuclear deterrent would be to make it fall under the "standard of necessity$_4$," that is, to allow it at times of supreme emergency. In order to do this, he might proceed in two steps, as James Burrell Dixon suggests he actually does: first, he would have to dispose of arguments that there is some property in nuclear threats that makes them morally unacceptable; second, he would have to argue that a nuclear deterrent strategy is morally defensible. Walzer's actual argument is somewhat more complicated than the "two steps" would lead one to believe.

Walzer does begin by redescribing the problem of nuclear deterrence which, he maintains, has been "misdescribed" by Ramsey in his analogy of regulating traffic by tying babies to car bumpers. Walzer suggests that the fact that we do not actually have such a traffic regulatory policy, but that we *do* have a nuclear deterrence policy, is evidence that there is something wrong with Ramsey's approach. Dixon faults Walzer on this point, saying that the fact that we do not in fact regulate traffic in this way "has nothing to do with its moral status."[152] However, Walzer does not seem to be making the mistake of moving from an "is" to an "ought;" rather, in keeping with his inductive and casuistic approach, he seems to be looking at society's actual behavior and policy-making in order to probe more deeply into the moral principles that may underlie these existing policies and laws. From this perspective, "what is" may well have bearing on moral status.

Walzer believes that Ramsey makes a more serious error in not distinguishing "direct" and "indirect" targets in his baby-bumper policy. In Ramsey's analogy, no one would set out intending to kill the babies, while in nuclear deterrent strategy, the intention is precisely that: to kill the innocent civilians, albeit regretfully. Walzer's argument here parallels what Grisez mentioned earlier. No one actually expects to kill these civilians since the goal of deterrence is to prevent actual nuclear attack, but the government policy demands that certain persons would carry out such a threat if the situation warrants it. "And from the perspective of morality," Walzer states, "readiness is all." Here he agrees with Ramsey that "Whatever is wrong to do is wrong to threaten, if the latter means 'mean to do'." The immorality lies in the threat, regardless of the consequences.[153]

Walzer seems right in his perception of the role noncombatants play in Ramsey's account. Even when they are to be considered indirect targets, they are indispensable in making the threat costly enough for deterrence to work. In this way, they seem close to being *direct* objects of attack. Ramsey wants to show that "collateral civilian damage" resulting from CF warfare in its maximum form would be sufficient to deter a potential aggressor. But he relies too heavily on their deaths, killing them without aiming at them. Second, if the deterrent threatens such damage, it will be radically disproportionate to the value of the military targets which are its direct objects and, Walzer argues, even to the ends of war, thereby violating the proportionality principle at both levels, *jus ad bellum* and *jus in bello*. Ramsey also argues that even if the threat is not a part of a nation's declaratory policy, the possession of the weapons alone is threat enough to deter since the enemy would be unsure of the intention to use it against population centers. But Walzer concludes, "[M]en and women are responsible for the threats they live by, even if they don't speak them out loud."[154]

There are some who say that nuclear deterrence violates the rights of noncombatants because these strategies fail to distinguish between combatants and noncombatants. Walzer clarifies this distinction. His argument may be expressed as Dixon sets it up:

(1) If an act violates the rights of a person, that act is morally wrong.
(2) Nuclear deterrence strategies violate the rights of noncombatants.
(3) Therefore, nuclear deterrence strategies are morally wrong.

But Walzer maintains the second premise is wrong: that making a deterrent threat does not amount to a "direct or physical violation of a person's rights."[155] Some might criticize Walzer by claiming that people do experience psychological harm because of the policy of nuclear deterrence.[156] Aside from the question whether the empirical evidence does or does not show this to be the case, "causing harm" is not necessarily a violation of rights. "Harm" as such does not render an act immoral. A dentist "harms" a patient in the sense that his/her actions result in physical pain, but the action is not immoral because of the physical evil that results. The dentist who causes pain *without the patient's consent* may or may not be acting immorally, however.

Another criticism of Walzer concerns the apparent inconsistency he shows in dealing with domestic law and with international convention. Dixon questions Walzer's conclusion concerning the morality of threats, for in keeping with Walzer's own method, Dixon notes that the domestic law does recognize cases where one may seek legal remedy to restrain another who threatens him if it is reasonable to believe these threats will be actualized. Has Walzer probed deeply enough into the moral principles which underlie such a social consensus? In case law, the intention to violate rights is recognized as an actual violation of rights, yet Walzer does not apply this to international policy. If the additional factor that makes the two different is simply the number of persons involved, then the argument cannot be said to rest on rights, but on the utilitarian notion of proportionality after all.

Walzer is aware, however, that the analogy between domestic and international conventions has its limits. In this case, the international situation does not provide enforceable means by which one state may seek legal remedy to restrain another state which is threatening harm. International society, Walzer states, "is unlike domestic society in that every conflict threatens the structure as a whole with collapse. Aggression challenges it directly and is much more dangerous than domestic crime, because there are no policemen." The rights of member states must be vindicated, Walzer maintains, since society exists only by virtue of these rights. If these rights are violated, then resistance is presumed, even military resistance.[157]

Walzer continues to probe the nature of "threat" to see why society does in fact approve of the policy of nuclear deterrence. He suggests that one look at the gravity of the danger which deterrence is supposed to prevent as opposed to the gravity of the traffic deaths which would be prevented in Ramsey's analogy. Nuclear war threatens "our common liberties and our common survival"; it guards against "atomic blackmail and foreign domination" and "nuclear destruction."[158] If these are the stakes, and one may assume Walzer is correct in saying that they are, and if the threat is indeed a "permanent condition," this situation qualifies for supreme emergency status.

Even in supreme emergency, however, Walzer has already precluded the possibility of a moral use of nuclear weapons. If threat implies use, as Walzer maintains it does, and all use of nuclear weapons is immoral, then the threat to use nuclear weapons is immoral and Walzer remains stuck on the horns of the nuclear dilemma, as he admits.

Ramsey arrived at the position that a nuclear deterrent policy might be moral by making the threat morally do-able with limited nuclear weapons. Walzer has ruled out the morality of using or threatening to use limited nuclear weapons and cannot take such a path. He criticizes Ramsey's account of the prevailing moral judgments on nuclear deterrence as "too complex and too devious," but useful in suggesting "the outer limits of the just war and the dangers of trying to extend those limits."[159]

Walzer's Solution

The first step of Walzer's argument is now complete. He finally rejects all attempts "[t]o draw insignificant lines, to maintain the formal categories of double effect, collateral damage, noncombatant immunity as corrupting the argument for justice as a whole.[160] His own argument, in order to be consistent with his overall just war theory, must be based on respect for individuals' rights, and so the argument for the morality of nuclear deterrence stands ultimately on the need to protect the rights of each individual to life and liberty. The only way of protecting those rights in the face of the nuclear war threat is through a policy of nuclear deterrence which then falls under the standard of supreme necessity. One is obliged to look for alternate means to peace; and if and when these possibilities are actualized, necessity will no longer apply and the deterrence policy will then be immoral. Walzer concludes that political leaders must choose the utilitarian side of the dilemma: "They must opt for collective survival and override those rights that have suddenly loomed as obstacles to survival."[161]

Walzer's justification of deterrence seems to be turning out not to be a moral justification after all if morality is based on rights and not on utility. There is need to look more closely at the state's options with regard to responses to aggression to see whether Walzer can make any argument for deterrence on the basis of rights.

Evidence has previously been given that in international society Walzer supports the state's right and even duty to defend itself against aggression. This gives the state the right and sometimes the duty to retaliate against an aggressor. Under certain conditions, a state even has the right to make a preemptive strike. An option to the preemptive strike would be the maintenance of a deterrent of such a nature that it could act as an immediate deterrent in a given situation or a general deterrent over a period of time.

These options, the preemptive attack and the immediate and general deterrent, are similar in that they are both responses intended to prevent the aggressor's attack. They differ, however, in that a preemptive policy states, in effect: "We will attack you and we will destroy you." The deterrence policy, on the other hand, states, "If you attack us, we will destroy you." Obviously, the latter policy is morally preferable to the former.

Here, too, however, Walzer meets the same moral obstacle: the actual use of nuclear weapons is immoral and, therefore, the threat to use them is immoral. On the basis of the states' rights to exist, Walzer has justified preemptive attacks. In cases where preemptive attacks would have to be nuclear, Walzer appears to desire to apply the same formula he used in justifying preemptive conventional attacks:

[S]tates may use [in this case, "maintain"] military [nuclear] force in the face of threats of war whenever failure to do so would seriously risk their territorial integrity or political independence. Under such circumstances it can fairly be said that they have been forced to fight [deter] and that they are the victims of aggression.[167]

There remains an inherent tension in Walzer's solution, however. If one must accept a plurality of states with "territorial integrity or political independence" in a nuclear age, then individual human rights to life and liberty will be violated because of the possibility of all-out nuclear war and the conditions of nuclear deterrence which accompany that possibility. Unless Walzer can move beyond that impasse, his position on nuclear war and deterrence may promote more morally considered policy making and war conduct, but, as John Langan states, it will remain an "ultimate theoretical failure."

If anything is to count as a "supreme emergency," i.e., a situation where "the heavens are (really) about to fall," it is the imminent threat of nuclear war. If the only way to prevent that war is to threaten counter-population destruction, Walzer concludes that political decision-makers must threaten what it is immoral to do, and immoral to threaten. He "justifies" the violation of the principle for the sake of averting a disaster to the political community, yet he holds "guilty" those who are thus justified. In chapter 3 it has been shown that Richard McCormick's concept of proportionate reason offers a possible way out for Walzer, at least in some instances of supreme emergency. However, it is not clear that Walzer has this way of escape in the case of nuclear war.

McCormick's third requirement for proportionate reason stated that the manner of protection of the higher value (the continuation of the political community), here and now, will not undermine it in the long run, for this would ultimately undermine the value of the individual human person. In the case of all-out nuclear war, the continuation of the political community is highly doubtful even if, as Herman Kahn asserts, "Most nuclear wars would probably not result in total destruction of even one side."[164] Proportionate reason, then, does not seem to offer a solution to Walzer's nuclear paradox.

But perhaps Walzer can be helped by Alan Donagan's assessment of "the problem of dirty hands." Donagan states, "Cases in which the choice of evils is between the destruction of a whole community or grave injury to it, and the death or grave injury to one of its members, are on a different footing from cases in which the choice is between the death or suffering of a larger or of a smaller number of individuals."[165] The "whole community" here may refer to either the global community or a significant part of it; for example, Western society. "One of its members" may refer to either Western society or to a nation or nations in one or other of the Western alliances.

Donagan observes that "[common morality] is outraged by the consequentialist position that, as long as human beings can remain alive, the lesser of two evils is always to be chosen." When resistance to tyrannical external force becomes impossible, common morality allows certain room for compliance but beyond a certain point, the line is drawn and compliance is excluded. One might even argue that there exists a kind of tacit agreement among the states that the welfare of the genuine international community is a good common to all members. Donagan draws examples from rabbinic teaching to show instances where states have acted as if this were the case. Thus in international affairs, even some unjust wars are allowed to proceed without intervention on another nation's part lest intervention lead to escalation and the threat of disaster to the larger political community.

When Walzer concludes that a political decision-maker must break with the moral precept by threatening the lives of large numbers of innocent persons in cases of supreme emergency, he is succumbing to the Machiavellian assumption "that in politics nobody succeeds except by getting his hands dirty." Donagan maintains that this idea is not seriously defensible.[166]

In taking the position he does, Walzer joins those who hold that common morality must be abrogated in cases of "necessity." Donagan describes the class of cases these moral philosophers offer as warranting a break with common morality as follows:

> All members of the class have a common form: a very powerful person or society (usually, a wicked dictator) threatens to bring a calamity upon a whole community (usually, its destruction by nuclear bombardment) unless it will do something abominable by the standards of common morality (say, to procure the judicial murder of an innocent man).[167]

In Walzer's case of nuclear deterrence, the "powerful society" is a state with nuclear weapons which threatens nuclear calamity upon another state or states unless the latter surrender their existence as political communities. The threatened states have the right and even the duty to resist in order to protect the rights of their citizens to live in political communities of their own choosing. Yet if they resist, the result spells disaster to their own and probably their adversary's political community as well; therefore, it would be immoral to retaliate and immoral to threaten to retaliate. There is a moral limit to what the threatened political leaders can do. They can threaten to strike CF or countercombatant targets in retaliation insofar as they take "due care" to minimize the deaths of innocent persons. To propose that they must also threaten to target the civilian population directly is to move beyond that point. It would be to agree with "Machiavelian arguments that a state may flourish more under rulers who do not regard themselves as bound by common morality than under rulers who do."[168]

If Walzer accepts Donagan's way out of the "dirty hands" dilemma, he still must deal with the morality of the risk that even CF targeting can lead to escalation to all-out nuclear war. It appears that, in the end, Walzer's real problem need not be the "paradox of dirty hands," but the prudential judgment that the risk of escalation to all-out nuclear war is inevitable. This belief prevents him from reaching a conclusion on nuclear deterrence that is consistent with his moral position: Walzer's conclusion is that there is no moral deterrent, yet he requires decision-makers to make the immoral decision to maintain such a deterrent in supreme emergency. However, the *risk* of nuclear war is, after all, not the *actual* waging of nuclear war. It may be that the risks to Walzer's highest values are less when deterrence policies are in effect than when one "Great Power" dominates, and there may be a way to justify his position through using the concept of proportionate reason.

Chapter 5

Nuclear War, Nuclear Peace, and the Bondedness of Peoples

Introduction: "In A Different Voice"

The question that has pervaded the analysis of the previous chapters has been whether the three contemporary theorists who are the subjects of this study have provided an adequate ethical framework to deal with the moral problems nuclear weapons pose. This question suggests a broader inquiry as well: does the just war tradition itself remain applicable to war and deterrence in the nuclear age? This latter question cannot be answered definitively by an examination of three American just war theorists. Although the three come from the major Western religious traditions and the academic disciplines chiefly involved in the nuclear debate, they do not exhaust the possibilities of interpreting and applying the just war tradition to contemporary warfare. Nevertheless, the answer to the first question provides insight into where just war thinking is heading as we approach the twenty-first century.

As I have tried to show, each theorist develops his own just war doctrine from within the broader tradition, but each looks at contemporary warfare "through a different window" and "across a different landscape." What each one sees, therefore, reflects his own point of view: each offers a different emphasis, a different combination of principles, and even a different stance on the same principles. Yet each one of the three treated in this work does not speak "in a completely different voice", if I may borrow Carol Gilligan's phrase; for each of the three is a member of an elite group: each is an American, each is white, each is male, and each has worked, for the most part, in an academic environment.[1] Changing even one of these characteristics will result in a shift to a different "window," a different "landscape," and will affect the way the argument is shaped and the conclusions to which it leads.

The work of this final chapter, then, will be to look through yet another window in order to examine the strengths and weaknesses, the contributions and omissions of the three theorists, and to speak in yet a different voice to the direction the just war tradition is taking and ought to take in the nuclear age.

In Search of Progress

My own reflection on the three theorists' work has repeatedly sent me back to a philosophical, more particularly an epistemological, "touchstone" that I find present throughout the nuclear debate. This touchstone has two sides: the one is the notion of knowledge as "being akin to;" the other is the notion of truth as *aletheia* or "unhiddenness." Both have their roots in Greek thought.

The Greeks contributed much to the beginnings of just war thinking, and it is fitting to turn to them to find greater clarity on the foundation of a just war theory for the nuclear age. The Greeks, notably Plato, understood reason as more than logic and clear thinking. Though reason *is* that, it is also a human reaching out to what one is "akin to."[2] When one truly knows, one establishes a bond with the object known. Truth lies in this "bonding" or "relating," this "kinship" with what is known.

It is somewhat ironic that stronger bonding often occurs only after separation: synthesis follows analysis. So, it seems, the twentieth century just war theorists have analyzed the just war tradition by separating out those principles they find applicable to a twentieth century setting. They have, in Martin Heidegger's interpretation of Plato, created a "clearing," a place where objects are "unhidden" and "dis-covered," where one may see more clearly the truth within the boundaries of *jus ad bellum* and *jus in bello* principles.[3] The just war theorist searches for truth, or unhiddenness, in this clearing; i.e., in this twentieth century "moral landscape." This is what all of us attempt to do as we analyze and reflect on the three American theorists. We each bring our own perspective to the task, and so we may be expected to make different discoveries.

Discovering an Old Principle

In this search for previously hidden just war principles, I have found support from one of the three, Michael Walzer, who says,

Insofar as we can recognize moral problems, it has less to do with the discovery or invention of new principles than with the inclusion under the old principles of previously excluded men and women.[4]

There is an "old principle" or "value" that has been overshadowed by other values and principles throughout the various political and social settings in which each just war theory has been articulated. The value that has begun to emerge from the clearing has been clothed in various names. (Like clothing, these names have partially revealed truth and partially covered it.) It has been hinted at variously by such names as "the principle of civilization, "the principle of humanity," "the interdependence of peoples." These terms help reveal a deeper truth that seems to lie close to the core of the just war tradition--the truth that the peoples of the world, though separated from one another by nationhood or culture, are, nevertheless, also bonded to one another. This truth is a value that may be called "the bondedness of peoples."

The bondedness of peoples may be understood on several different levels. Three of these levels are particularly significant in relation to the just war tradition: bondedness which we experience by virtue of our common humanity, bondedness which contributes to national identity, and bondedness which is a cosmopolitan ideal.

Bondedness of peoples refers in its primary sense to our kinship that exists among us by virtue of our common humanity. This fundamental notion of kinship seems to form the basis for the condemnation of war made by Erasmus and the humanitarian thinkers who followed him. For these thinkers, the sufferings and deaths inflicted by some human beings on others provided sufficient grounds for condemning war. As Michael Howard points out in *War and the Liberal Conscience*, Erasmus and, later, Rousseau and others in the seventeenth and eighteenth centuries thought the evils of war "could be cured only by severing the bonds which held society together"; in other words, Rousseau believed returning to a "state of nature" would lead to peace, not to war, as Hobbes theorized. The desirability of returning to a state of nature is not a conclusion just war theorists have entertained. They accept the more complex political realities that have evolved over the course of human history; and for the nation-state system that has prevailed for more than two hundred years war has seemed inescapable.

The societal bonds to which Rousseau refers indicate still another sense of the bondedness of peoples. It is only within the context of society that human beings can fulfill their needs and pursue happiness. Yet Rousseau uncovers the irony that societal bonds which create national identity can also cause tension and lead to violence among different societies as well as within one's own society. Excesses in nationalism lead to a bondedness that is promoted by selfish interests. They permit the vested interests of certain profit-seeking or power-seeking groups to exploit others in order to promote their own economic or political gain. Such "bondedness" runs counter to the foundational notion of bondedness as kinship.

The bondedness in society that is more consistent with the primary sense of bondedness of peoples is the close relationship that exists among a people bonded together by shared values and culture, a situation particularly characteristic of the contemporary Western world. Howard notes that the world system as a whole still lacks "a homogeneity of values" and "a coincidence of perceived values." He points out that the United States "virtually alone among nations, found and to some extent still finds its identity not so much in ethnic community or shared historical experience as in dedication to a value system."[6] A shared history may lead to a more exclusive bondedness, one close to the concept of "statism." While statism acknowledges and values certain aspects of internationality, it places a higher value on the state as the institution that guarantees the self-determination and territorial integrity of a people. The goal of more widely shared values, on the other hand, is consistent with a more inclusive notion of bondedness, a more "cosmopolitan" ideal than that of the statist position.

The cosmopolitan sense of bondedness is articulated by Immanuel Kant in his work, *Perpetual Peace*, written in 1795. Kant's views suggest the cosmopolitan view is closely allied to the concept of law. The bonds or the "relationships" between and among states are kept intact by virtue of principles of law agreed to by the contracting parties. Kant believes, contrary to Rousseau, that left to themselves, human beings would naturally resort to war. "Thus," says Kant, "a state of peace must be established."[7] Peace will be the result of human choice and a result of a bondedness that is chosen; it does not come "naturally."

Kant specifies three different types of law which we may consider relevant to the bondedness which each is meant to support. First, there is the *jus civitatis*, whereby a constitution is formed in accordance with the right of citizenship of individuals who constitute a nation; second, the *jus gentium* exists according to which a constitution is agreed upon whose principles form international law and determine the relations of states; third, is the *jus cosmopoliticum* which is formed in accordance with cosmopolitan law, in so far as individuals and states, standing in an external relation of mutual reaction, may be regarded as citizens of one world-state.[8]

Writing in 1795, Kant describes the ideal of the *jus cosmopoliticum*:

> The intercourse, more or less close, which has been everywhere steadily increasing between the nations of the earth, has now extended so enormously that a violation of right in one part of the world is felt all over it. Hence, the idea of a cosmopolitan right is no fantastical, high-flown notion of right, but a complement of the unwritten code of law--constitutional as well as international law--necessary for the public rights of mankind in general and thus for the realization of perpetual peace. For only by endeavoring to fulfill the conditions laid down by this cosmopolitan law can we flatter ourselves that we are gradually approaching that idea.[9]

The *jus cosmopoliticum* was not a political reality in Kant's time any more than it is today, but Kant uses an argument from nature to support his position that the *jus cosmopoliticum* is an ideal worth pursuing. First, says Kant, human beings *can* live in all parts of the globe; second, they *do* live in all parts of the globe; and, third, they are forced to enter into relations more or less controlled by law. The "principle of public right," as Kant calls this third constitution, "must be in harmony with the universal end of mankind, which is happiness, [and it] must be in harmony with the right of the people, for a union of the ends of all is only possible in harmony with this right."[10]

The cosmopolitan sense of the bondedness of peoples demands an expanded account of rights and duties. John Rawls' section on "Natural Duties" in *A Theory of Justice* may be helpful in understanding the implications this concept has for the contemporary world situation.

In an expanded version of the origin of the social contract, Rawls considers the parties in the "original position" as representatives of different nations. These parties are ignorant of their own nationality when they meet to choose fundamental principles they will need to adjudicate conflicting claims among states. Rawls believes these original contractors would choose certain "natural duties" that will play a role in making social cooperation stable. Such principles include the principle of equality, the principle of self-determination, the right of self-defense against attack, the duty to keep treaties, and, most importantly, the duty to support and to further just institutions. Rawls grounds the latter duty in the claim that everyone benefits from a society where the duty of mutual respect is honored, saying, "[T]he cost to self-interest is minor in comparison with the support for the sense of one's own worth."[11] The duty of mutual aid which follows from the more comprehensive view of the bondedness of peoples is similarly grounded in Rawls. His reasoning closely resembles Kant's grounding of the duty of beneficence in *The Foundations of the Metaphysics of Morals*; that is, to deny the principle of mutual aid would be to deprive one's society of assistance in time of need.[12]

The parties in the original position would, according to Rawls, accept the possibility of the just war. They would recognize the need for the *jus ad bellum* and *jus in bello* limitations. According to these limitations, the original parties, being "blind" to their own national situation, would not permit nations to fight wars for world power, national glory, economic gain, or the acquisition of territory, nor would they employ means that would show contempt for human life or put humanity in jeopardy. The reason for this is that they themselves could be among the most vulnerable or the least advantaged nations and such "justifications" for war would jeopardize their own self-interest.

It is this cosmopolitan sense of the bondedness of peoples that, I suggest, lies at the core of the just war tradition. Within that tradition, the principle and the value of the bondedness of peoples may be grounded according to a Kantian or Rawlsian theory of justice and "enlightened self-interest." The bondedness of peoples entails the duty to respect all peoples and to foster mutual aid.

Both the value and the principle of the bondedness of peoples are an acknowledgment of the likeness or "kinship" among all men and women across divisions of race and nationality. Unlike animals of the same genus and species, human "kin" differ from one another in language, custom, and worldview despite the natural kinship among races and nationalities. Unlike animals of the same genus and species, human persons relate to each other by choice, not by instinct. They may choose to enter (or not) into "covenants," agreements which establish bonds among peoples who are more alike than not, as well as among peoples who are unlike in significant ways. The possibility of choice offers both a positive and a negative side: negatively, human persons have the capacity to destroy their own kind in ways and to an extent other creatures cannot. But the possibility of choice offers human persons the opportunity to enhance the lot of others, enabling them not only to survive but to flourish.

It is this tension and this choice that just war theorists continue to focus on during our times. The tension gave birth to the just war tradition and to the pacifist tradition: two different responses to the results of the negative choices. Both seek peace, yet seek it differently; however, it seems that peace, like happiness, is more likely to be found not in seeking it directly, but in finding it "by the way." Perhaps it would be more correct, then, to say that the theorists of both traditions seek justice and *hope* to find peace. If so, they might contribute to policy formation at this time by focusing less on the limits of war and more on what is in the clearing; namely, the values that keep influencing the just war framework. Debates could contine on "supreme emergency" conditions and policies, but meanwhile the world must operate in a period of nuclear deterrence, or "nuclear peace." It would be of benefit to policy-makers at this time to hear the just war thinking on the values that continue to affect and effect the *jus ad bellum* and *jus in bello* limitations. In Heideggerian terms, if the theorists would come away from the edges into the clearing itself and expand further on the values that are having an impact on their thinking, they may be able to affect policy in ways that move the nations away from nuclear military options. Henry Shue espresses the possibilities well when he states that "how the philosophical questions with which we have wrestled are resolved does make a difference for how public policy should proceed."[13] We need to ensure that we are asking the right questions: not only, "how do we fight a just war," but also, "what makes for a just peace, a peace that encourages human flourishing."

Human flourishing is a natural good and therefore ought to be pursued. From the very nature of the human person as a social being, however, it cannot be pursued in isolation. Flourishing takes place in an environment where persons are cared for, where resources and knowledge are shared, where suffering is alleviated, and where there is capacity for empathy and love as well as a challenge to grow and to move beyond oneself. It usually takes place in an atmosphere of *eirene*, "peace," or as Roland Bainton has translated *eirene*, "linkage."[14] This term conceals an important truth related to the bondedness of peoples. It is the duty of one's kin to provide such an environment, but eventually it becomes the duty of human persons in the broader society to foster conditions where human flourishing can take place.

As human persons move beyond themselves and, subsequently, as societies also move beyond the capacity of their abilities and resources to meet the needs of their people, the bonds among all peoples become more evident and significant. These bonds entail the duty to care for those one is "akin to" and to foster social, political, and economic environments within which people may flourish.

The political structure that has evolved to accomplish this end in the twentieth century is the nation-state system. The nations have become so interdependent that the efforts of one nation to effect such an environment for its own people has either enhanced or had disastrous effects on other nations in their pursuit of similar goals. This is not without precedent in other centuries, but the extent of interdependence today greatly magnifies the effects one nation's actions have on the other nations. For this reason wars that may well have been justified in former times may not be justified today.

It is this twentieth century reality that offers the first glimpse of the value that was present in the just war tradition from the beginnings but that remained hidden until the smoke of modern wars began to clear. In order to illuminate this principle or value "in shadow" we may find it useful first, to locate it in the philosophical foundations and methodologies just war theorists have employed. Next, we may search for it within the clearing created by the *jus ad bellum* and *jus in bello* boundaries the classic and contemporary theorists have set. Finally, we will try to see whether the principle of the bondedness of peoples, long visible only in shadow, offers any solutions to the contemporary difficulties the three just war theorists have encountered and whether it clears the way through the moral impasse each seems to reach.

Classic Just War Theorists: Foundations and Methodologies

Ramsey, Walzer and O'Brien engage in the often tedious process of unwrapping the complexities that nuclear weapons have introduced in order to determine whether one can wage a just war in a nuclear age. What they have succeeded in doing has been to bring into sharp relief the boundary-setting principles of proportionality and discrimination. Setting these boundaries opens up the space or forum that offers the opportunity to see and to discuss realities that may hold the key to the solution of current perplexing issues. Yet these realities have their roots in prior centuries.

Chapters 1 through 3 have shown that the three contemporary theorists are linked to the classic just war theorists in the broader tradition. It is not surprising, then, that the centuries that have separated the two groups have covered over some of the truths the classic thinkers had caught sight of. William O'Brien provides an opening through which one gets a glimpse of the principle Suarez gave expression to in the sixteenth century. Although I have cited it before, it is worth repeating here.

> The reason for the Law of Nations, under this aspect, is, that the human race, though divided into no matter how many different peoples and nations, has for all that a certain unity, a unity nor merely physical, but also in a sense political and moral. This is shown by the natural precept of mutual love and mercy, which extends to all men, including foreigners of every way of thinking. Wherefore, though any one state, republic or kingdom be in itself a perfect community and constant in its members, nevertheless each of the states is also a member, in a certain manner, of the world, so far as the human race is concerned. For none of these communities are ever sufficient unto themselves to such a degree that they do not require some mutual help, society or communication, either to their greater advantage or from moral necessity and need, as is evident from custom.[15]

Suarez uncovers a particular truth here. It is that there is a "natural precept" that obliges nations to acknowledge the kinship among all peoples. As Plato and Heidegger suggest, the search for truth involves a search to uncover what is alien and foreign in order to find likeness or kinship. The natural law truth that begins to become "unhidden" in Suarez involves the knowledge of the proper relationship *among persons*, and this is the paradigm notion of kinship. Kinship among persons entails obligations: responsibility *to* the other, but also responsibility *for* and *with* the other. In the just war tradition it is this very responsibility that justifies defense or intervention and the decision to go to war in the first place.

Warfare took on a different appearance to classic just war theorists from the appearance it assumes today, however. The combatants Aquinas speaks of are a "discrete functional class within a rational kingdom," pursuing the common good, a view "rooted in the nature of human communities."[16] Aquinas puts the safety of the community ahead of the safety of the single individual. This attitude reveals respect for the underlying value and the necessary condition that makes human flourishing possible: the bondedness of peoples and the necessity to respect and nurture kinship among peoples. It is this sense of mutual care and responsibility that bears particular importance for international conduct, and it re-surfaces in the thought of the sixteenth and seventeenth century classic just war theorists.

Vitoria (1492-1546) marks, according to Walters, a renaissance within scholasticism--a reaffirmation of the human found in Aquinas--with an emphasis on the integrity of human nature and natural *human community*.[17] Accordingly, Vitoria urges that the "means of war should not exceed the quality and nature of the wrong, result in 'great evils for both sides' or cause the 'ruin' of the enemy. He urges 'equity and *humanity*,'"[18] thus acknowledging the duty to look beneath "enemy" status for the common bond among allies and enemies alike, the "kinship" that is the bond among all peoples.

The same principle is evident in Grotius (1583-1645), who emphasizes keeping faith with *all* enemies, "even pirates," thus acknowledging the "bondedness of peoples" as a consideration of *humanity*. James Johnson has reminded us that Grotius reached back beyond the medieval to the classical world for secular roots of principles to limit war. Before the dictates of Christian charity Grotius finds that the duty to care for other peoples was considered as part of the perfection of natural law. It has been expressed as the "humanitarian principle" or the "principle of civilization," names that help to uncover the "bondedness of peoples."

Even as the principle begins to come to light in the sixteenth and seventeenth centuries, it becomes overshadowed by another principle of war: military necessity, and by a new reality, the appearance of the nation-state.

The separate, sovereign nation-state is the outcome of the break-up of the unified Christian world of the medievals. This development did much to influence subsequent just war thinking. J. Bryan Hehir expresses the long-term effects this period has had. Hehir describes the nation-state as "a qualitatively new center of secular political authority which challenged both the idea of a wider Christian commonwealth and the binding power of any universal moral authority higher than the state. ... The impact of the Reformation eroded *the spiritual and moral bonds* which Augustine and Aquinas had taken for granted."[19] [Emphasis added]

The "bondedness of peoples," covered over with the devastation of holy wars, followed by national wars and ideological wars did not completely disappear, however. Even the destruction of the Napoleonic wars, the revolutions and the civil wars of the eighteenth and nineteenth centuries could not obliterate either the idea or the reality of the bonds of kinship among peoples on a global scale. Through the centuries the bonds have been stretched thin among some peoples; they have been strengthened among others. But today some of them threaten to be permanently broken. The latter half of the twentieth century is a unique period in history; it is the only period in history in which the complete destruction of the possibility of bonds of kinship among peoples, "total war," has become possible.

It is the potential for unprecedented death and destruction that has forced contemporary just war theorists to reflect on the conditions and values that once informed the thinking of classic just war theorists. Weapons technology forces one to look again at *jus in bello* conditions, and the prolonged attention given to these conditions tends to absorb the attention of theorists and to cover over the ultimate values that are at stake in modern war.

The question contemporary just war theorists must ask is the one Aquinas asked, but it must embrace a much broader human community: to what extent must the safety of the global community be put ahead of the values of a single nation? Is it time for the *jus cosmopoliticum* to replace the *jus gentium*? Or, in a different voice: to what extent does kinship, the bondedness of peoples, take precedence over even the otherwise legitimate self-interest of a nation-state or alliance? Just as the principle of military necessity served as the impetus to revise the just war framework from the sixteenth century on, so this principle in shadow is surfacing today and it is the contemporary just war theorists' task to discover it.

Contemporary Just War Theorists

The classic theorists, as shown in chapters 2 and 3, have as their foundation a natural law-law of nations base. Of the three contemporary theorists, only William O'Brien openly declares that his theory is based on natural law, that he is, in fact, a "twentieth century Grotian" who uses the *jus naturale-jus gentium* to identify moral principles. His realist-natural law-law of nations view of international relations suggests he may be on the way to uncovering a value whose time has come, for he says that strong nations have a right, "maybe an obligation, to protect smaller nations."[20] Paul Ramsey, on the other hand, chooses *agape*, or Christian love, as the foundation of his theory; and Michael Walzer builds on the foundation of human rights. Ramsey's later works indicate a willingness to recognize natural law through the "prism" of actual cases, and to find it manifested in the *jus gentium*. Michael Walzer, too, while maintaining that he cannot know the foundations of morality gives reason to believe that a "deeper theory" may underlie his doctrine of human rights. The deeper theory that seems to be guiding Walzer's thinking may indeed be consonant with a natural law theory, though Walzer himself suggests his own view is that morality is more like an on-going argument than a law set in nature.[21]

The three use different approaches in their handling of the questions posed by nuclear war and deterrence. Paul Ramsey's approach is deductive, arguing as he does from a single first principle, *agape*, and deriving from it further general principles of *lex*, *ordo*, and *jusititia* as well as the particular *jus in bello* principles of discrimination and proportionality. For Ramsey *agape* is the whole of morality. Its formalistic dimension establishes bounds within which its discretionary dimension functions. Walzer and O'Brien use predominantly an inductive and casuistic method, analyzing the history of belligerents' practice and positive international law in their attempts to identify the principles that govern and have governed the conduct of war. In this way they hope to determine moral guidelines for policy on warfare in the nuclear age. Given their philosophical foundations and the methodology they use, what, then, would be the effect of having them focus on a principle like the bondedness of peoples?

The Bondedness of Peoples and *Jus ad bellum* Doctrines

The three theorists are in basic agreement on the conditions necessary to justify the use of military force. The differences among them are evident in the degree of emphasis they give to *jus ad bellum* as a whole as well as the emphasis each gives to certain principles and values or combinations of these. We might look to see if the bondedness of peoples is hidden there.

Though Ramsey begins with *agape*, his *jus ad bellum* doctrine emphasizes the limits set by justice, order and law. He assigns responsibility to political decision-makers for discerning the good that *ought to be done* from the pool of total humanitarian good that also *ought to be*. Just what those goods are is not spelled out by Ramsey, and it is this weakness that, in the end, prevents him from framing a just war theory that adequately protects noncombatants. Whether a more adequate treatment of the bondedness of peoples could have overcome this weakness in Ramsey remains to be seen.

O'Brien's *jus ad bellum* analysis emphasizes the balance needed to preserve the values of Western democracy, especially respect for political freedom, with the concern for respecting the interdependence of peoples, or the "principle of civilization." Of the three, O'Brien comes closest to identifying the principle that would provide the limits to war that he seeks. Instead, the principle gets buried again in *jus in bello* concerns: military necessity, prudence, and the general qualitative effects in proportionality. In Walzer, vindictive justice, which sets right the wrong that has been suffered by punishing the offender, receives emphasis, particularly in Walzer's revised legalist paradigm. Walzer's supreme emergency endangers the hope of preserving any value, as he is willing to risk the destruction of even his highest values in conditions of supreme emergency. The recognition or omission of the bondedness of peoples has significant potential for influencing the *jus ad bellum* doctrine of Ramsey and O'Brien; and if Walzer were to recognize such a value, the individual's right to life and liberty is more likely to be preserved in the long run.

PAUL RAMSEY

In selecting *agape* as his ultimate norm, Ramsey follows Augustine in holding that war is justified, primarily, because of the necessity to protect noncombatants. Of the three theorists, however, Ramsey devotes least attention to *jus ad bellum*. He relegates the determination of just cause and reasonable hope of success to the discretionary domain of *agape*, subjecting their determination to the prudential judgment of political decision-makers. These "magistrates" are presumed to be in a better position, with more complete information, to make such decisions than is the general public. Aside from telling them to operate within the limits set by *ordo, justitia,* and *lex,* Ramsey offers little other moral guidance. He does not specify a hierarchy of values to be sought nor does he offer an external absolute standard to evaluate the balance of good and evil. He seems to posit, but does not show how he derives, the values O'Brien identifies as "'minimum world public order,' presumption against aggression, ...and a 'fundamental human dignity' presumption in favor of the kinds of human rights that exist in what some of us can still call the Free World and against *regimes* that deny those rights."[22]

Despite Ramsey's scant attention to *jus ad bellum* concerns, however, the "principle in shadow" does not lie far from the surface in his thought. Ramsey's ultimate validating norm, in fact, relates closely to the bondedness of peoples. Ramsey appeals to Christian *agape,* the "Augustinian insight... that from love we should restrain an enemy who would injure the innocent."[23] Seen from a different perspective, *agape* is the bond among peoples that gives rise to the Christian's duty to love. Ramsey himself, however, derives the principle from the *individual's* bondedness in love to Christ: "Anyone *who for the love of Christ* is *morally bonded* to *both* the oppressor and the oppressed and to the bystanders (e.g., the children) of both, is not likely to come through with hands unclean only from the suffering of others that might have been prevented by sounder understanding"[24] [Emphasis added].

The "sounder understanding" that Ramsey speaks of is just one of those values that require dialogue at the present time. Discussion of what such understanding requires moves us away from the boundaries to the area where argument and action are needed in order to prevent warfare in these days. If Ramsey paid closer attention to the bond among "oppressor" and "oppressed," and the "sounder understanding" needed, he might have been moved to give more emphasis to *jus ad bellum* requirements. Instead he seems not to acknowledge nor to advocate that the people of a nation be involved in the debate that ought to precede the decision to go to war. However, open and broad debate is advisable even if such a decision is never to be put to a popular vote. One is reminded of Walzer's words that new discoveries will be made "under the old principles of previously excluded men and women." People who may have been excluded from debate in former days now have the opportunity and the duty to make themselves informed and to contribute to that debate. By relying almost completely on the prudence of the decision-makers, Ramsey limits the information brought to bear on matters of war, especially since the military establishment has ease of access to government officials not enjoyed by the wider population. Thus, even within one's own nation, the principle of the bondedness of peoples could play a key role in providing stronger limits in Ramsey's *jus ad bellum* policy.

O'Brien summarizes Ramsey's *jus ad bellum* concept as follows: "[J]ust war derives from the right and duty in social charity (love) of the strong to defend the weak and threatened from aggressors."[25] In defending "the weak and threatened," one wonders if enough attention has been given to the bonds that also bind the just defender to the "strong and threatening" aggressor. Bonds of kinship with the aggressor require that before a nation goes to war, it must meet the *jus ad bellum* requirement of having a "right intention." The bondedness of peoples must enter into the formation of that right intention and will act as a further restriction on entering into warfare. In addition, the bondedness of peoples strengthens the *jus in bello* restrictions because the nation contemplating war must also assess the injuries and destruction that might be anticipated in war. Ramsey allows for a large number of collateral noncombatant deaths and injuries, and this is one of the weaknesses of his position. The bondedness of peoples would place greater limitations on such "collateral" effects. Ramsey's lack of attention to *jus ad bellum* concerns relative to the attention he gives to *jus in bello* matters, may be attributed to an outdated political worldview as we have seen.

In not specifying the hierarchy of values to be sought, I believe Ramsey fails to give adequate attention to the *jus ad bellum* principle that could have provided an external standard to evaluate the balance of good and evil. This may be traced to his "sixteenth century understanding" about defense and arms[26] that also sheds light on his skepticism concerning the ability of people to be adequately informed to engage in public debate. The protection and fostering of the bondedness of peoples could have provided the standard against which *jus ad bellum* and *jus in bello* decisions should be made.

WILLIAM V. O'BRIEN

O'Brien criticizes contemporary just war theorists, including Ramsey and the U.S. Bishops, for not paying more attention to *jus ad bellum* concerns. As O'Brien enters the uncharted waters of international law in the nuclear age, he turns to Thomistic-Suarezian deductive natural law to supplement his "state of nature-natural law" approach. O'Brien acknowledges that natural law is based upon "a metaphysical appreciation of human nature, not upon relativistic social norms of any particular society of men"[27]--a position consistent with the notion of kinship among peoples. In probing *jus naturale* for first principles, O'Brien identifies "respect for the dignity of the human person" as an ultimate principle. This principle accounts for limitations on military necessity and *raison d'état*. These limits are discovered, he argues, through acknowledgment of a hierarchy of values which subordinate the value of the State to that of the individual person. The principles that give rise to this conclusion concern the three-fold relationship between the Human Person, the State, and International Society. The minimum requirements of human dignity become what O'Brien terms an "internal immanent limitation" on military necessity.

It is when O'Brien speaks of the "external immanent limitation" or military necessity that he comes closest to unwrapping the principle that Suarez began to uncover three hundred years ago. Suarez's concept of international society presumed an interdependence of peoples. Notions of international common good and the "higher necessities" are derived from this principle. The subordinate place of the State in the natural law hierarchy of values thus has implications for the determination of O'Brien's *jus ad bellum* doctrine and his *jus in bello* doctrine: no war can be undertaken which would result in disproportionate injury to the earth, its resources and humankind.

According to O'Brien, just cause, which must be determined prior to any decision to engage in war, must be evaluated within the domain of prudence, which is bound to respect the limitations set by the interdependence of peoples. Elsewhere, O'Brien expresses his concept this way: "My view, reflecting my natural law background, is that the law of nations arises out of natural law, or the principle of humanity or the universal conscience of mankind."[28]

O'Brien posits the interdependence of peoples as a *necessary condition* for "respect for the human person." It is true that the human person is dependent on the resources and labor of others to satisfy even basic needs. This is perhaps more true today than it ever was in the past: no American, for example, can satisfy his or her own needs without relying on the policies, the products, the labor of Europeans, Asians, Africans, Arabs; nor can any European, Asian, African, or Arab satisfy his or her own needs without relying upon the policies, products and labor of Americans. "Interdependence," however, does not equate to "bondedness among peoples." In fact, the bondedness of peoples antedates the interdependence of peoples, since interdependence is a response to the needs of peoples that bondedness entails, especially in today's economically sophisticated world. Interdependence can, and often does, result in disparity among nations in ways that respecting the bondedness of peoples would not permit. Henry Shue speaks of this when he urges the nations to respond to a minimal requirement, "the subsistence needs of peoples."[29] In the name of interdependence, the twentieth century has introduced conditions where once self-sufficient peoples have actually been prevented from satisfying their own basic needs--much less from flourishing. These conditions include changes in the environment caused by industrial development and changes in trade between the "first world countries" and the so-called "developing" countries brought about by the manufactured "needs" of first world peoples that result in shortages of resources to fill the real needs of other peoples.

Thus, O'Brien comes very close to identifying the principle that could be the decisive factor in determining *jus ad bellum*. O'Brien's stress of interdependence ought to provide sufficient reason for a nation to resist entering into warfare on any large scale. It does not go far enough, however. Nations might still be inclined to enter into warfare that could "benefit" themselves either because defense spending and the manufacture of wartime goods might offer economic benefits or because war might effect a favorable change in alliances. Both of these national "benefits" could, however, come at great cost to other peoples of other nations. If O'Brien appealed to the more fundamental principle of the bondedness of peoples rather than to the interdependence of nations alone, he would be able to establish stronger *jus ad bellum* limits and his *jus in bello* doctrine would allow for fewer wars fought for "national interests," for there would be greater emphasis on national responsibility *to*, *with*, and *for* other nations.

MICHAEL WALZER

Michael Walzer, like O'Brien, devotes significant attention to *jus ad bellum* concerns. In setting forth his *jus ad bellum* doctrine, he relies less on the concepts and vocabulary of classic just war theorists to which O'Brien often refers, than on the concepts and vocabulary of contemporary political, legal and moral theorists.

Walzer proceeds with his analysis of *jus ad bellum* from examining the limitations and allowances recognized by international law. There he identifies the legalist paradigm, certain rules pertaining to aggression that are operative in international society. Walzer accepts without evaluation the existence of a pluralist international society of independent states each with rights to territorial integrity and political sovereignty. He revises the rest of the legalist paradigm, however, in an attempt to make international law more consonant with the prevailing concept of justice. These revisions make it possible to classify more wars as "defensive" rather than aggressive since Walzer allows for intervention in situations where there is no "fit" between a government and its people (secession), in states where a single political community is disrupted by civil war, and in cases where "humanitarian intervention" is warranted. In addition, Walzer recognizes the "collective character" of the states as members of the international society. This recognition entails that "punishment of an aggressor state" be reinterpreted and limited because the effects of war are felt over a wide geographical and political area.

Through his revisions, Walzer hopes to enhance the rights of the individual to life and liberty and the rights of states to political sovereignty and territorial integrity. The right to life and liberty sometimes requires that nation-states go to war and this is the primary justification for war and/or deterrence in Walzer's *jus ad bellum* doctrine.

Walzer considers the state valuable because it is the necessary condition for the individual's right to life and liberty. If the state does not foster an environment where the individual can flourish, Walzer would say that civil war is justified, but intervention by another state may not be. Even in the case of civil war, however, without having to reckon with the value of the bondedness of peoples, one side may determine it is in a state of "supreme emergency" and "justify" the elimination of the rebels. Charles Beitz's criticism of Walzer strikes me as correct: Walzer fails to appreciate the extent of interdependence among states and fails to see that changes within states come from without as well as from within. If Walzer recognized the bondedness of peoples as a fundamental value, its preservation might justify intervention according to *jus in bello* restrictions. In either case, a war among nations or a civil war, in focusing on the individuality of states and their rights *vis a vis* one another, Walzer is prevented from paying adequate attention to the bonding that ought to be the goal of the existing "pluralist international society" if that society is ultimately to survive and to flourish. Thus, though Walzer resists utilitarian justifications throughout most of his theory, he resorts to a utilitarian justification for even nuclear war in times of supreme emergency. He bases this justification on the claim that the survival and freedom of political communities are the highest values in international societies.[30] As long as supreme emergency can be applied to the survival of a single political community, a single nation-state, Walzer's just war doctrine allows the possible destruction not only of that nation-state and/or its aggressor, but he permits the endangering of many or even all other nation-states as well. This ultimate failure of Walzer's can be traced to his positing the individual and separate state or the "political community" as the highest value, and to his overlooking the value that underlies even the existence of the state: the bondedness of peoples. If Walzer is forced to say the decision-maker must do the immoral in cases of supreme emergency, he might justify such extreme measures even if he were to accept the bondedness of peoples as a value to be fostered. According to Walzer's logic, in order to "save" a more ultimate value, a nation might have to risk destroying it. But this logic only convinces me further that Walzer's position on supreme emergency is, as he himself says of Ramsey's position, "hard to take and not a plausible moral doctrine."

The emphasis the contemporary just war theorists have placed on different principles and values, as well as their omission of certain values, in their *jus ad bellum* doctrines have significance for war in *every* age. The possibility of *nuclear* war makes the values and principles the theorists emphasize and omit in their *jus in bello* doctrines particularly significant.

The Bondedness of Peoples and *Jus in bello* Doctrines

As the bondedness of peoples is applicable to *jus ad bellum*, it applies perhaps even more broadly to the actual conduct of war. As has been noted earlier, *jus in bello* has absorbed most of the attention of contemporary just war theorists.

PAUL RAMSEY

This change in focus is clearly the case with Paul Ramsey, whose emphasis throughout is on the *jus in bello* principle of discrimination. For Ramsey, the permission to harm combatants in the first place follows from the need to protect noncombatants.[31]

As the discretionary dimension of *agape* dominates Ramsey's treatment of *jus ad bellum*, so the formalistic dimension of *agape* dominates his treatment of *jus in bello*. The principle of discrimination marks the "outer limit" within which discretion, or prudence, determines right and wrong actions, and it is the principle of discrimination, "the moral immunity of noncombatants from direct attack," that places the most stringent limits on the conduct of war.[32] Justification for the "indirect" killing of injuring of noncombatants is based on the principle of double effect.

For Ramsey the principle of discrimination is an *absolute* moral principle that may not be violated no matter what the circumstance. The principle of discrimination is lexically prior to the principle of proportionality; i.e., if the principle of discrimination cannot be observed, the principle of proportionality cannot even be applied.

Yet the principle of discrimination threatens to allow too many collateral noncombatant deaths. This is especially evident in Ramsey's defense of the possible justice of CF nuclear strikes against deeply buried military targets, fifty or more miles in diameter. However, proportionality can transform *jus ad bellum* into *jus contra bellum* "in the face of the destructiveness of modern war that imposes severe limits upon the states' use of violent means,"[33] and it is in the area of proportionality that Ramsey comes closer to acknowledging the value of the bondedness of peoples.

David Little speaks of the principle of discrimination as the formalistic side of agape revealed by "covenantal fidelity." The concept of covenant is an important one for Ramsey, one that plays a significant role in his medical ethics as well. Yet, he appears to believe that the possibility of *peoples* or *nations* living in convenant with one another is an unrealistic hope. Even among nations which have not entered into formal agreements with one another, there is the possibility of the unwritten convenant. This convenant could be considered the recognition of the "natural precept" of mutual obligation to care for other peoples in a way that fosters and preserves an environment in which all the peoples of the earth may flourish.

Yet Ramsey speaks of this as "the time between times:" we live in the trust-system (City of God) and the distrust-system (City of Man),[34] the "already/not yet" of his final book on war.[35] For Ramsey it is unrealistic to think in terms of the nations of this fallen world living in covenant, that is, bonded together. And yet, in this "time between times," nuclear weapons have in fact hastened the necessity for such a covenantal relationship even if nations are motivated by self-interest.

Once again a sixteenth century view of the political world proves inadequate to deal with present realities; yet Ramsey continues to compare the two eras: "The notion of comparative justice comes from the "simultaneous ostensible justice" of those Spanish scholastics who sought to preserve the just war restraints in a world of sovereign states. This is precisely the sort of world to which the restraints have *now* to be addressed, not to hierarchical political authorities in a supposed Christian Empire (if such ever existed)."[36] The twentieth century has witnessed a rapidity of change never before experienced: the speed of communications, the speed of intercontinental travel, the increased level of education among many peoples, to name a few. These changes have resulted in increased possibilities for significant developments for growth in peoples' understanding and concern for one another--even and perhaps, especially, of the desire of people to work for a better understanding of others most unlike themselves. Yet Ramsey appears not to recognize this.

It is more in the area of proportionality where Ramsey touches upon values closely related to the bondedness of peoples. For example, in *Deeds and Rules*, Ramsey states, "The Christian who thinks of himself as an act-agapist has, or should have, concern for the *social consequences* that are not in the direct line of his action, *for the social fabric in which all men must dwell*, for the *most fellowship-producing* general rules of action."[37] [Emphasis added]

At the same time, Ramsey cites the need for a "far deeper world community if there is to be sustained collective use of force, supplanting the nation-state, and the sacrifice of the finite individual to the on-going assuredly continuous life of some future 'United Nations' [to be] worth it,"[38] but he doubts any such transition is taking place and believes that in a defective international order, military intervention must be retained as a last resort.

The two principles of proportionality and discrimination are individually necessary and jointly sufficient to justify military actions in Ramsey, such that even though a military action satisfies the requirements of discrimination, it still may be immoral to perform. Ramsey clearly limits the "range of applicability" of proportionality to quantitative, that is, "commensurable," effects of an action, such as the comparison of the number of lives lost in different military actions. Qualitative effects, such as the level of suffering, the value of freedom, etc., are excluded from his calculation since they entail the comparison of very different types of things which are incommensurate. Presumably, Ramsey includes something resembling the value of the bondedness of peoples in these qualitative effects. Yet, as a necessary condition for the flourishing of the human person, it would better serve if it were lexically prior to others in the hierarchy of values Ramsey considers, at least in the sense that severing the possibility of establishing such bonds among peoples ought never to be permitted. While his principle of discrimi-nation is a powerful restraint against harming individual noncombatants, it is not powerful enough to prevent their being put at great risk in conditions of countercombatant nuclear warfare which Ramsey permits. The likely conditions of counterforce warfare, I believe, also violate the bondedness of peoples. The magnitude of destruction as described in chapter 1, including the severity of injuries among combatants and noncombatants alike, the long-lasting effects of radiation on individuals and on the environment made more likely by the use of nuclear weapons is sufficient to cause excessive suffering and even to destroy the environment necessary to support a people's survival and flourishing.

WILLIAM V. O'BRIEN

William O'Brien is particularly critical of Ramsey's absolute stance on the principle of discrimination. This principle in O'Brien's *jus in bello* doctrine is *relative*, not absolute. He locates its historical origins in the chivalric code, in the principle of utility and in military necessity. Noncombatant deaths and injuries, direct and indirect, enter into the proportionality calculus, according to O'Brien, although he, too, recognizes the distinction between the morality of directly targeting noncombatants and of allowing their deaths and injuries as incidental to targeting military forces and other military resources. O'Brien does not need to appeal to the principle of double effect to justify the violation of noncombatant immunity but appeals instead to the non-absolute character of the principle of discrimination and to the demands of legitimate military necessity and, consequently, to proportionality.

In asking whether a nation is justified in entering into war, O'Brien has insisted that there is no hierarchy among the conditions that will need to be met. "They form a comprehensive whole."[39] Underlying the principle of discrimination, which O'Brien expands to include nonmilitary targets, is the deeper principle of "humanity." In fact O'Brien calls the principle of discrimination "a subordinate principle of the principle of humanity and as a natural law principle in just-war doctrine."[40] Yet O'Brien claims the principle has collapsed in practice under the pressures of modern wars. The "relative ease" with which some claim that O'Brien is able to permit the principle to be overridden parallels the decreased emphasis O'Brien gives to the related general principle of the "interdependence of peoples" used frequently in his writings of the 1950's and early 1960's but not at all in his *Conduct of Just and Limited Wars* (1981). O'Brien says that he has moved in these decades from looking at war from an international law point of view towards considering it almost entirely from the just war point of view. A further return to the values underlying the just war tradition may bring about a reconsideration of such ideas as O'Brien discussed in "The Meaning of Military Necessity" (1957); that is, respect for human life and dignity as required by the "'higher necessities,' the necessities of the entire international community, the ultimate supremacy of natural law and divine law."[41] Since O'Brien notes that the principle of discrimination must be debated in the context of modern warfare and the possibility of widespread destruction, he considers it in the context of proportionality.

In O'Brien *jus in bello* proportionality plays a central role in determining legitimate military necessity, the principle which, he maintains, embraces all the elements of just war and international law *jus in bello*. O'Brien defines the principle of proportionality as a principle of humanity and as a principle of natural law, while the principle of discrimination is a subordinate principle of the principle of humanity.[42] His dissatisfaction with Ramsey's *jus ad bellum* had come because the principle of proportionality is "meaningless without a referent in the category of ends"[43]; that is, Ramsey never adequately addresses the reasons for which a nation may justly engage in war. One such end is state sovereignty; another might be the fostering of the bondedness of peoples. Thus, O'Brien could justify undertaking a war of self-defense or defense of an unjustly attacked weaker nation. He could conceivably justify such wars because a hostile opponent actually threatens to break these bonds. The stronger nation might then be called on to fight to defend the bondedness of peoples.

State sovereignty challenges the obligation to foster the bondedness of peoples. Often it is an end O'Brien calls "the most serious obstacle to a truly effective law of nations,"[44] yet he disagrees with McDougal and Feliciano, who tend "to judge all issues of proportionality... in terms not only of the ultimate *raison d'état* of belligerents but in transcendent perspectives that could be called '*raison du monde*.'"[45] O'Brien exhibits a more "cosmopolitan" view than either Ramsey or Walzer. It is clear that while state sovereignty and territorial integrity are values for O'Brien, they may be sacrificed when higher values are at risk. This is not true according to Walzer's view of "statism."

O'Brien, while denying *raison du monde*, affirms the concept of an international society and the mutual dependence among states. He may be stating what *is* or can be expected as opposed to what he believes *ought to be*. While individuals are members of a state, they share membership in the human race, and therefore, share a common destiny. In our time, however, O'Brien believes the best that can be hoped for is a "less-than global community outside the areas of Communist control." Even so he would prohibit a nation's acting from merely *national* military necessity, or even the necessities of an alliance if disproportionate injuries threatened the higher good of international society.[46] O'Brien thus acknowledges the hidden principle that ought to be recognized as the ultimate limiting *jus in bello* principle in his theory. As in his *jus ad bellum* doctrine, recognition of the value of the bondedness of peoples would force national decision-makers to give greater weight to the legitimate interests of all other peoples than would be the case if O'Brien's interdependence of peoples were the deciding norm. The concept of interdependence without the more inclusive emphasis the bondedness of peoples introduces, places greater value on "nation-blocs" and on the mutual interests of the nation-states that composed such political, economic and/or military alliances. The more inclusive bondedness of peoples forces nations to give more weight to the interests of the non-allied nations and to the opposing nation-blocs in terms of duties to, with, and for all peoples while considering the duty to look out for their own long-term self-interest as well. Practically speaking, this broader view may result in greater economic involvement in less developed countries than is presently considered advantageous, with a view toward assisting those countries in their development rather than in achieving shorter term benefits for the more advantaged nations. O'Brien himself seems to recognize the obligations that follow upon the responsibility to, with and for other peoples. A more clear articulation of the principle of the bondedness of peoples would give greater support and impetus to nations to realize further this ideal.

Michael Walzer

Walzer strives to avoid relying on proportionality in his *jus in bello* doctrine. He comes closer to Ramsey's absolutist position on noncombatant immunity than does O'Brien. However, Walzer finds Ramsey's absolutist stance, as we have seen, "hard to take [and] not for most people a plausible moral doctrine." Instead, Walzer treats concombatant immunity more as a *prima facie* duty to protect noncombatants--one which may be overridden under certain circumstances. Like Ramsey, Walzer uses the principle of double effect as "a way of reconciling the absolute prohibition against attacking noncombatants with the legitimate conduct of military activity."[47] He argues, however, that this reconciliation has traditionally come too easily and he amends the third condition of double effect to include a "due care" clause; i.e., "aware of the evil involved [the actor] seeks to minimize it, accepting costs to himself."[48] Walzer does not, however, spell out exactly what is entailed by "minimizing" the evil nor how much "cost" is required; and although his amended version is probably of doubtful value in determining *particular* tactical decisions, political and military leaders will reduce the levels of destruction and death in war if they reflect on the implications of Walzer's amended version.

Walzer "succeeds" to some extent in providing moral guidelines for military and political decision-making; he also "fails" to achieve a consistent just war theory. Walzer's ultimate theoretical "failure" has been attributed to his willingness to abandon his highest values in conditions of supreme emergency. Even his "due care" clause explodes here along with every other principle he has stuggled to uphold. Yet even in Walzer's supreme emergency one can find the shadow of the principle of the bondedness of peoples. This principle hinges upon Walzer's reference to the principle of civilization. He considers the violation of noncombatant immunity a violation of the principle of civilization, a principle very close to the "bondedness of peoples." "Civilization," for Walzer, encompasses the conditions under which individuals exercise their rights to life and liberty in a shared life with others in political community.[49] In Walzer, civilization is valued for the sake of the individual person. Yet, Walzer can say, "But the social union is something more than a pact for the preservation of life; it is also a way of living together and (inevitably) of *living with other peoples and other unions*, and there is comething here that needs to be preserved as well"[50] [emphasis added].

In Walzer, then, the right to individual life is a value that must be preserved, but, at the same time, it may be sacrificed if the right to liberty and the right to live in a civilized society is at risk. In recognizing the value of civilization, however, Walzer remains consistent in attributing the highest value to the individual human person, for this is the reason civilization itself is a value: it provides the environment and the conditions that sustain the individual.

Walzer's "something to be preserved as well" may well be the value of the bondedness of peoples. One might conclude that this value is radically present in Walzer, for his concept of the individual as possessor of rights is linked to the concept of the social contract, a kind of "bonding" among people: a community of "the living, the dead, and those who are yet to be born."[51] It must be remembered, however, that Walzer's community is a community of *nations*, not of *humanity*[52] and so the bondedness of peoples does not play a part in his *jus in bello* limits to war. If it did, Walzer's theory as a whole would be made more consistent, and his conclusions necessarily different.

Walzer states that he has not discovered where individual rights are founded; they are "somehow... entailed by 'human being,'" and human beings are bonded together horizontally, not vertically as governments are bonded to people. Such a horizontal notion of bonding would support a more comprehensive view of community than the bonding Walzer subscribes to in a given political grouping or state. Yet Walzer limits himself to the political community as an ultimate underlying value to be protected; and he insists that bondedness within single political communities or states is the most we can hope for "for a long time." Shared history, communal sentiment and accepted conventions are, for Walzer, indispensable for such bonding to take place and these he finds "hardly conceivable on a global scale."[53] He claims that political communities have not been nor should be transcended, as others like Charles Beitz have advocated. Thus, Walzer's is a decidedly "anti-cosmopolitan" view.

Doppelt's criticism of Walzer is applicable here. Ultimately Walzer places the rights of *de facto* states above those of individuals.[54] The possibility exists for the tyrannical state to possess legal authority over the individual whose rights are denied, although individuals' rights are the foundation of Walzer's moral theory. Ought not the rights of tyrannical governments be limited by the even broader human community in order to preserve individual rights? It is the bondedness among *all* peoples that underlies the right of the state to exist. People united in their particular communities must act collectively to satisfy their own needs and then must rely on other communities to provide what they lack. The bondedness of peoples also allows proportionate intervention against the state that promotes terror and deprives its people of the goods and conditions necessary to support their pursuit of happiness. The terrorist state must surrender its "right" to exist when its people are prevented from sharing the resources that they need from other peoples in order to flourish as human beings. "[Walzer's] theory is not grounded on any consensus among the disparate peoples, classes, or political groups of the world. Therefore, it amounts to a statism without foundations, a statism that cannot even ground the exceptions to statism it would like to allow."[55]

It is this very weakness, however, that moves one from *jus in bello* boundaries to the open space. Even as Walzer claims that the peoples of the world lack a common history and culture necessary to bond them into one human community, the work to create a global community is already underway, though it must be granted that it is in its very beginning stages. It is the work that must continue if the desired goal of genuine peace is to be achieved. Wars continue to separate, but the building of ties continue to occur through other means: cultural exchanges, satellite transmissions of international athletic and cultural events, global travel, international business negotiations all transcend a single nation's interests. What Walzer does is to alert us to the space where dialogue must occur about how to effect a global culture, a culture that supports and takes delight in *diverse* cultures. The creation of this culture has already begun. As it continues to take hold, "supreme emergency" will consist in the imminent threat not to the survival of a single nation but to the survival and flourishing of the human community. As the peoples of the world gain an increasing share in determining the limits of states' power over individual rights to life and liberty, military intervention will remain morally permissible. However, it will always need to be limited by a proportionality principle that includes the qualitative effects on the entire human community.

Walzer's alternative to Ramsey and O'Brien is summed up in his maxim, "Do justice unless the heavens are (really) about to fall." He concedes that this is a "utilitarianism of extremity," but he believes it is superior to the "sliding scale" basis for observing proportionality which he attributes to O'Brien.[56] The moral advantage of Walzer's position over the sliding scale argument is that it is not so likely to erode the war convention bit by bit. The war convention does not reveal a *range* of actions over which the sliding scale moves, for Walzer, but it distinguishes one act from another, barring certain inadmissible acts. A sliding scale, Walzer maintains, acts more like a utilitarian ruler in a manner effectively contrary to the reason the rules were originally set up; namely, to limit the destructiveness of war. The individual's right to life and liberty remains standing even as it is being overridden at times of supreme emergency. Nevertheless, Walzer concludes that the person who overrides these rights must bear the guilt for such action--he ends by saying, "Yes--and no."

If Walzer had used McCormick's notion of "proportionate reason," as suggested in Chapter 3, and if he could accept the value of the bondedness of peoples, he would be obliged to respect the *ordo bonorum*, the order of goods or values. McCormick's third requirement of proportionate reason includes the obligation not to undermine the value in the long run in an effort to protect it here and now. So it would seem that in an effort to defend the nation-state, proportionate reason would require refraining from war when the human community is in danger of being severely devastated. Walzer has argued that national leaders must opt for collective survival and he has denied the likelihood or even the desirability of a global community. Yet he acknowledges a higher good: not the global *state*, but global *order*: "There is every reason to work for such [a universal] order. The difficulty is that we sometimes have no choice but to fight for it."[57]

"Order" is not "bonding," although bonding recognizes a certain order, for it involves respect for the proper relationship among persons. If it is the bondedness of peoples that is desired and not merely global order, then the desired end cannot be achieved by "fighting for it." Bonds may be forged among comrades in battle, but they are only forged with the "enemy" after the "enemy" is recognized as "friend," "ally," or "kin," as has been the post-World War II experience among the Western allies and the Axis powers. One wonders what the Western world would be like today without the cultural exchanges, cooperation in trade, the opportunities for travel between the former "Allies" and West Germany and Japan, for example. One wonders what the world will be like tomorrow without the wall that has separated Eastern Europe from the rest of the world for more than forty years.

A "New-Clearing" for Nuclear War and Nuclear Peace

What of the bondedness of peoples and the particular concern of contemporary just war theorists--the appearance of nuclear weapons in the twentieth century? If failing to give adequate attention to the bondedness of peoples is a weakness in the three theorists, it may be expected to affect thier recommendations on the *jus in bello* principles relevant to nuclear war and deterrence. I believe it does. Ultimately, Ramsey and O'Brien have to join Walzer in saying, "Yes--and no," to some degree. This is evident in the summary of their conclusions on the use of nuclear weapons in war-fighting and deterrence below.

Each of the deterrence policies has a weakness stemming from the theorists' position that threat implies a willingness to do. A major criticism is that these policies permit a CF declaratory policy which includes an inherent CV threat from escalation that would involve too many "collateral" noncombatant deaths while they oppose CV use as immoral. Ramsey permits a CF deterrent but relies too heavily on the "collateral" effects, the deaths and injuries to the very noncombatants he wishes to protect. Ramsey risks the possibility, many would say, the probablility, of escalation to countervalue warfare, which he acknowledges. Because he denies the possibility for a broader bonding of peoples than occurs in a single political community or alliance, Ramsey is able to risk the widespread destruction that would follow upon CV warfare.

Figure 1. On the Use of Nuclear Weapons.

	CF	CV	First Use	Retaliation	Recommended Policy
Ramsey	Yes	No	Yes*	Yes	"CF-plus avoidance"
O'Brien	Yes	No	No	Yes	"CF-just defense"
Walzer	No	No	No	No	
but	Yes*	Yes*	Yes*	Yes*	CF/CV permissible in Supreme Emergency

*with qualifications

*Ramsey's qualification of first use leaves open the moral possibility of first use defensively, with CF (the term he indicated he wished to change to "counter-combatant" in his last work)[58] tactical weapons, over one's own country. O'Brien had once included a qualification stemming from his allowance for "selective strategic CV" use in a nuclear war already underway. However, he has now abandoned this. Walzer gives no moral justification for use, yet concludes CV or CF targeting is permissible in supreme emergencies, thereby ending up with the "dirty hands" paradox.

Figure 2. Deterrence.

	Bluff	CF	CV	Recommended Policy
Ramsey	No	Yes	No*	"Graduated Deterrent"
O'Brien	No	Yes	No	"Deterrence/Just Defense"
Walzer	No	No	No	
but	Yes*	Yes*	Yes*	CF or CV in Supreme Emergency

*The "qualified no" of Ramsey to CV targeting refers only to declaratory policy, for Ramsey recognizes the "dual use" inherent in certain nuclear weapons: the enemy cannot be certain that the weapons will not be used in CV targeting and is therefore deterred by this "inherent threat." Walzer permits even the CV deterrent when conditions of supreme emergency are met.

If the necessity to be responsible *to*, *with*, and *for* the "aggressor" as well as the "defended" were recognized more clearly; i.e., if Ramsey recognized the value of the bondedness of peoples as a stronger just war limiting principle, he would have to say, "No," to first use because of the risk of escalation and the endangering of neighboring peoples. O'Brien's allowance for tactical use during war also presents the danger of the risk of escalation, especially in Europe where such tactical use of nuclear weapons is considered a possibility, and is subject to moral criticism because the stakes are so high. O'Brien also recognizes that the enemy, realizing that CV targeting is off-limits to the other side, may not be deterred by a CF deterrent, thereby increasing the risk of counterpopulation attack.[59] On the other hand, O'Brien himself points out that a *moral* threat may be more credible to the enemy if it doubts that the other side would actually act on an immoral threat. Actual war-fighting conditions make escalation all the more likely, however, because of the emotional, mental, and physical strain under which political and military decision-makers are working. The "deterrent/just defense" position, therefore, also threatens the principles of civilization and humanity, O'Brien's highest values. O'Brien's decision to move back from allowing selective CV attacks is an indication that he does acknowledge the still insufficiently articulated principle of the bondedness of peoples. O'Brien's recommended policy on use comes closest to what the bondedness of peoples might require at the present time. Walzer receives the most criticism of the three because his conditions of supreme emergency make it impossible for him to guarantee the saving of any values in conditions of supreme emergency, as he realizes.

The three American theorists struggle with the framework of their just war positions because the threat to the values they try to protect keeps challenging the limits they set. The value that clamors for attention today seems to me to be the value that I have called the bondedness of peoples. Those working within the just war tradition must pay attention to the limiting conditions of warfare; however, they must not remain at the boundaries. They must, at the same time, listen closely to the value they are trying to preserve and point out the implications recognition of this value has for public policy. They will then need to adjust their just war frameworks to be more responsive to the demands the value makes. Some of these demands will involve national self-examination and a stronger critique of economic policy as well as of military policy as Shue suggested; nations must look to their contribution to the underlying unjust conditions that spawn war as well as to the conditions they must maintain while fighting it.

So it seems that the three American just war theorists have opened a "new clearing," or a new forum, for the just war tradition. They have succeeded and they have failed. Their arguments are not strong enough to escape the horns of the nuclear dilemma--the risks are too great and the stakes are too high to accept the morality of all their conclusions. They have succeeded, however, in highlighting the tension of the nuclear age: the nation's duty to defend its people or to defend an unjustly attacked weaker nation vs. the nation's duty to be responsible for, with and to other nations to establish and to foster conditions that enhance human flourishing throughout the world. Just war conclusions demand, at this time in history and under present conditions, a period of "nuclear peace," if we may call "nuclear deterrence" that. While it is a peace of questionable duration (a weapon once developed is seldom a weapon never used), it offers time to move into the forum, away from the *jus ad bellum* and *jus in bello* boundaries, to consider the issues and values that are the best hope for rendering the nuclear dilemma moot. There are indications in the theories we have been considering that those at work within the just war tradition are actually engaged in the process of un-covering an aspect of the global reality that has been only dimly visible for several centuries. William O'Brien speaks as a true realist when he states that "[the international system] is only about five centuries old and it will probably change."[60] The change advocated in this chapter is not necessarily a change in governmental structure, but a change in the way people think about their responsibilities to, with and for one another. That change can bring about a "recognition," or a perception of "kinship," the likeness that comes from a "corrected way of looking." Ramsey is quite correct when he says that the peace of the City of God will never be the peace of the City of Man. And he does uncover a significant truth: that the state needs to look at itself more critically than it has ever had to do before. "The argument that, since the state is a necessary condition, the safety of the state *functions* as the supreme value *even if it is not* can no longer serve when that will likely *contradict* all the values it conditions."[61]

Ramsey is undoubtedly correct as well when he says that "nuclear death" is not really part of "the last things" of Christian eschatology.[62] I find this truth far from reassuring, however, and cannot be satisfied with restricting the just war debate to the limiting conditions of war and peace; i.e., with remaining at the edge of the "new clearing." There in that open space lies the principle glimpsed early on in the just war tradition but covered over through the centuries only to emerge again in our own time. While the principle of the bondedness of peoples has always been valid, its application to policy has never been so necessary.

The just war tradition, then, does remain relevant and applicable in an age of nuclear weapons: how the philosophical questions it raises are resolved does make a difference in how public policy should proceed. The three American perspectives have contributed to a clearer understanding of the issues involved in the nuclear debate. Indeed, one might expect that Americans will continue to contribute much more to the uncovering of the important principle and value of the bondedness of peoples because America is a "nation of nations" and a "people of peoples." Therefore, they might be expected to be sensitive to the demands the bondedness of peoples makes. It would seem that Americans, particularly, ought to be able to find kinship in the faces of people of every race, nationality and creed.

The just war tradition continues to challenge men and women to take new perspectives and to take the "long view" of national self-interest. Challenge does not guarantee achievement, but responding to the challenge to leave the edges and to enter into the forum of dialogue about the values that continue to inform and transform *jus ad bellum* and *jus in bello* principles, is the most realistic means of achieving *eirene*, translated "linkage"--genuine peace.

Endnotes

Notes for Chapter 1

1. Raymond Aron, *Peace and War: A Theory of International Relations* (New York: Doubleday, 1966), 1.
2. Francis X. Winters, S.J., "Ethics, Diplomacy, and Defense," in *Ethics and Nuclear Strategy?*, ed. Harold P. Ford and Francis X. Winters, S.J. (Maryknoll, N.Y.: Orbis Books, 1977), 15.
3. Raymond Aron, *Peace and War*, 16.
4. James T. Johnson, *Can Modern Wars Be Just* (New York: Yale University Press, 1984), 95.
5. See the list Ford gives in John C. Ford, S.J., "The Morality of Obliteration Bombing," *Theological Studies* 5 (September 1944):284.
6. Pierce S. Corden, "Ethics and Deterrence. Moving Beyond the Just War Tradition," in *Ethics and Nuclear Strategy*, ed. Harold P. Ford and Francis X. Winters, S.J. (Maryknoll, N.Y.: Orbis Books, 1977), 156-57.
7. Stockholm Peace Research Institute, *Nuclear Radiation in Warfare* (London: Taylor and Francis, Ltd., 1981), 1.
8. The Joint Commission on Peace, *To Make Peace* (Cincinnati: Forward Movement Publications, 1982), 17.
9. Stockholm Peace Research Institute, *Nuclear Radiation in Warfare*, 19.
10. Desmond Ball, "U.S. Strategic Forces: How Would They Be Used?" *International Security* 7 (Winter 1982-83):34.
11. Ibid., 31.
12. Stockholm Peace Research Institute, *Nuclear Radiation in Warfare*, 33.
13. Ibid., 32-37.
14. *Webster's Universities Dictionary*, rev. ed. (1941), s.v. "deter."
15. Francis X. Winters, "Ethics, Diplomacy, and Defense," 19.
16. James T. Johnson, *Just War Tradition and the Restraint of War: A Moral and Historical Inquiry* (Princeton: Princeton University Press, 1981), 9.
17. William V. O'Brien, *The Conduct of Just and Limited War* (New York: Praeger, 1981), 23-24.
18. James T. Johnson, "Toward Reconstructing the *Jus ad Bellum*," *The Monist* (October 1973):461.

19. William V. O'Brien, "The Failure of Deterrence and the Conduct of War," in *The Nuclear Dilemma and the Just War Tradition*, ed. William V. O'Brien and John Langan, S.J. (Lexington, Mass.: D.C. Heath and Co., Lexington Books, 1986), 153-97.

20. Stanley Hauerwas, "Epilogue: A Pacifist Response to the Bishops," in *Speak Up for Just War or Pacifism*, by Paul Ramsey (University Park: The Pennsylvania State University Press, 1988), 154 (hereafter cited as "Epilogue"). Hauerwas cites John Howard Yoder, *Nevertheless* (Scottdale, Pa: Herald Press, 1971).

21. Louis J. Swift, *The Early Fathers on War and Military Service* (Wilmington, Del.: M. Glazier, 1983), 149-57.

22. Roland H. Bainton, *Christian Attitudes toward War and Peace: A Historical Survey and Critical Re-evaluation* (Nashville: Abingdon Press, 1960), 253.

22. Ibid., 88. Bainton cites *Theodosiani Libri* XVI, XVI, 10, 21, 7 December, 416.

23. Ibid., 120.

24. L. Bruce van Voorst, "The Churches and Nuclear Deterrence," *Foreign Affairs* 61 (Spring 1983):839-40.

25. Ibid., 840.

26. Ibid.

27. Stanley Hauerwas, "Epilogue," 154-59.

28. National Conference of Catholic Bishops, *The Challenge of Peace: God's Promise and Our Response*. Washington, D.C.: United States Catholic Conference, 1983), par. 74.

29. James T. Johnson, *Ideology, Reason, and the Limitation of War: Religious and Secular Concepts 1200-1740* (Princeton: Princeton University Press, 1975), 266.

30. Roland Bainton, *Christian Attitudes toward War and Peace*, 44.

31. Ibid., 143-51.

32. LeRoy Walters, "The Just War and the Crusade: Antithesis or Analogies?" *The Monist* 57 (October 1973):589 and 591.

33. See Thomas Aquinas, *Summa Theologica*, II-II, 40.

34. James Johnston, *Ideology, Reason, and the Limitation of War*, 12.

35. Ibid., 22.

36. Ibid., 18. See note 7.

37. Donald L. Davidson, *Nuclear Weapons and the American Churches: Ethical Positions on Modern Warfare* (Boulder: Westview Press, 1983), 167-77. L. Bruce van Voorst, "The Churches and Nuclear Deterrence," 843.

38. L. Bruce Van Voorst, "The Churches and Nuclear Deterrence," 845.

39. Donald Davidson, *Nuclear Weapons and the American Churches*, 142.

40. John C. Ford, S.J., "The Morality of Obliteration Bombing," *Theological Studies* 5 (September 1944):261-309.

41. Paul Ramsey, *War and the Christian Conscience: How Shall Modern War be Conducted Justly?* (Durham, N.C.: Duke University Press, 1961), 147 (hereafter cited as WCC).

42. Ibid., 141-42.

43. Ibid., 156.

44. Ibid., 142. Ramsey cites John Courtney Murray, S.J., "Remarks on the Moral Problem of War," *Theological Studies* 20 (March 1959):54.

45. Stanley Hauerwas, "Epilogue," 150.

46. The Commission of the Churches on International Affairs, "Documents of the World Council of Churches," in *Peace and Disarmament: Documents of the World Council of Churches on International Affairs and the Roman Catholic Church presented by the Pontifical Commission "Justitia et Pax," 1982* (Geneva and Vatican City, 1982), 1.

47. Ibid., 1-13. See especially the citation from the Report of the Public Hearing on Nuclear Weapons and Disarmament.

48. L. Bruce van Voorst, "The Churches and Nuclear Deterrence," 842.

49. The Joint Commission on Peace, "To Make Peace," 23. The Commission quotes the *Statement of the Anglican Primates*, 1981.

50. Ibid., 3-4.

51. Ibid., 14 and 20.

52. L. Bruce van Voorst, "The Churches and Nuclear Deterrence," 840.

53. Paul Ramsey, WCC, 141.

54. L. Bruce van Voorst, "The Churches and Nuclear Deterrence," 842.

55. James T. Johnston, "Toward Reconstructing the *Jus ad Bellum*," 475-77. See note 26 on 477.

56. Ibid., 468.

57. J. Bryan Hehir, "The Teaching of the Church on War and Peace," *Catholic Standard and Times*, Special Supplement (Washington, D.C.), 3 June 1982, 2.

58. Francis X. Winters, "The Bow or the Cloud? American Bishops Challenge the Arms Race," *America* (18-25 July, 1982):28.

59. Francis X. Winters, "Nuclear Deterrence Morality: Atlantic Community Bishops in Tension," *Theological Studies* 43 (1982):431, 444.

60. Richard A. McCormick, S.J., "Notes on Moral Theology: 1983," *Theological Studies* 45 (March 1984):134-35.

61. The German bishops say the following:

By virtue of this decision we are choosing from among various evils the one which, as far as it is humanly possible to tell, *appears as the smallest* (par. 4.4) [emphasis added].

Out of Justice, Peace: The Church in the Service of Peace, joint pastoral letter of the West German bishops, English translation of the German bishops' pastoral, *Gerechtigkeit schafft Frieden*, prepared by Irish Messenger Publications, and *Winning the Peace*, joint pastoral letter of the French bishops, ed. James V. Schall, S.J. (San Francisco: Ignatius Press, 1984).

The French bishops' statement read as follows:
> Affronté à un choix entre deux neux quasiment imparables, la capitulation ou la contremenace... *on choisit le moindre* sans prétendre en faire un bien (par. 20) [emphasis added].

"Gagner La Paix: Document de la Conférence episcopale française," *La Documentation catholique* 21 (4 décembre 1983):1093-1129.

The Irish bishops say:
> According to Catholic moral teaching, the possession of nuclear weapons is tolerable only to deter their use by others as the *lesser of two evils*, and only under certain conditions (sec. 5) [emphasis added].

The Storm That Threatens: Conference on War and Peace in the Nuclear Age Joint pastoral letter of the Irish bishops, *The Furrow* 34 (1983):589-95.

The Belgian bishops state:
> Elle est tout au plus "*un moindre mal*," une solution de détresse strictement provisoire, et à maintenir dans les limites les plus rigoureuses" (sec 4) [emphasis added].

Désarmer pour construire la paix: La déclaration des évêques de Belgique, *La libre belgique* (20-21 juillet, 1983:1-3).

62. "The Storm That Threatens," sec. 5.

63. Richard A. McCormick, S.J., "Notes on Moral Theology: 1983," 133.

64. Ibid., 128.

65. John Langan, S.J., "The Debate Identified," *The Washington Quarterly* (Autumn 1982):126.

66. Richard A. McCormick, S.J., "Notes on Moral Theology: 1983," 127. McCormick cites Charles Curran, "Analyse américaine de la lettre pastorale sur la guerre et la paix," Supplement to *Theological Studies* 147 (November 1983):569-92.

67. Kenneth Himes, O.F.M., "Deterrence and Disarmament: Ethical Evaluation and Pastoral Advice," *Cross Currents* 33 (Winter 1983-1984):427.

68. Richard A. McCormick, S.J., "Notes on Moral Theology," 136.

69. William V. O'Brien, "The Failure of Deterrence and the Conduct of War," 1-3.

70. Richard A. McCormick, S.J., "Notes on Moral Theology: 1983," 133.

71. William V. O'Brien, "The Failure of Deterrence and the Conduct of War," 1.

Notes for Chapter 2

1. LeRoy Brandt Walters, Jr., "Five Classic Just-War Theories: A Study in the Thought of Thomas Aquinas, Vitoria, Suarez, Gentili, and Grotius" (Ph.D. dissertation, Yale University, 1971), 4.

2. Thomas Aquinas, *Summa Theologica* II-II, 64, 7, and 5 (hereafter cited as ST).

3. LeRoy B. Walters, "Five Classic Just-War Theories," 118. Walters cites the following references from Aquinas: ST II-II. 105, 3 ad 3; 64, 6 ad 3. See also 159, notes 290 and 291 in Walters.

4. Ibid., 318-20. Cf. 320, n. 158. Walters cites Grotius, *De jure belli ac pacis libri tres* II, 24, 7, ed. Francis W. Kelsey, et al., Classics of International Law (Oxford: Clarendon Press, 1925), II, 24, 7 (hereafter cited as JBP). Walters also cites Francisco Suarez, *De bello* in *Selections from Three Works*, trans. Gladys L. Williams, Classics of International Law (2 vols; Oxford: Clarendon Press, 1944), IV, 10 (hereafter cited as DB).

5. Ibid., 318. Walters cites Grotius, JBP, II, 24, 5, 2-3.

6. Ibid., 364. Walters cites the following: Suarez, DB, VII, 6, 15-17; Grotius, JBP, II, 1, 2, title; III, 1, 4, 1; Francisco de Vitoria, *De Indis et de jure belli relectiones*, ed. Ernest Nys and trans. John Bawley Pate, Classics of International Law (Washington, D.C.: Carnegie Institution of Washington, 1917), *De jure belli*, 37, 35, 41, 42, 52 (hereafter cited as DJB); Alberico Gentili, *De jure belli libri tres*, trans. John C. Rolfe, Classics of International Law (2 vols; Oxford: Clarendon Press, 1933), III, 12, 2; II, 23.

7. James T. Johnson, *Ideology, Reason and the Limitations of War: Religious and Secular Concepts 1200-1740* (Princeton: Princeton University Press, 1975), 193-95.

8. LeRoy B. Walters, "Five Classic Just-War Theories," 367-68. Cf. n. 366; cf. n. 281. Walters cites Vitoria, DJB, 58, 33, 60. See also 367 and 368; cf. n. 282, 283 and 285. Walters cites Suarez, DB, VII, 7; I, 7. Walters also cites Gentili, DJB, II, 4 and Grotius, JBP, II, 11-16, title of each chapter.

9. Ibid., 368. Walters cites Suarez, DB, IV, 8-9; Vitoria, DJB, 37, 51, and 58; Grotius, JBP, III, 1, 4, 2.

10. Ibid., 369; cf. n. 290. Walters cites Grotius, JBP, III, 1, 4, 2.

11. Ibid., 370-71.

12. James T. Johnson, *Just-War Tradition and the Restraint of War: A Moral and Historical Inquiry* (Princeton: Princeton University Press, 1981), 277.

13. Ibid., 268.

14. John R. Connery, "The Teleology of Proportionate Reason," *Theological Studies* 44 (September 1983):495.

15. Ibid.

16. LeRoy B. Walters, "Five Classic Just-War Theories," 368.

17. Paul Ramsey, *War and the Christian Conscience: How Shall Modern War be Conducted Justly?* (Durham, N.C.: Duke University Press, 1961), 66 (hereafter cited as WCC).

18. Paul Ramsey, *The Just War: Force and Political Responsibility* (New York: Charles Scribner's Sons, 1968), 408, 430. Hereafter cites as JW. Also cf. Paul Ramsey, "A Political Ethics Context for Strategic Thinking," in *Strategic Thinking and Its Moral Implications*, ed. Morton A. Kaplan (Chicago, 1973), 132.

19. Paul Ramsey, JW, 429.

20. Ramsey, "A Political Ethics Context for Strategic Thinking," 132.

21. David Little, "The Structure of Justification in the Political Ethics of Paul Ramsey," in *Love and Society: Essays in the Ethics of Paul Ramsey*, ed. James Johnson and David Smith (Missoula, Mont.: Scholars Press, 1974), 139-62.

22. Paul Ramsey, "The Case of the Curious Exception," in *Norm and Context in Christian Ethics*, ed. Gene H. Outka and Paul Ramsey (New York: Charles Scribner's Sons, 1968), 75.

23. David Little, "The Structure of Justification," 145.

24. Paul Ramsey, *Basic Christian Ethics* (New York: Charles Scribner's Sons, 1950), 32 (hereafter cited as BCE).

25. Ibid., 1-17.

26. William I. Frankena, *Ethics* (Englewood Cliffs, N.J.: Prentice-Hall, 1973), 56.

27. Don Thomas O'Connor, "War in a Moral Perspective: A Critical Appraisal of the Views of Paul Ramsey" (Ph.D. dissertation, Claremont Graduate School, 1972), 266.

28. BCE, 46-91; Ramsey cites Augustine, *De Libero Arbitrio*, I, 5.

29. Charles Curran, "Paul Ramsey and Traditional Roman Catholic Natural Law Theory," in *Love and Society: Essays in the Ethics of Paul Ramsey*, ed. James Johnson and David Smith (Missoula, Mont.: Scholars Press, 1974), 57-59. For evidence of a rejection of universal norms, Curran cites Ramsey, "The Case of the Curious Exception," 120-35.

30. Paul Ramsey, *Deeds and Rules in Christian Ethics* (New York: Charles Scribner's and Sons, 1967), 108-9. (hereafter cited as DR).

31. Ibid., 121-25.

32. Little, "The Structure of Justification," 146.

33. See especially Ramsey's conclusions in "Incommensurability and Indeterminacy in Moral Choice," in *Doing Evil to Achieve Good*, ed. Richard A. McCormick and Paul Ramsey (Chicago: Loyola University Press, 1978), 69-144.

34. Little, "The Structure of Justification," 147.

35. Ibid; cf. Ramsey, DR, 108.

36. Little, "The Structure of Justification," 148.

37. Ramsey, JW, 12.

38. Ramsey, WCC, 59.

39. Ramsey, JW, 144-45.

40. Ibid., 190-91. Ramsey quotes Edvard Kardelj, *Socialism and War* (Beograd: Jugoslavia Publishing House, 1960), 89.

41. Paul Ramsey, JW, 191.

42. Little, "The Structure of Justification," 151; cf. Ramsey, JW, 11.

43. Ramsey, *Speak Up for Just War or Pacificism*, 56.

44. Richard A. McCormick, "A Commentary on Commentaries," in *Doing Evil to Achieve Good* (Chicago: Loyola University Press, 1978), 261.

45. Ramsey, "Incommensurability and Indeterminacy," 71.

46. Ibid.

47. Rawls describes lexical ordering as setting principles in order, ranking them from left to right and moving to the right only to break ties. John Rawls, *A Theory of Justice* (Cambridge: The Belknap Press of Harvard University, 1971), 42, note 23.

48. Ramsey, JW, 408, n. 6.

49. Ramsey, "A Political Ethical Context," 135.

50. William V. O'Brien, "Morality and War: The Contribution of Paul Ramsey," in *Love and Society: Essays in the Ethics of Paul Ramsey*, ed. James Johnson and David Smith (Missoula, Mont.: Scholars Press, 1974), 179; William V. O'Brien, "Legitimate Military Necessity in Nuclear War," in *World Polity, The Yearbook of the Institute of World Polity*, 2 (Washington, D.C.: Georgetown University/Utrecht-Antwerp: Spectrum Publishers, 1957), 55; William V. O'Brien, *The Conduct of Just and Limited War* (New York: Praeger, 1981), 41; hereafter cited as CJLW.

51. O'Brien, "Legitimate Military Necessity in Nuclear War," 55.

52. William V. O'Brien, "The Meaning of 'Military Necessity' in International Law," in *World Polity, The Yearbook of the Institute of World Polity*, 1 (Washington, D.C.: Georgetown University/Utrecht-Antwerp: Spectrum Publishers, 1957), 148; cf. also O'Brien, CJLW, 41 on "reasonable commander."

53. O'Brien, "Legitimate Military Necessity in Nuclear War," 71.

54. O'Brien is reflecting the interpretation of necessity as "economy of force," as given in Myers McDougal and Florentino Feliciano, *Law and Minimum World Political Order* (New Haven: Yale University Press, 1961), 243: "It [the principle of economy of force] prescribes that in the use of armed force as an instrument of national policy no greater force should be employed than is necessary to achieve the objectives toward which it is directed; or, stated in another way, the dimensions of military force should be proportioned to the value of the objectives at stake."

55. William V. O'Brien, *War and/or Survival* (Garden City, N.Y.: Doubleday, 1969), 238.

56. O'Brien, CJLW, 320.

57. O'Brien, "The Meaning of Military Necessity," 121.

58. Ibid., 128.

59. Ibid.

60. William V. O'Brien, "Nuclear Warfare and the Law of Nations," in *The State of the Question: Morality and Modern Warfare*, ed. William J. Nagle (Baltimore: Helicon Press, 1960), 143.

61. O'Brien, "The Meaning of Military Necessity," 138.

62. Ibid., 142.

63. O'Brien, "Legitimate Necessity in Nuclear War," 68.

64. Ibid., 40.

65. O'Brien, CJLW, 65.

66. O'Brien, "Legitimate Military Necessity in Nuclear War," 59 and 60.

67. Ibid.

68. Ibid., 62.

69. Ibid., 101.

70. Ibid., 105.

71. Ibid., 107.

72. Judith A. Dwyer, S.S.J., "An Analysis of Nuclear Warfare in Light of the Traditional Just War Theory: An American Roman Catholic Perspective (1945-1981)" (Ph.D. dissertation, Catholic University of America, 1983), 353. Dwyer cites Germain Grisez and Joseph M. Boyle, *Life and Death with Liberty and Justice: A Contribution to the Euthanasia Debate* (Notre Dame, Ind.: Notre Dame Press, 1979), 399.

73. O'Brien, CJLW, 21-27.

74. Ibid., 39.

75. William V. O'Brien, "Just-War Doctrine in a Nuclear Context," *Theological Studies* 44 (June 1983): 201.

76. O'Brien, CJLW, 22.

77. O'Brien, "Legitimate Military Necessity in Nuclear War," 75.

78. Ibid., 39.

79. Ibid., 51.

80. O'Brien defines "tactical" and "strategic" means as follows: "Tactical means will normally be judged in terms of their proportionality to tactical [specific] military ends. ... Strategic means will normally be judged in terms of their proportionality to the political/military goals of war." CJLW, 40.

81. O'Brien, CJLW, 41.

82. O'Brien, "Legitimate Military Necessity in Nuclear War," 71.

83. Ramsey, WCC, 160; cf. n. 42.

84. O'Brien, CJLW, 38.

85. O'Brien, "Nuclear Warfare and the Law of Nations," 142.

86. O'Brien, "The Meaning of Military Necessity," 27.

87. Michael Walzer, *Just and Unjust Wars: A Moral Argument with Historical Illustrations* (New York: Basic Books, 1977), 44 (hereafter cited as JUW).

88. Ibid., 153.

89. Ibid., 130.

90. *Encyclopedia of Philosophy*, 1972 ed., s.v. "Rules," by Newton Garver.

91. Walzer, JUW, 129.

92. Ibid., 130.

93. Ibid., 120.

94. Michael Walzer, "Political Action: The Problem of Dirty Hands," *Philosophy & Public Affairs* 2 (Winter 1973): 169.

95. James Burrell Dixon, "A Critical Analysis of Michael Walzer's Just War Theory" (Ph.D. dissertation, University of Arizona, 1980), 169.

96. Walzer, JUW, 131.

97. Ibid., 133.

98. Ibid., xvi.

99. Stanley Hauerwas, review of *Just and Unjust Wars: A Moral Argument with Historical Illustrations*, by Michael Walzer. *Review of Politics* 41 (January 1979): 148.

100. Michael Walzer, "World War II: Why Was This War Different?" *Philosophy & Public Affairs* 1 (Fall 1971): 13.

101. Walzer, JUW, 54.

102. Michael Walzer, "The Moral Standing of States: A Response to Four Critics," *Philosophy & Public Affairs* 9 (Spring 1980): 224.

103. Walzer, JUW, 135.

104. Charles R. Beitz, review of *Just and Unjust Wars: A Moral Argument with Historical Illustrations*, by Michael Walzer. *International Organization* 33 (January 1979): 413.

105. Ibid., 227.

106. Ibid., 246.

107. Walzer, JUW, 320.

108. Ibid., 231.

109. Ibid., 325.

110. Ibid., 192.

111. Ibid. See 144-51 for Walzer's view on "Necessity$_1$."

112. Ibid., 144. Walzer cites M. Greenspan, *The Modern Law of Land Warfare* (Berkeley, 1959), 313-14.

113. Ibid. See 239-42 for "Necessity$_2$."

114. Ibid. See 251-66 for "Necessity$_3$." Walzer cites Angus Calder, *The Peoples' War 1939-1945* (New York, 1969), 491.

115. Ibid. See 264 for "Necessity$_4$."

116. James F. Childress, review of *Just and Unjust Wars*, by Michael Walzer. *Bulletin of the Atomic Scientists* 34 (October 1978): 45.

117. Walzer, JUW, 231-32.

118. Ibid., 254.

119. Ibid., 326.

Notes for Chapter 3

1. David Alan Rosenberg, "The Origins of Overkill: Nuclear Weapons and American Strategy, 1945-1960," *International Security* 7 (Spring 1983): 44. Rosenberg cites A.J. Goodpaster, Memorandum for Admiral Arthur W. Radford, Feb. 29, 1956, Joint Chiefs of Staff, January-April 1956, Folder 2. Subject Series, Defense Dept., Box 4, WHOSS, DDEL.

2. Carole A. Shifrin, "Army to Begin Flight Testing Tactical Missile System," *Aviation Week and Space Technology* 128 (18 April, 1988): 21.

3. Theresa M. Foley, "SDIO May Test Nuclear DEW Concept in Pop-Up Launch," *Aviation Week and Space Technology* 128 (16 May, 1988): 23.

4. Richard Shelley Hartigan, "Noncombatant Immunity: An Analysis of Its Philosophical and Historical Origins" (Ph.D. dissertation, Georgetown

University, 1964), 287. Hartigan cites Lester Nurick, "The Distinction between Combatants and Noncombatants in the Law of War," *The American Journal of International Law*, 39 (October 1945): 680-97 at 690.

5. Ibid., 295.

6. James T. Johnson, *Just War Tradition and the Restraint of War: A Moral and Historical Inquiry* (Princeton: Princeton University Press, 1981), 147.

7. James T. Johnson, *Ideology, Reason, and the Limitation of War: Religious and Secular Concepts 1200-1740* (Princeton: Princeton University Press, 1975), 8 (hereafter cited as IRLW).

8. James T. Johnson, *Just War Tradition*, 127. Johnson quotes *Corpus Juris Canonici*, Pars Secunda, *Decretalium*, Lib. 1, Tit. XXXIV (hereafter cited as CJC, *Decretalium*).

9. Ibid., 124.

10. Ibid., 131 and 132. Johnson quotes CJC, *Decretalium*, Quaest. VIII, Cans. IV, XIX.

11. Ibid., 122.

12. Frederick H. Russell, *The Just War in the Middle Ages*, 55 and 56. See also 86, note 1 on the "Decretalists" as well as 136 and 179.

13. Ibid., 300.

14. Ibid., 222 and 234.

15. James T. Johnson, *Just War Tradition*, 139.

16. Ibid., 137-39.

17. Ibid., 141. Johnson quotes Bonet, *The Buke of the Law of Armys or Buke of Battalia*. Trans. from the French *L'Arbre des battails*, vol. 1 of Gilbert the Haye's Prose Manuscript, ed. J.H. Stevenson (Edinburgh and London: William Blackwood and Sons, 1901), 237-39.

18. Ibid., 139.

19. Ibid., 143.

20. Augustine, *City of God* 1.21; cf. *Against Faustus* 22.70. Cited in Louis J. Swift, *The Early Fathers on War and Military Service* (Wilmington, Del.: M. Glazier, 1983), 129.

21. Paul Ramsey, *WCC*, 33.

22. Ibid., 96.

23. Frederick H. Russell, *The Just War in the Middle Ages*, 16 and 17. Russell cites Augustine, *Contra Faustum Manichaeum*, xxii, 74.

24. James T. Johnson, *Just War Tradition*, 145.

25. Richard Shelley Hartigan, "Noncombatant Immunity," 96.

26. Frederick H. Russell, *The Just War in the Middle Ages*, 19.

27. Thomas Aquinas, *Summa Theologia* II-II, 40 (hereafter cited as ST).

28. LeRoy Brandt Walters, Jr., "Five Classic Just-War Theories: A Study in the Thought of Thomas Aquinas, Vitoria, Suarez, Gentili, and Grotius." See 176, note 326. Walters cites Steven Runciman in *The Later Crusades*, ed. Wolff and Hazard, 578.

29. Frederick H. Russell, *The Just War in the Middle Ages*, 258 and 267.

30. LeRoy B. Walters, "Five Classic Just-War Theories," 172-76 and 188. See note 317 on 172-73.

31. Thomas Aquinas, ST II-II, 64, 6.2.

32. Frederick H. Russell, *The Just War in the Middle Ages*, 273-75. Russell cites Aquinas, ST II-II, 64, 6, and 7; 188, 3 and 1.

33. Richard Hartigan, "Noncombatant Immunity," 127. Hartigan cites Emile Chenon, "Saint Thomas D'Aquin et la guerre," in *L'Eglise et le droit de guerre* (Paris: Blond and Gay, 1920), 102.

34. Ibid., 151-58.

35. James T. Johnson, *Just War Tradition*, 143.

36. Richard Hartigan, "Noncombatant Immunity," 161.

37. Ibid., 226.

38. LeRoy B. Walters, "Five Classic Just-War Theories," 325. Walters cites *De Potestate civili*, 12 (Williams translation, lxxx-lxxxi).

39. Richard Shelley Hartigan, "Noncombatant Immunity," 240.

40. Ibid., 264. Hartigan cites Vitoria, JB, 13 (426-30), liv.

41. LeRoy B. Walters, "Five Classic Just-War Theories," 383 and 375. Walters cites Vitoria, DJB, 36 and 48.

42. Ibid., 327.

43. James T. Johnson, IRLW, 197. Johnson cites Vitoria, DJB, sec. 37.

44. Ibid. Johnson cites Suarez, *On War*, sect. VII, 15.

45. Richard Shelley Hartigan, "Noncombatant Immunity," 273. Hartigan cites DTVT, sec. VII, para. 10. Trans. 843 and *Decretals*, Bk. I, title xxxiv, chapter ii. See also 280-81. Hartigan cites DJB, sec. XX. Trans., 735 and 281; sec. x, trans. 736, and secs. xi and xii, trans. 737.

46. LeRoy B. Walters, "Five Classic Just-War Theories," 376-83. Walters cites DJB, II, 21 (261-66) and see note 337 on 383 re: capability of bearing arms; 376, Walters cites DJB, 1, 3, 22-4.

47. Ibid., 384. Walters cites Vitoria, DJB, 38; Suarez, DB, VII, 16. Gentili and Grotius did not address the problem, but probably would not agree with Vitoria and Suarez, Walters concludes. He cites Gentili, DJB, II, 2 (p. 260).

48. Ibid. Walters cites Vitoria, DI, III, 6; DJB, 32, 48, and 49; Grotius, JBP, III, 11, 3-5.

49. Ibid., 384. See note 339.

50. Augustine, *Questions on Heptateuch* 6.10. In Louis J. Swift, *The Early Fathers*, 111-38.

51. Richard S. Hartigan, "Noncombatant Immunity," 91.

52. Ibid., 135-36.

53. LeRoy B. Walters, "Five Classic Just-War Theories," 209. Walters cites ST II-II, 10, 8 obj. 1 and ad 1; 11, 3, obj. 3 and ad 3; 64, 2, obj. 1 and ad 1; 198, 1, obj. 5; 108, 3, obj. 1 and ad 1; SCG, III, 146.

54. Ibid., 198.

55. Ibid., 160. Walters cites ST, II-II, 64, 7, obj. 5.

56. Richard Hartigan, "Noncombatant Immunity," 99.

57. Joseph Mangan, S.J., "An Historical Analysis of the Principle of Double Effect," *Theological Studies* X (March 1949): 52.

58. Ibid., 56.

59. Richard Hartigan, "Noncombatant Immunity," 253.

60. LeRoy B. Walters, "Five Classic Just-War Theories," 386. Walters cites DJB, 37.

61. James T. Johnson, *Just War Tradition*, 201. Johnson cites Vitoria, DJB, sec. 37.

62. Richard Hartigan, "Noncombatant Immunity," 277.

63. LeRoy B. Walters, "Five Classic Just-War Theories," 366. Walters cites DB, VII, 17.

64. Ibid., 88. Walters cites DB, VII, 7.

65. Ibid., 387. Walters cites DB, VII, 16.

66. Ibid. Walters cites JBP, III, 12, 8, 4. (Walters' italics added.)

67. Richard Hartigan, "Noncombatant Immunity," 282.

68. LeRoy B. Walters, "Five Classic Just-War Theories," 365. Walters cites JBP, III, i, 2 title; III, 1, 4, 1.

69. Ibid. Walters cites JPr, VIII, 112 and VIII, 109.

70. Ibid., 370, 385. Walters cites JBP, III, 1, 4, 1 (Walters' italics). The basis of violating noncombatant immunity is indirect intention as evident in JBP II, 26, 6; IV, 1, 4, 1,; III, 11, 8; JPr, VIII, (p 10).

71. Ibid., 263. Walters cites Grotius, JBP, II, 26, 6; III, 1, 4, 1; III, 2, 6; III, 11, 8; JPr, VIII (p. 10).

72. Joseph Mangan, S.J., "An Historical Analysis," 44.

73. LeRoy B. Walters, "Five Classic Just-War Theories," 389. Walters cites Gentili, JBP, III, 11, 16, 1; III, 11, 17, title.

74. Ibid., 378.

75. Ibid., 373. Walters cites Grotius, JBP, 26, 6, 1 and 2.

76. Ibid., 388.

77. Ibid., 385.

78. Ibid., 384.

79. Geoffrey Best, *Humanity and Warfare* (New York: Columbia University Press, 1980), 76.

80. Ibid., 221. For a more complete treatment of "total war," see Best's chapter IV, 216-85.

81. Jeffrie G. Murphy, "The Killing of the Innocent," *The Monist* (October 1973): 527-50.

82. Paul Ramsey, JW, 429.

83. James T. Johnson, *Just War Tradition*, 196.

84. Paul Ramsey, "A Political Ethics Context for Strategic Thinking," 133 (hereafter cited as PEC).

85. Paul Ramsey, WCC, 144.

86. Ibid., 69. Ramsey cites John C. Ford, "The Morality of Obliteration Bombing," *Theological Studies* 5 (September 1944): 281-82.

87. Ibid., 144-45, note 18.

88. Ibid., 69-72.
89. Ibid., 143-44.
90. Paul Ramsey, JW, 145.
91. Ibid., 502, and PEC, 133.
92. Paul Ramsey, WCC, 503.
93. Paul Ramsey, PEC, 133.
94. Paul Ramsey, WCC, 64-65 and PEC, 134.
95. Paul Ramsey, JW, 144-45, 164. David Little, "The Structure of Justification in Paul Ramsey," in *Love and Society: Essays in the Ethics of Paul Ramsey*, ed. James Johnson and David Smith (Missoula, Mont.: Scholars Press, 1974), 154.
96. Paul Ramsey, "The Case of the Curious Exception," 102, and David Little, "The Structure of Justification," 154.
97. James T. Johnson, *Just War Tradition*, 206, and BCE, 172.
98. Paul Ramsey, *Deeds and Rules*, 113.
99. Paul Ramsey, WCC, 39.
100. Ibid., 40. Ramsey cites ST II-II, 64, art. 7.
101. Ibid., 46-48.
102. Ibid., 57.
103. Paul Ramsey, WCC, 94.
104. Such would be the case where the fetus was developing in a *cancerous* uterus, for example. In this instance, the argument is made that the diseased organ may be removed for the sake of the whole, even though the operation will cause the death of the fetus as a secondary and "indirect" effect. Bouscaren also used this argument with tubal pregnancies in which the tube becomes impaired and becomes the proximate cause of danger to the mother's life. "The pathology of the tube becomes '*entitatively distinct* from the present and future growth of the child.'" (Paul Ramsey, WCC, 172. Ramsey cites Bouscaren, *Ethics of Ectopic Operations* (Milwaukee: Bruce Publishing Co., 2d ed., 1944), 151.) The operation can then be brought under the rule of double effect as an action done and intended directly to save the mother's life while a foreknown secondary effect is the death of the child.
105. Paul Ramsey, WCC, 178.
106. Ibid., 179.
107. Ibid., 185-88.
108. Paul Ramsey, PEC, 132.
109. Paul Ramsey, "The Case of the Curious Exception," 102.
110. Paul Ramsey, JW, 350.
111. Ibid., 349 and 351.
112. Paul Ramsey, "Farewell to Christian Realism," *America* 114 (1966): 619.
113. Paul Ramsey, JW, 351-53.
114. Ibid., 353.
115. Ibid., 355.

116. William V. O'Brien, "Legitimate Military Necessity in Nuclear War," 83 (hereafter cited as LMN), and CJLW, 43.

117. William V. O'Brien, LMN, 83.

118. William V. O'Brien, WS, 247.

119. William V. O'Brien, LMN, 83.

120. William V. O'Brien, "Nuclear Warfare and the Law of Nations," 135.

121. William V. O'Brien, CJLW, 55. O'Brien cites the U.S. Air Force Protocol 110-31, 5-6.

122. William V. O'Brien, CJLW, 46.

123. Ibid., 42.

124. William V. O'Brien, "The Failure of Deterrence," 170.

125. Ibid.

126. William V. O'Brien, "Just War in a Nuclear Context," 211.

127. Ibid.

128. Ibid., 210.

129. William V. O'Brien, "Nuclear Warfare and the Law of Nations," 135.

130. William V. O'Brien, CJLW, 45.

131. Ibid., 43.

132. Ibid., 65 and 43.

133. William V. O'Brien, WS, 248.

134. William V. O'Brien, "Morality and War," 167.

135. William V. O'Brien, LMN, 86.

136. William V. O'Brien, "The Meaning of Military Necessity," 171-74.

137. William V. O'Brien, CJLW, 44.

138. William V. O'Brien, WS, 25.

139. William V. O'Brien, "Morality and War," 168.

140. William V. O'Brien, LMN, 41.

141. Richard Hartigan, "Noncombatant Immunity," 341.

142. Thomas O'Connor, "War in a Moral Perspective: A Critical Appraisal of the Views of Paul Ramsey" (Ph.D. dissertation, Claremont Graduate School, 1972), 191.

143. William V. O'Brien, "Just War in a Nuclear Context," 211.

144. William V. O'Brien, LMN, 84.

145. William V. O'Brien, "The Meaning of Military Necessity," 138.

146. William V. O'Brien, CJLW, 312 (all underlined). O'Brien cites James R. McCarthy and George B. Allison, *Linebacker II: A View from the Rock*, ed. Robert E. Rayfield, USAF Southeast Asia Monograph Series, vol. 6, Monograph 8 (Maxwell AFB, Ala.: Air Power Research Institute, 1979), 46-47.

147. William V. O'Brien, CJLW, 146. This is affirmed, according to O'Brien, in U.S. Department of Air Force, *International Law--The Conduct of Armed Conflict and Air Operations*, 19 November 1976, AFP 110-31 (Washington, D.C.: Department of the Air Force, 1976) 5-6-14.

148. William V. O'Brien, "Just War in a Nuclear Context," 212.

149. William V. O'Brien, CJLW, 204. O'Brien cites Sir Charles Webster and Noble Frankland, *The Strategic Air Offensive against Germany, 1939-1945*, 4 vols. (London: Her Majesty's Stationery Office, 1961), 2:12.

150. Ibid., 304.

151. Ibid., 83-85.

152. Ibid., 86.

153. Ibid., 86-87.

154. Michael Walzer, JUW, 111.

155. Ibid., 138 and 151.

156. Ibid., 43.

157. Michael Walzer, "World War II: Why Was This War Different?", 12-13 (hereafter cited as WWII).

158. Ibid., 13.

159. Michael Walzer, JUW, 43.

160. Ibid., 143.

161. Michael Walzer, WWII, 12.

162. Michael Walzer, JUW, 146. See G.E.M. Anscombe, "War and Murder," in *Nuclear Weapons and Christian Conscience*, ed. Walter Stein (London, 1863); and John C. Ford, S.J. "The Morality of Obliteration Bombing," *Theological Studies* 5 (September 1944): 261-309.

163. Michael Walzer, WWII, 13.

164. Michael Walzer, JUW, 145.

165. Michael Walzer, WWII, 20.

166. Ibid., 12. Walzer quotes Gerald Vann, *Morality and War* (London, 1939), 50.

167. Ibid.

168. Michael Walzer, JUW, 151.

169. Ibid., 135.

170. Michael Walzer, WWII, 8.

171. Ibid., 21.

172. Ibid., 12.

173. James B. Dixon, "A Critical Analysis of Michael Walzer's Just War Theory," 49.

174. James T. Johnson, *Just War Tradition*, 223.

175. Michael Walzer, WWII, 12.

176. Ibid., 17-18.

177. Ibid., 13.

178. Ibid., 18.

179. Ibid., 19.

180. Michael Walzer, JUW, xvi.

181. Michael Walzer, WWII, 10.

182. Michael Walzer, JUW, 54.

183. Michael Walzer, *Obligations*, 21.

184. Michael Walzer, JUW, 156.

185. Ibid., 153.

186. Ibid.
187. Ibid.
188. Ibid., 155.
189. Michael Walzer, WWII, 11-12.
190. Michael Walzer, JUW, 253.
191. Ibid., 143-45. Walzer quotes from *Instructions for the Government of Armies of the U.S. in the Field*, General Order 100, April 1863 (Washington, D.C., 1898), Article 69.
192. Ibid., 168. Walzer quotes from W.E. Hall, *International Law*, 398.
193. Ibid., 174.
194. Ibid., 193.
195. Ibid., 254.
196. James F. Childress, review of *Just and Unjust Wars*, by Michael Walzer. *The Bulletin of Atomic Scientists* 34 (October 1978): 46.
197. Richard A. McCormick, "Ambiguity in Moral Choice," in *Doing Evil to Achieve Good*, ed. Richard A. McCormick and Paul Ramsey (Chicago: Loyola University Press, 1978), 46.
198. Ibid., 47.
199. Ibid., 29.
200. Ibid., 40.
201. Ibid., 45.

Notes for Chapter 4

1. David Alan Rosenberg distinguishes preventive war from preemptive war by saying that preventive war is "waged in the belief that war is inevitable, although not imminent, and that delay would be a disadvantage. Preemption occurs in the expectation of an imminent enemy attack." From David Alan Rosenberg, "A Smoking Radiating Ruin at the End of Two Hours," *International Security* 6 (Winter 1981-1982): 15.

2. Bruce Russett, ed., *Power and Community in World Politics* (San Francisco: W.H. Freeman, 1974), 242.

3. In the SALT II Treaty, ICBM launchers are defined for the purposes of the treaty as land-based launchers of ballistic missiles "capable of a range in excess of the shortest distance between the northeastern border of the continental part of the territory of the United States of America and the northwestern border of the continental part of the territory of the Union of Soviet Socialist Republics, that is, a range in excess of 5,500 kilometers." From "Treaty Between the United States of America and the Union of Soviet Socialist Republics on The Limitation of Strategic Offensive Arms," in United States Arms Control and Disarmament Agency, *Arms Control and Disarmament Agreements: Texts and Histories of Negotiations* (Washington, D.C.: U.S. Government Printing Office, 1982), Article II, 247 and 249.

4. Herman Kahn, "Thinking about Nuclear Morality," *The New York Times Magazine* (13 June 1982): 48.
5. Bernard Brodie, *War and Politics* (New York: Macmillan, 1973), 377. Brodie cites an earlier paper, "The Atomic Bomb and American Security, Memorandum No. 18," Yale Institute of International Studies, 1945. This is later included in expanded form in Bernard Brodie, ed., *The Absolute Weapon* (New York: Harcourt, Brace, 1946), 76.
6. Leon Wieseltier, "The Great Nuclear Debate," *New Republic* 188 (10-17 January 1983): 7.
7. Patrick M. Morgan, *Deterrence: A Conceptual Analysis* (Beverly Hills, Calif.: SAGE Publications, 1983), 20.
8. Ibid., 11.
9. Ibid., 29.
10. Ibid., 30.
11. Leon Wieseltier, "The Great Nuclear Debate," 12.
12. Ibid., 32.
13. William Kneale, "Natural Laws and Contrary-to-Fact Conditionals," in *Philosophical Problems of Causation*, ed. Tom L. Beauchamp (Encino and Belmont, Calif.: Dickenson Publ. Co., Inc., 1974), 46-49, at 47.
14. Carl G. Hempel, *Philosophy of Natural Science* (Englewood Cliffs, N.J.: Prentice-Hall, 1966).
15. Patrick Morgan, *Deterrence*, 25.
16. Bruce Russett, *Power and Community*, 202.
17. Ibid., 430.
18. See, for example, Germain Grisez, "The Moral Implications of a Nuclear Deterrent," *Center Journal* 2 (Winter 1982): 13.
19. See, for example, Leon Wieseltier, "The Great Nuclear Debate," 30: "In fact, deterrence does not require your enemy to believe that you will strike back; it requires only that he not believe that you will not. Deterrence does not, in other words, require certainty. Doubt is quite enough." See also Bernard Brodie, *War and Politics*, 404: "We do not need repeatedly to threaten that we will use them in case of attack.... Their being there is quite enough." See also David Hollenbach, S.J., *Nuclear Ethics: A Christian Moral Argument* (New York: Paulist Press, 1983), 69, where he cites Cardinal John Krol's testimony to the U.S. Senate that the *possession* of these weapons is compatible with an intention *not* to employ them.
20. Paul Ramsey held this view for a time but soon abandoned it. See Paul Ramsey, "Letters to the Editor," *Newsweek* (5 July 1982): 11.
21. David Hollenbach, *Nuclear Ethics*, 73.
22. Ibid.
23. Ibid.
24. Germain Grisez, "The Moral Implications of a Nuclear Deterrent," *Center Journal* 2 (Winter 1982): 13.
25. Paul Ramsey, WCC, 162.
26. Ibid., 163.

27. Ibid.
28. Paul Ramsey, JW, 253.
29. Paul Ramsey, WCC, 154.
30. Paul Ramsey, JW, 328.
31. Paul Ramsey, WCC, 154.
32. Ibid., 292-95.
33. Paul Ramsey, JW, 237.
34. Ibid., 235.
35. Ibid., 236.
36. Ibid., 246. Ramsey cites William O'Brien, "Nuclear War and the Law of Nations," in *Morality and Modern Warfare*, ed. William J. Nagle (Baltimore: Helicon Press, 1960), 140.
37. Ibid., 247.
38. Ibid., 214.
39. Ibid., 214-15.
40. Ibid., 215.
41. Ibid., 226.
42. Ibid. Ramsey cites *Limited Strategic War*, ed. Klaus Knorr and Thornton Read (New York: Frederick A. Praeger, 1962), 11.
43. Ibid., 234.
44. Ibid., 231.
45. Ibid., 248.
46. Ibid., 416.
47. Ibid., 215.
48. Ibid., 244-45.
49. Ibid., ix.
50. Paul Ramsey, WCC, 162.
51. Paul Ramsey, "A Political Ethics Context," 134-35.
52. Paul Ramsey, "The Case of the Curious Exception," 89.
53. Paul Ramsey, JW, 251.
54. Paul Ramsey, "Letters to the Editor," 11.
55. Philip Green, *Deadly Logic: The Theory of Nuclear Deterrence* (Columbus: Ohio State University Press, 1966), 167.
56. Paul Ramsey, "A Political Ethics," 131.
57. Ibid.
58. Ibid., 144, see note 44.
59. Paul Ramsey, JW, 259-78.
60. Ibid., 269. Ramsey cites from *On Escalation* (New York: Frederick N. Praeger, 1965).
61. Michael Walzer, JUW, 280.
62. Paul Ramsey, JW, 303. Ramsey refers to *Peace, the Churches and the Bomb*, in James Finn, ed., pamphlet issued by the Council on Religion and International Affairs, 1965.
63. Paul Ramsey, "A Political Ethics," 145.
64. Michael Walzer, JUW, 281.

65. Paul Ramsey, "A Political Ethics," 146.
66. Walter Stein, "The Limits of Nuclear War: Is a Just Deterrence Strategy Possible?" 73-84, in James Finn, ed. *Peace, the Churches and the Bomb.*
67. William V. O'Brien, "Aggression and National Self-Interest," in *Christian Ethics and Nuclear Warfare,* ed. Ulrich S. Allers and William V. O'Brien (Washington, D.C.: Institute of World Polity, 1961), 8-11.
68. William V. O'Brien, *The Conduct of Just and Limited War,* 40 (hereafter referred to as CJLW).
69. William V. O'Brien, "Legitimate Military Necessity," 75 (hereafter referred to as LMN).
70. CJLW, 135.
71. Ibid., 137.
72. LMN, 68-69.
73. William V. O'Brien, "Aggression and National Self-Interest," 1.
74. Ibid., 9.
75. Ibid., 11.
76. Ibid., 18-19.
77. William V. O'Brien, *War and/or Survival,* 258 (hereafter cited as WS).
78. William V. O'Brien, "Aggression and National Self-Interest," 19.
79. LMN, 103.
80. CJLW, 75-85.
81. WS, 128.
82. CJLW, 86.
83. William V. O'Brien, *Nuclear War, Deterrence and Morality,* 79 (hereafter referred to as NDM).
84. WS, 127.
85. NDM, 80.
86. William V. O'Brien, "Just-War Doctrine in a Nuclear Context," *Theological Studies* 44 (June 1983): 213.
87. WS, 129.
88. LMN, 110.
89. Ibid., 107-8; O'Brien cites Suarez, *De Legibus as de Deo Legislatore,* Lib. II, Cap. XIX, par. 9, as cited in John Eppstein, 265.
90. Ibid., 109.
91. Ibid., 115-16.
92. Ibid., 116-17.
93. WS, 127.
94. Ibid., 130.
95. Ibid., 129.
96. CJLW, 135.
97. William V. O'Brien, "Just War in a Nuclear Context," 212.
98. CJLW, 137.

99. William V. O'Brien, "The Future of the Nuclear Debate," in *The Nuclear Dilemma and the Just War Tradition*, ed. William V. O'Brien and John Langan, S.J. (Lexington, Mass.: D.C. Heath Co., Lexington Books, 1986), 236-37.

100. CJLW, 136.

101. William V. O'Brien, "The Future of the Nuclear Debate," 238.

102. William V. O'Brien, "The Peace Debate and American Catholics," *The Washington Quarterly* (Spring 1982): 140.

103. William V. O'Brien, "The Failure of Deterrence and the Conduct of War," in *The Nuclear Dilemma and the Just War Tradition*, 170.

104. Ibid., 171.

105. William V. O'Brien, "Just War in a Nuclear Context," 209. O'Brien lists CF weapons, including strategic nuclear weapons used against missile bases in the wilderness of Siberia, theater weapons against a heavy concentration of attacking enemy forces on the battlefield or an enemy airfield, and tactical weapons against advancing tank formations in open country.

106. NDM, 78.

107. CJLW, 134.

108. Ibid., 135.

109. Ibid., 136.

110. William V. O'Brien, "Just War in a Nuclear Context," 209.

111. CJLW, 340-41.

112. William V. O'Brien, "Just War in a Nuclear Context," 203-6.

113. William V. O'Brien, "A Just-War Deterrence/Defense Strategy," *Center Journal* 3 (Winter 1983): 19.

114. WS, 127, 110 and 129.

115. William V. O'Brien, "A Just-War Deterrence/Defense Strategy," 13 (hereafter referred to as JWDD).

116. Walter Stein, "The Limits of Nuclear War," 74.

117. CJLW, 127.

118. William V. O'Brien, "Relevant Knowledge and Moral Issues," in *Peace, the Churches and the Bomb*, 95-100, at 99.

119. CJLW, 128.

120. William V. O'Brien, "The Peace Debate and American Catholics," *The Washington Quarterly* (Spring 1982): 221.

121. WS, 111.

122. JDD, 11.

123. William V. O'Brien, "Just War in a Nuclear Context," 215.

124. Ibid., 109.

125. Ibid., 166.

126. Ibid., 109.

127. Ibid., 110. O'Brien refers to Raymond Aron, *The Century of Total War* (New York: Doubleday, 1954); Walter Lippman, *The Public Philosophy*

(Boston: Little, Brown, 1955); Major-General J.F.C. Fuller, *The Second World War* (New York: Duell, Stran and Pearce, 1949).
128. Ibid., 105.
129. William V. O'Brien, "Just War in a Nuclear Context," 214.
130. WS, 250.
131. William V. O'Brien, "Just War in a Nuclear Context," 216.
132. William V. O'Brien, "The Future of the Nuclear Debate," 236.
133. CJLW, 135.
134. William V. O'Brien, "The Future of the Nuclear Debate," 236-37.
135. CJLW, 141.
136. JDD, 23.
137. JDD, 25.
138. William V. O'Brien, "Just War in a Nuclear Context," 218-19.
139. William V. O'Brien, "The Future of the Nuclear Debate," 241.
140. LMN, 110.
141. JUW, 263-64.
142. JUW, 269.
143. JUW, 264.
144. JUW, 268.
145. JUW, 274.
146. JUW, see 275-78 for this discussion in Walzer.
147. JUW, 277.
148. Ibid.
149. JUW, see 274-83 for Walzer's treatment of deterrence.
150. JUW, 269.
151. JUW, 278.
152. James Burrell Dixon, "A Critical Analysis of Michael Walzer's Just War Theory," 172.
153. JUW, 272. Walzer refers to Paul Ramsey, "A Political Ethics," 134-35.
154. JUW, 281.
155. James Dixon, "A Critical Analysis," 167.
156. Dr. Robert J. Lifton, a psychiatrist and member of the "Physicians for Social Responsibility," has given evidence of psychological harm related to the threat of nuclear war in his talk, "Experiencing Nuclear Holocaust," International Student Pugwash Conference, 17 June 1981, Yale University, New Haven, Conn.
157. JUW, 59.
158. JUW, 273.
159. JUW, 289.
160. JUW, 283.
161. JUW, 326.
162. JUW, 85.

163. John Langan, S.J., review of *Just and Unjust Wars: A Moral Argument with Historical Illustrations*, *Theological Studies* 40 (September 1979): 566.
164. Herman Kahn, "Thinking about Nuclear Morality," 56.
165. Alan Donagan, *The Theory of Morality* (Chicago: University of Chicago Press, 1977), 180.
166. Ibid., 180-84.
167. Ibid., 181.
168. Ibid., 183.

Notes for Chapter 5

1. For a different point of view, see John Finnis, Joseph M. Boyle, Jr. and Germain Grisez, *Nuclear Deterrence, Morality and Realism* (Oxford: Clarendon Press, 1987), 143-57. These writers oppose all CV and CF strategies on the basis that even a pure CF nuclear strategy would fail to deter, and, even if effective, would involve an immoral intention. They place an absolute prohibition against killing the "innocent," understood in the technical sense of "noncombatant." For a fuller critique of their view, see Gerald J. Hughes, "Philosophical Debate on Nuclear Disarmament," *The Heythrop Journal* 29 (April 1988): 222-31.
2. See Plato's *Republic*, Book VII, for a fuller account of knowledge as "kinship", based on Plato's play on the words, *philo* and *sophia*.
3. Martin Heidegger, "Plato's Doctrine of Truth," in *Philosophy in the Twentieth Century: An Anthology*, vol. 3, ed. William Barrett and Henry D. Aiken (New York: Random House, 1962), 265.
4. Michael Walzer, *Interpretation and Social Criticism* (Cambridge, Mass.: Harvard University Press, 1987), 27.
5. Henry Shue, *Basic Rights, Subsistence, Affluence and U.S. Foreign Policy* (Princeton: Princeton University Press, 1980), 155.
6. Suarez, *De Legibus as de Deo Legislatore*, Lib. II, Cap. XIX, par. 9, as cited in John Eppstein, 265.
7. Frederick H. Russell, *The Just War in the Middle Ages* (London: Cambridge University Press, 1975), 291 and 272.
8. Leroy B. Walters, "Five Classic Just War Theories," 222.
9. Ibid., 366. Walters cites Vitoria, DJB, 134.
10. J. Bryan Hehir, "The Just-War Ethic and Catholic Theology: Dynamics of Change and Continuity," in *War in Peace*, ed. Thomas A. Shannon (Maryknoll, N.Y.: Orbis Books, 1980), 15-39, at 17.
11. William V. O'Brien, *War and/or Survival*, 126.
12. Michael Walzer, *Interpretation and Social Criticism* (Cambridge, Mass.: Harvard University Press, 1987), 30-32.

13. William V. O'Brien, "Morality and War: The Contribution of Paul Ramsey," in *Love and Society: Essays in the Ethics of Paul Ramsey*, ed. James Johnson and David Smith (Missoula, Mont.: Scholars Press, 1974), 180.

14. Paul Ramsey, with an epilogue by Stanley Hauerwas, *Speak Up for Just War or Pacificism: A Critique of the United Methodist Bishops' Pastoral Letter, "In Defense of Creation"* (University Park: Pennsylvania State University Press, 1988), 72.

15. Ibid., 73.

16. William V. O'Brien, "Morality and War," 164.

17. Thomas O'Connor, "War in a Moral Perspective: A Critical Appraisal of the Views of Paul Ramsey (Ph.D. dissertation, Claremont Graduate School, 1972), 225.

18. William V. O'Brien, "The Meaning of 'Military Necessity' in International Law," in *World Polity, The Yearbook of the Institute of World Polity*, vol. 1 (Washington, D.C., Georgetown University/Utrecht-Antwerp: Spectrum Publishers, 1957), 153.

19. William V. O'Brien, *War and/or Survival*, 220.

20. Henry Shue, *Basic Rights, Subsistence, Affluence, and U.S. Foreign Policy*, 155.

21. Michael Walzer, JUW, 193.

22. James T. Johnson, *Just War Tradition and the Restraint of War: A Moral and Historical Inquiry* (Princeton: Princeton University Press, 1981), 5.

23. James T. Johnson, "The Cruise Missile and the Neutron Bomb: Some Moral Reflections," *Worldview* 12 (December 1977): 25.

24. Paul Ramsey, JW, 408. See especially footnote 6.

25. Paul Ramsey, "A Political Ethics Context for Strategic Thinking," in *Strategic Thinking and Its Moral Implications*, ed. Morton A. Kaplan (Chicago: University of Chicago Center for Policy Study, 1973), 111.

26. Paul Ramsey, *Speak Up for Just War or Pacificism*, 48.

27. Ibid., 91.

28. Paul Ramsey, *Deeds and Rules in Christian Ethics* (New York: Charles Scribner's Sons, 1967), 126.

29. Paul Ramsey, JW, 15.

30. William V. O'Brien, CJLW, 35.

31. Ibid., 67.

32. William V. O'Brien, "The Meaning of 'Military Necessity,'" 172.

33. Ibid., 67.

34. William V. O'Brien, "Morality and War," 177.

35. William V. O'Brien, "The 'Meaning of Military Necessity,'" 109.

36. William V. O'Brien, "Morality and War," 179.

37. William V. O'Brien, "Legitimate Military Necessity in Nuclear War," in *World Polity, The Yearbook of the Institute of World Polity*, vol. 2 (Washington D.C., Georgetown University/Utrecht-Antwerp: Spectrum Publishers, 1960), 109.

38. Michael Walzer, JUW, 153.

39. Ibid., 155.

40. Michael Walzer, "World War II: Why Was This War Different?" *Philosophy and Public Affairs* (Fall 1971): 19.

41. Ibid., 10.

42. Michael Walzer, "The Moral Standing of States: A Response to Four Critics," *Philosophy and Public Affairs* (Spring 1980): 211.

43. Michael Walzer, JUW, 226.

44. Michael Walzer, "The Moral Standing of States," 228.

45. Gerald Doppelt, "Walzer's Theory of Morality in International Relations," *Philosophy and Public Affairs* (Fall 1978): 26.

46. Gerald Doppelt, "Statism without Foundations," *Philosophy and Public Affairs* (Summer 1980): 403.

47. Michael Walzer, JUW, 231.

48. Ibid., 327.

49. Paul Ramsey, *Speak Up for Just War or Pacifism*, 58.

50. William V. O'Brien, "The Future of Nuclear Debate," in *The Nuclear Dilemma and the Just War Tradition*, ed. William V. O'Brien and John Langan, S.J. (Lexington, Mass.: D.C. Heath and Co., Lexington Books, 1986), 236.

51. William V. O'Brien, *War and/or Survival*, 11.

52. Paul Ramsey, JW, 419.

53. Paul Ramsey, *Speak Up for Just War or Pacifism*, 29.

Selected Bibliography

Primary Sources

Books and Articles by William V. O'Brien

Books

O'Brien, William V. *The Conduct of Just and Limited War.* New York: Praeger, 1981.
____. *Nuclear War, Deterrence and Morality.* Westminster, Md.: Newman Press, 1967.
____. *War and/or Survival.* Garden City, N.Y.: Doubleday and Co., 1969.

Articles

____. "Aggression and National Self-Interest." In *Christian Ethics and Nuclear Warfare*, edited by Ulrich S. Allers and William V. O'Brien, 1-24. Washington, D.C.: Institute of World Polity, 1961.
____. "The Failure of Deterrence and the Conduct of War." In *The Nuclear Dilemma and The Just War Tradition*, edited by William V. O'Brien and John Langan, S.J., 153-97. Lexington, Mass.: D.C. Heath and Co., Lexington Books, 1986.
____. "The Future of the Nuclear Debate." In *The Nuclear Dilemma and the Just War Tradition*, edited by William V. O'Brien and John Langan, S.J., 223-48. Lexington, Mass.: D.C. Heath and Co., Lexington Books, 1986.
____. "A Just-War Deterrence/Defense Strategy." *Center Journal* 3 (Winter 1983): 9-29.
____. "Just-War Doctrine in a Nuclear Context." *Theological Studies* 44 (June 1983): 191-220.
____. "Legitimate Military Necessity in Nuclear War." In *World Polity, The Yearbook of the Institute of World Polity*. Vol. 2, 35-120. Washington, D.C., Georgetown University/Utrecht-Antwerp: Spectrum Publishers, 1960.
____. "The Meaning of 'Military Necessity' in International Law." In *World Polity, The Yearbook of the Institute of World Polity*, vol. 1, 109-76.

Washington, D.C., Georgetown University/Utrecht-Antwerp: Spectrum Publishers, 1957.

____. "Morality and War: The Contribution of Paul Ramsey." In *Love and Society: Essays in the Ethics of Paul Ramsey*, edited by David Smith and James T. Johnson, 163-67. Missoula, Mont.: Scholars Press, 1974.

____. "Nuclear Warfare and the Law of Nations." In *The State of the Question: Morality and Modern Warfare*, edited by William J. Nagle, 126-49. Baltimore: Helicon Press, 1960.

____. "The Peace Debate and American Catholics." *The Washington Quarterly* 5 (Spring 1982): 219-22.

____. "Relevant Knowledge and Moral Issues." In *Peace, The Churches and the Bomb*, 95-100. The Council for Religion and International Affairs, 1965.

____. "A Response." *The Washington Quarterly* 5 (Autumn 1982): 137-42.

Books and Articles by Paul Ramsey

Books

Ramsey, Paul. *Basic Christian Ethics*. New York: Charles Scribner's Sons, 1950.

____. *Deeds and Rules in Christian Ethics*. New York: Charles Scribner's Sons, 1967.

____. *Ethics at the Edges of Life*. New Haven: Yale University Press, 1978.

____. *The Just War: Force and Political Responsibility*. New York: Charles Scribner's Sons, 1968.

____. *Nine Modern Moralists*. Englewood Cliffs, N.J.: Prentice-Hall, 1962.

____. *Speak Up for Just War or Pacifism: A Critique of the United Methodist Bishops' Pastoral Letter "In Defense of Creation."* With an epilogue by Stanley Hauerwas. University Park: The Pennsylvania State University Press, 1988.

____. *War and the Christian Conscience: How Shall Modern War be Conducted Justly?* Durham: Duke University Press, 1961.

Articles

____. "The Case of the Curious Exception." In *Norm and Context in Christian Ethics*, edited by Gene H. Outka and Paul Ramsey, 67-135. New York: Charles Scribner's Sons, 1968.

____. "Farewell to Christian Realism." *America* 114 (1966): 618-22.

____. "Incommensurability and Indeterminacy in Moral Choice." In *Doing Evil to Achieve Good*, edited by Richard A. McCormick, S.J. and Paul Ramsey, 69-144. Chicago: Loyola University Press, 1978.

____. "Letter to the Editor." *Newsweek*, 5 July 1982: 11.
____. "Love and Law." In *Reinhold Niebuhr: His Religious, Social, and Political Thought*, edited by Charles W. Kegley and Robert W. Bretail, 80-123. New York: Macmillan and Co., 1961.
____. "A Political Ethics Context for Strategic Thinking." In *Strategic Thinking and Its Moral Implications*, edited by Morton A. Kaplan, 101-47. Chicago: University of Chicago Center for Policy Study, 1973.

Books and Articles by Michael Walzer

Books

Walzer, Michael. *Just and Unjust Wars: A Moral Argument with Historical Illustrations*. New York: Basic Books, 1977.
____. *Obligations: Essays on Disobedience, War and Citizenship*. Cambridge, Mass.: Harvard University Press, 1970.
____. *Interpretation and Social Criticism*. Cambridge, Mass.: Harvard University Press, 1987.

Articles

____. "The Moral Standing of States: A Response to Four Critics." *Philosophy & Public Affairs* 9 (Spring 1980): 209-29.
____. "Nuclear Deterrence and Democratic Politics." In *The Nuclear Dilemma and the Just War Tradition*, edited by William V. O'Brien and John Langan, S.J., 209-20. Lexington, Mass.: D.C. Heath and Co., Lexington Books, 1986.
____. "Political Action: The Problem of Dirty Hands." *Philosophy & Public Affairs* 2 (Winter 1973): 160-80.
____. "Response to Lackey." *Ethics* 92 (April 1982): 547-48.
____. "World War II: Why Was This War Different?" *Philosophy & Public Affairs* 1 (Fall 1971): 5-21.

Secondary Sources

Books

Anscombe, G.E.M. *The Collected Philosophical Papers of G.E.M. Anscombe*, vol. 3: *Ethics, Religion and Politics*. Minneapolis: University of Minnesota Press, 1981.
Aquinas, Thomas. *Summa Theologia*. Translated by Fathers of the English Dominican Province. London: Burns, Oates and Washbourne, Ltd., 1916.

Aron, Raymond. *Peace and War: A Theory of International Relations*. New York: Doubleday, 1966.

Bainton, Roland H. *Christian Attitudes toward War and Peace*. New York: Abingdon Press, 1960.

Bennet, John C. *The Radical Imperative*. Philadelphia: Westminster Press, 1975.

Best, Geoffrey. *Humanity in Warfare*. New York: Columbia University Press, 1980.

Brodie, Bernard. *War and Politics*. New York: The Macmillan Co., 1973.

Curran, Charles E. *Politics, Medicine, and Christian Ethics: A Dialogue with Paul Ramsey*. Philadelphia: Fortress Press, 1973.

Davidson, Donald L. *Nuclear Weapons and the American Churches: Ethical Positions on Modern Warfare*. Boulder, Colo.: Westview Press, 1983.

Donagan, Alan. *The Theory of Morality*. Chicago: University of Chicago Press, 1977.

Douglass, James. *Nonviolent Cross: A Theology of Revolution and Peace*. New York: Macmillan, 1966.

Finn, James, ed. *Peace, the Churches and the Bomb*. New York: The Council on Religious and International Affairs, 1965.

Finnis, John, Joseph M. Boyle, Jr., and Germain Grisez. *Nuclear Deterrence, Morality and Realism*. Oxford: Clarendon Press, 1987.

Ford, Harold P., and Francis X. Winters, S.J., eds. *Ethics and Nuclear Strategy*. New York: Orbis Books, 1977.

Frankena, William K. *Ethics*. Englewood Cliffs, N.J.: Prentice-Hall, 1973.

Gilligan, Carol. *In a Different Voice: Psychological Theory and Women's Development*. Cambridge, Mass.: Harvard University Press, 1982.

Green, Philip. *Deadly Logic: The Theory of Nuclear Deterrence*. Columbus: Ohio State University Press, 1966.

Hempel, Carl G. *Philosophy of Natural Science*. Englewood Cliffs, N.J.: Prentice-Hall, 1966.

Hoffmann, Stanley. *Duties beyond Borders: On the Limits and Possibilities of Ethical International Politics*. Syracuse: Syracuse University Press, 1981.

Hollenbach, David, S.J. *Nuclear Ethics: A Christian Moral Argument*. New York: Paulist Press, 1983.

Howard, Michael. *War and the Liberal Conscience*. New Brunswick, N.J.: Rutgers University Press, 1978.

Johnson, James T. *Ideology, Reason, and the Limitation of War: Religious and Secular Concepts 1200-1740*. Princeton: Princeton University Press, 1975.

____. *Just War Tradition and the Restraint of War: A Moral and Historical Inquiry*. Princeton: Princeton University Press, 1981.

____. *Can Modern War Be Just*. New Haven: Yale University Press, 1984.

Johnson, James T., and David Smith, eds. *Love and Society: Essays in the Ethics of Paul Ramsey*, 47-65. Missoula, Mont.: Scholars Press, 1974.

Kahn, Herman. *On Thermonuclear War*. Princeton: Princeton University Press, 1960.

_____. *Thinking about the Unthinkable.* 2d ed. New York: Avon Books, 1966.

Kant, Immanuel. *Foundations of the Metaphysics of Morals.* Translated and with an introduction by Lewis White Beck. Indianapolis: Bobbs-Merrill Co., 1939.

_____. *Perpetual Peace: A Philosophical Essay.* Translated with introduction and notes by M. Campbell Smith. New York: Garland Publishing, 1972.

Kaplan, Morton A., ed. *Strategic Thinking and Its Moral Significance.* Chicago: University of Chicago Center for Policy Study, 1973.

Morgan, Patrick M. *Deterrence: A Conceptual Analysis.* 2d ed. Beverly Hills, Calif.: SAGE Publications, Inc., 1983.

Murphy, Jeffrie G. *Retribution, Justice, and Therapy.* Dordrecht: D. Reidel Publishing Co., 1979.

Murray, John Courtney. *Morality and Modern War.* The Council on Religion and International Affairs, 1959.

Murray, Thomas E. *Nuclear Policy for War and Peace.* Cleveland and New York: The World Publishing Co., 1960.

Nagle, William J., ed. *Morality and Modern Warfare.* Baltimore: Helicon Press, 1960.

Niebuhr, Reinhold. *The Structure of Nations and Empires.* New York: Charles Scribner's Sons, 1959.

Osgood, Robert E., and Robert W Tucker. *Force, Order and Justice.* Baltimore: Johns Hopkins University Press, 1967.

Potter, Ralph B. *War and Moral Discourse.* Richmond, Va.: John Knox Press, 1969.

Rawls, John. *A Theory of Justice.* Cambridge: Belknap Press of Harvard University Press, 1971.

Russell, Frederick H. *The Just War in the Middle Ages.* London: Cambridge University Press, 1975.

Russett, Bruce, ed. *Power and Community in World Politics.* San Francisco: W.H. Freeman, 1974.

Shannon, Thomas A., ed. *War or Peace? The Search for New Answers.* Maryknoll, N.Y.: Orbis Books, 1982.

Shue, Henry. *Basic Rights: Subsistence, Affluence and U.S. Foreign Policy.* Princeton: Princeton University Press, 1980.

Stockholm Peace Research Institute. *Nuclear Radiation in Warfare.* London: Taylor and Francis, 1981.

Swift, Louis J. *The Early Fathers on War and Military Service.* Wilmington, Del.: M. Glazier, 1983.

Tucker, Robert W. *The Just War: A Study in Contemporary American Doctrine.* Baltimore: Johns Hopkins Press, 1960.

Von Clausewitz, Carl. *On War.* 3 vols. Translated by J.J. Graham. London: Routledge and Kegan Paul, 1962.

Wasserstrom, Richard, ed. *War and Morality.* Belmont, Calif.: Wadsworth Publishing Co., 1970.

Articles

Anscombe, G.E.M. "Modern Moral Philosophy." *Philosophy* 33 (January 1958): 1-19.

Augustine, Norman R. "Brilliant Missiles on the Horizon." *IEEE Spectrum* 19 (October 1982): 96-97.

Ball, Desmond. "U.S. Strategic Forces: How Would They Be ... Used?" *International Security* 7 (Winter 1982-1983): 31-60.

Beitz, Charles R. Review of *Just and Unjust Wars: A Moral Argument with Historical Ideas*, by Michael Walzer. *International Organization* 33 (Summer 1979): 405-24.

_____. "Nonintervention and Communal Integrity." *Philosophy & Public Affairs* 9 (Summer 1980): 385-91.

Bennet, John C. "Christian Realism in Vietnam." *America* 114 (1966): 616-17.

_____. "Niebuhr's Ethics: The Later Years." *Christianity and Crisis* 42 (12 April 1982): 91-95.

Bennet, Jonathan. "Whatever the Consequences." *Analysis* 26:3 (January 1966): 83-102.

Brandt, Richard. "Utilitarianism and the Rules of War." *Philosophy & Public Affairs* 2 (Winter 1971/1972): 145-65.

Brittain, Vera. "Massacre by Bombing." *Fellowship* 10 (March 1944): 50-63.

Brody, Baruch. "The Problem of Exceptions in Medical Ethics." In *Doing Evil to Achieve Good: Moral Choice in Conflict Situations*, edited by Richard A. McCormick, S.J. and Paul Ramsey, 54-68. Chicago: Loyola University Press, 1978.

Childress, James F. "Just-War Criteria." In *War or Peace? The Search for New Answers*, edited by Thomas A. Shannon, 40-58. Maryknoll, N.Y.: Orbis Books, 1980.

_____. Review of *Just and Unjust Wars*, by Michael Walzer. *The Bulletin of Atomic Scientists* 34 (October 1978): 44-48.

Connell, Francis J. "Is the H-Bomb Right or Wrong?" *The Sign* (March 1950): 11-13.

Connery, John R. "Morality of Nuclear Armament." *Theology Digest* 5 (Winter 1957): 9-12.

_____. "The Morality of Nuclear Warfare." *America* 14 (10-17 July, 1982): 25-28.

_____. "The Teleology of Proportionate Reason." *Theological Studies* 44 (September 1983): 489-96.

Curran, Charles. "Paul Ramsey and Traditional Roman Catholic Natural Law Theory." In *Love and Society: Essays in the Ethics of Paul Ramsey*, edited by James Johnson and David Smith, 47-65. Missoula, Mont.: Scholars Press, 1974.

Deats, Paul. "Protestant Social Ethics and Pacificism." In *War and Peace? The Search for New Answers*, edited by Thomas A. Shannon, 75-92. Maryknoll, N.Y.: Orbis Books, 1980.

Doppelt, Gerald, "Statism without Foundations." *Philosophy & Public Affairs* 9 (Summer 1980): 398-403.

———. "Walzer's Theory of Morality in International Relations." *Philosophy & Public Affairs* 8 (1): 3-26.

Encyclopedia of Philosophy, 1972 ed. S.v. "Rules," by Newton Garver.

Feinstein, Joseph. "Research Thrusts of the U.S. D.o.D." *IEEE Spectrum* 10 (October 1982): 91-93.

Foley, Theresa M. "SDIO May Test Nuclear DEW Concept in Pop-Up Launch." *Aviation Week and Space Technology* 128 (16 May 1988): 23.

Ford, John C. "The Hydrogen Bombing of Cities." *Theology Digest* (Winter 1957): 6-9.

———. "The Morality of Obliteration Bombing." *Theological Studies* 5 (September 1944): 261-309.

Frankena, William K. "McCormick and the Traditional Distinction." In *Doing Evil to Achieve Good*, edited by Richard A. McCormick and Paul Ramsey, 145-64. Chicago: Loyola University Press, 1978.

Gannon, Michael V. "The Question of Deterrence: All Our Eggs in One Basket?" *Catholic World* 185 (August 1957): 364-70.

Gilligan, Carol. *In a Different Voice: Psychological Theory and Women's Development*. Cambridge, Mass.: Harvard University Press, 1982.

Grisez, Germain. "The Moral Implications of a Nuclear Deterrent." *Center Journal* 2 (Winter 1982): 9-24.

Hare, R.M. "Rules of War and Moral Reasoning." *Philosophy & Public Affairs* 1 (1971-1972): 166-81.

Hauerwas, Stanley. Review of *Just and Unjust Wars: A Moral Argument with Historical Ideas*, by Michael Walzer. *Review of Politics* 41 (January 1979): 147-53.

Hehir, J. Bryan. "The Catholic Church and the Arms Race." *Worldview* 21 (July/August 1978): 13-18.

———. "The Just-War Ethic and Catholic Theology: Dynamics of Change and Continuity." In *War or Peace? The Search for New Answers*, edited by Thomas A. Shannon, 15-39. Maryknoll, N.Y.: Orbis Books, 1982.

———. "The Teaching of the Church on War and Peace." *Catholic Standard and Times*, Archdiocese of Washington, D.C., Special Supplement, 3 June 1982, n.p.

Heidegger, Martin. "Plato's Doctrine of Truth," In *Philosophy in the Twentieth Century: An Anthology*, vol. 3, 251-69. Translated by John Barlow. Edited and with an introduction by William Barrett and Henry D. Aiken. New York: Random House Publishers, 1962.

Hellwig, Monika K. "American Catholics and the Peace Debate." *The Washington Quarterly* 5 (Autumn 1982): 120-23.

Himes, Kenneth. "Deterrence and Disarmament: Ethical Evaluation and Pastoral Advice." *Cross Currents* 23 (Winter 1983-1984): 421-31.

Holmes, Robert L. "On Pacifism." *The Monist* 5 (October 1973): 489-507.

Hughes, Gerard J. "Notes and Comments: Philosophical Debate on Nuclear Disarmament." *The Heythrop Journal* 29 (April 1988): 222-31.

Johnson, James T. "The Cruise Missile and the Neutron Bomb: Some Moral Reflections." *Worldview* 22 (December 1977): 20-26.

____. "Ideology and the Jus ad Bellum." *Journal of the American Academy of Religion.* June 1973: 212-28.

____. "Just War, the Nixon Doctrine and the Future Shape of American Military Policy." *The Year Book of World Affairs 1975*: 139-54.

____. "Morality and Force in Statecraft: Paul Ramsey and the Just War Tradition." In *Love and Society: Essays in the Ethics of Paul Ramsey*, edited by James Johnson and David Smith, 93-112. Missoula, Mont.: Scholars Press, 1974.

____. "Reader's Response: Rationalizing the Hell of War." *Worldview* 1 (January 1974): 43-47.

____. "Toward Reconstructing the *Jus ad Bellum*." *The Monist* 57 (October 1973): 461-88.

____. "Two Issues in Contemporary Defense: A Just War Critique." (Typewritten.)

Johnson, James T., and Gordon Zahn. "Reader's Response: Rationalizing the Hell of War." *Worldview* 17 (January 1974): 43-47.

Kahn, Herman. "Thinking about Nuclear Morality," *New York Times Magazine* (13 June 1982): 42-50+.

Kneale, William. "Natural Laws and Contrary-to-Fact Conditionals." In *Philosophical Problems of Causation*, edited by Tom L. Beauchamp, 46-49. Encino and Belmont, Calif.: Dickenson Publishing Co., 1974.

Lackey, Douglas. "A Modern Theory of Just War: Review Essay." *Ethics* 92 (April 1982): 533-46.

Langan, John P. "The American Hierarchy and Nuclear Weapons." *Theological Studies* 43 (September 1982): 447-67.

____. "BUT IF NOT..." An address given at the Naval College, Newport, R.I., 23 May 1984. (Typewritten.)

____. Review of *Just and Unjust Wars: A Moral Argument with Historical Illustration*, by Michael Walzer. *Theological Studies* 40 (September 1979): 564-66.

____. "The Debate Identified." *The Washington Quarterly* 5 (Autumn 1982): 123-27.

Lawler, Justus George. "Moral Issues and Nuclear Pacifism." In *Peace, the Churches and the Bomb*, edited by James Finn, 85-94. A pamphlet issued by The Council on Religion and International Affairs, 1965.

Luban, David. "Just War and Human Rights." *Philosophy & Public Affairs* 9 (Winter 1980): 160-81.

____. "The Romance of the Nation-State." *Philosophy & Public Affairs* (Summer 1980): 392-97.

McCormick, Richard A., S.J. "A Commentary on the Commentaries." In *Doing Evil to Achieve Good*, edited by Richard A. McCormick, S.J. and Paul Ramsey, 193-267. Chicago: Loyola University Press, 1978.

____. "Ambiguity in Moral Choice." In *Doing Evil to Achieve Good*, edited by Richard A. McCormick, S.J. and Paul Ramsey, 7-53. Chicago: Loyola University Press, 1978.

____. "Notes on Moral Theology." *Theological Studies* 45 (March 1984): 80-138.

____. "Notes on Moral Theology." *Theological Studies* 27 (December 1966): 607-54.

Mangan, Joseph T., S.J. "An Historical Analysis of the Principle of Double Effect." *Theological Studies* 10 (March 1949): 41-61.

Muelder, Walter G. "Concerning Power in the State." *The Philosophical Forum* 5 (Spring 1947): 6.

Murphy, Jeffrie G. "The Killing of the Innocent." *The Monist* 57 (October 1973): 527-50.

Murray, John Courtney, S.J. "Remarks on the Moral Problems of War." *Theological Studies* 20 (March 1959): 40-67.

Nagel, Thomas. "War and Massacre." *Philosophy & Public Affairs* 2 (Winter 1971/1972): 123-44.

Novak, Michael. "Moral Clarity in the Nuclear Age." *National Review* 30 (1 April 1983): 354-70+.

Pangle, Thomas L. Review of *Just and Unjust Wars: A Moral Argument with Historical Illustrations*, by Michael Walzer. *The American Political Science Review* 72 (1978): 1393-95.

Rosenberg, David Alan. "The Origins of Overkill: Nuclear Weapons and American Strategy, 1945-1960." *International Security* 7 (Spring 1983): 3-71.

____. "A Smoking Radiating Ruin at the End of Two Hours." *International Security* 6 (Winter 1981-1982): 3-38.

Russett, Bruce M. "Short of Nuclear Madness." *Worldview* 15 (April 1972): 31-37.

Schall, James V., S.J. "The Political Consequences." *The Washington Quarterly* 5 (Autumn 1982): 127-32.

Schüller, Bruno, S.J. "The Double Effect in Catholic Thought: A Reevaluation." In *Doing Evil to Achieve Good*, edited by Richard A. McCormick, S.J. and Paul Ramsey, 165-92. Chicago: Loyola University Press, 1978.

Shifrin, Carole A. "Army to Begin Flight Testing Tactical Missile System." *Aviation Week and Space Technology* 128 (18 April 1988): 20-21.

Stein, Walter. "The Limits of Nuclear War: Is a Just Deterrence Strategy Possible?" In *Peace, the Churches and the Bomb*, edited by James Finn, 73-84. A pamphlet issued by The Council on Religion and International Affairs, 1965.

Van Voorst, L. Bruce. "The Churches and Nuclear Deterrence." *Foreign Affairs* 61 (Spring 1983): 827-52.

Walters, LeRoy. "Historical Applications of the Just War Theory: Four Case Studies in Normative Ethics." In *Love and Society: Essays in the Ethics of Paul Ramsey*, edited by James Johnson and David Smith, 115-38. Missoula, Mont.: Scholars Press, 1974.

_____. "The Just War and the Crusade: Antithesis or Analogies?" *The Monist* 57 (October 1973): 584-94.

Wasserstrom, Richard. Review of *Just and Unjust Wars*, by Michael Walzer. *Harvard Law Review* 92 (December 1978): 536-45.

Weber, Theodore R. "'To Deter or Not to Deter' ... Is Not the Only Question." In *Peace, the Churches and the Bomb*, edited by James Finn, 67-72. A pamphlet issued by the Council of Religion and International Affairs, 1965.

Wieseltier, Leon. "The Great Nuclear Debate." *New Republic* 188 (10-17 January 1983): 7-12+.

Winters, Francis X., S.J. "The Bow or the Cloud? American Bishops Challenge the Arms Race." *America* (18-25 July 1982): 26-30.

_____. "Ethics, Diplomacy and Defense." In *Ethics and Nuclear Strategy?*, edited by Harold P. Ford and Francis X. Winters, S.J., 14-50. Maryknoll, N.Y.: Orbis Books, 1977.

_____. "A Fair Hearing for the Bishops." *The Washington Quarterly* 5 (August 1982): 132-37.

_____. "Nuclear Deterrence: Atlantic Community Bishops in Tension." *Theological Studies* 43 (1982): 428-36.

_____. "The Violence of Truth." *Worldview* 17 (January 1974): 21-26.

Zamayon, Pelayo, O.F.M. Cap "Morality of War Today and in the Future." *Theology Digest* (Winter 1957): 2-5.

Church Statements

The Challenge of Peace: God's Promise and Our Response: A Pastoral Letter on War and Peace. National Conference of Catholic Bishops. Washington, D.C.: United States Catholic Conference, 1983.

"Désarmer pour construire la paix. La déclaration des évêques de Belgique." *La libre Belgique*, 20-21 juillet 1983, 1-3.

"Faith, Arms and Peace: Biblical, Theological and Ethical Perspectives." Committee of inquiry appointed by the Episcopal Bishop of the Diocese of Washington. Washington, D.C.: n.d. (Typewritten.)

"Gagner La Paix: Document de la Conférence épiscopale française." *La Documentation catholique* 1893 (4 decembre 1983): 568-94.

In Defense of Creation: The Nuclear Crisis and a Just Peace: Foundation Document. United Methodist Bishops. Nashville, Tenn.: Graded Press, 1986.

Out of Justice, Peace: Joint Pastoral Letter of the West German Bishops. English translation of the German Bishops' pastoral, *Gerechtigkeit schafft Frieden*, prepared by Irish Messenger Publications. *Winning the Peace: Joint Pastoral Letter of the French Bishops.* English translation of the French Bishops' pastoral by Rev. Michael Wrenn and copyrighted in 1983 by the *Wanderer*. Edited and with an introduction by James V. Schall, S.J. San Francisco: Ignatius Press, 1984.

Pacem in Terris. John XXIII. In *Vatican II: The Conciliar and Post-Conciliar Documents*, edited by A. Flannery. Collegeville, Minn.: Liturgical Press, 1975.

Peace and Disarmament: Documents of the World Council of Churches and Roman Catholic Church. The Commission of the Churches on International Affairs and the Pontifical Commission "Justitia et Pax." Geneva and Vatican City, n.p., 1982.

"Some Definitions Related to the Struggle for Social Justice by Nonviolent Action." Report of the Consultation at Cardiff, Wales, World Council of Churches. "Appendix. Department of Church and Society," n.p., 20 November 1972, 30-31.

"The Storm That Threatens: Statement by the Irish Bishops' Conference on War and Peace in the Nuclear Age." *The Furrow* 34 (1983): 589-95.

"To Make Peace." Report of the Joint Commission on Peace (Episcopal Church). Cincinnati: Forward Movement Publications, 1982.

Related Dissertations

Dixon, James Burrell. "A Critical Analysis of Michael Walzer's Just War Theory." Ph.D. dissertation, University of Arizona, 1980.

Dwyer, Judith A., S.S.J. "An Analysis of Nuclear Warfare in Light of the Traditional Just War Theory: An American Roman Catholic Perspective (1945-1981)." Ph.D. dissertation, Catholic University of America, 1983.

Ebenreck, Sara Van Raalte. "An Evaluation of Paul Ramsey's Approach to Just-War Theory by Way of Plato, Augustine, and the Theory of Non-Violent Action." Ph.D. dissertation, Fordham University, 1976.

Hartigan, Richard Shelley. "Noncombatant Immunity: An Analysis of Its Philosophical and Historical Origins." Ph.D. dissertation, Georgetown University, 1964.

O'Connor, Don Thomas. "War in a Moral Perspective: A Critical Appraisal of the Views of Paul Ramsey." Ph.D. dissertation, Claremont Graduate School, 1972.

Walters, LeRoy Brandt, Jr. "Five Classic Just-War Theories: A Study in the Thought of Thomas Aquinas, Vitora, Suarez, Gentili, and Grotius." Ph.D. dissertation, Yale University, 1971.